Interdisciplinary Education in the Age of Assessment

Interdisciplinary Education in the Age of Assessment addresses a prevalent need in educational scholarship today. Many current standards-driven curricula follow strict subject-specific guidelines, leaving educators little room for interdisciplinary innovation. This book gears itself toward developing assessment models specific to interdisciplinary education, positioning itself as a seminal volume in the field and a valuable resource to educators across the disciplines. Each chapter covers a major subject area (literacy, science, math, social studies, bilingual education, foreign language, educational policy) and discusses methods of assessing integrated/interdisciplinary curriculum and instruction.

David M. Moss is an Associate Professor in the Neag School of Education at the University of Connecticut.

Terry A. Osborn is Professor and Chair of the Division of Curriculum and Teaching in the Graduate School of Education, Fordham University.

Douglas Kaufman is an Associate Professor of Curriculum and Instruction in the Neag School of Education at the University of Connecticut.

Interdisciplinary Education in the Age of Assessment

Edited by

David M. Moss, University of Connecticut

Terry A. Osborn, Fordham University

Douglas Kaufman, University of Connecticut

Routledge
Taylor & Francis Group

NEW YORK AND LONDON

First published 2008
by Routledge
270 Madison Ave, New York, NY 10016

Simultaneously published in the UK
by Routledge
2 Park Square, Milton Park, Abingdon, Oxon OX14 4RN

Routledge is an imprint of the Taylor & Francis Group, an informa business

© 2008 Taylor & Francis

Typeset in Minion and Trade Gothic by
Florence Production Ltd, Stoodleigh, Devon
Printed and bound in the United States of America on acid-free paper by
Walsworth Publishing Company, Marceline, MO

Library of Congress Cataloging in Publication Data
Interdisciplinary education in the age of assessment/
    edited by David M. Moss, Terry A. Osborn, Douglas Kaufman.
        p. cm.
    1. Educational evaluation.   2. Interdisciplinary approach in
    education—Evaluation.   3. Curriculum evaluation.   I. Moss,
    David M.   II. Osborn, Terry A., 1966–.   III. Kaufman, Douglas,
    1963–.
    LB2822.75.I5624 2008
    371.26—dc22   2007038936

ISBN10: 0–8058–5377–4 (hbk)
ISBN10: 0–8058–5378–2 (pbk)
ISBN10: 0–203–92944–6 (ebk)

ISBN13: 978–0–8058–5377–3 (hbk)
ISBN13: 978–0–8058–5378–0 (pbk)
ISBN13: 978–0–203–92944–5 (ebk)

From David – for my parents, Michael and Carol Moss
From Terry – for Jennifer, Kevin, and Kelly
From Doug – for Judy, Paul, and Lisa

Contents

Illustrations

Preface

This book affords the reader a contemporary perspective on curriculum, learning, and accountability beyond the overly narrow and prescribed lens of single-subject standardized testing that has dominated our profession for too many years. Recent trends in assessment have habitually demanded that educators refine and reduce curriculum into the smallest possible elements to facilitate the generation of corresponding test items. Further compounding the issue, the resulting veneer of accountability drives everything from professional preparation of teachers to local real estate values. Reversing this dangerous trend, this book presents a fresh and timely perspective on assessment and interdisciplinary learning and teaching.

Intended for reform minded K-16 professional educators who are seeking theory supported strategies to counter the madness of poorly conceived curriculum and assessment models, which serve neither our students nor society, this book offers comprehensive and compelling vignettes and research about learning environments which break the bounds of traditional disciplines. Acknowledging that most educators are well steeped within a discipline and that curriculum is organized in this fashion, we take a realistic approach to this topic by framing this work from the starting point of familiar content areas which are central to most of our work. Our final chapter offers readers a practical guide derived from our interpretation of the contributors' work to aid in the development of assessment systems which promote interdisciplinary and transdisciplinary inquiry in the classroom.

Our first chapter, which was developed by the Editors, *The Promise of Interdisciplinary Assessment*, frames the ideas underpinning this book by acknowledging that we are in the throes of a profession driven by policies obsessed with assessment. Citing various national standards across the disciplines, it frames the ideas underpinning this book.

In Chapter 2, *Assessment is Not a Dirty Word: Measuring Knowledge, Attitudes, and Behaviors in Interdisciplinary Learning Environments*, Scott W. Brown presents a three-pronged assessment approach for interdisciplinary learning environments within which educators at any level can conceptualize assessment, and its role and value in education. Additionally, he advocates that teaching and learning should be guided by the instructional design and curriculum goals, not the assessment. He hopes to convince you that "assessment" and "test" are, in fact, not dirty words.

In our third chapter, *Assessment as Process: Transdisciplinary Self Evaluation from a Writer's Point of View*, Douglas Kaufman draws on concepts developed within the disciplines of writing and writing instruction to place assessment – and self-assessment, in particular – at the center of the act of learning. He argues that if the purpose for transdisciplinary studies is to engender a more holistic, useful concept of the world through a richer, more multifaceted exploration of it, then assessment should be at the heart of that exploration – and, in fact, an exploration itself. He concludes the search for the answers to profound questions and our definition of assessment become, in effect, one and the same.

Following, David M. Moss, John Settlage, and Catherine Koehler present *Beyond Trivial Science: Assessing Understandings of the Nature of Science*, in which they argue science education is still dominated by a coverage of content mentality supported by simplistic recall assessments. They contend all citizens should develop informed scientific perspectives while embracing a willingness to engage in social discourse necessary for a free and open society. They denote *Science for Democratic Participation* and *Science for Promoting Quality of Life* as essential constructs for promoting literacy in science.

In *Re-Solving the Tension Between Interdisciplinarity and Assessment: The Case of Mathematics* Jean McGivney-Burelle, Katherine McGivney, and Jane M. Wilburne discuss the challenge of preparing students to know and understand mathematics, and to be able to apply mathematical knowledge within and beyond the discipline. They advocate for learning opportunities which stretch students' basic understandings, encourage them to make cross-curricular connections, and ultimately solve real-life problems. They conclude that applying and assessing mathematics in interdisciplinary settings offers opportunities for genuine learning and understanding to take place.

In Chapter 6, *Hello Dolly!: Interdisciplinary Curriculum, Authentic Assessment, and Citizenship*, Alan S. Marcus argues that citizenship education is at the core of social studies, and of education more generally, and that the creation of interdisciplinary curricula with authentic assessments are best suited to support the goals of citizenship education. He presents two possible scenarios in which citizenship education could play out in classrooms and notes that although various standards and curricular guidelines may include citizenship education as an important goal, these goals may not trickle down into daily classroom activities. He invites readers not to shy away from this challenging work.

Terry A. Osborn authored *Language Learning as an Interdisciplinary Endeavor* in which he argues interdisciplinary work in world languages provides students with opportunities to examine the social and cultural worlds that they shape and are shaped by, specifically as it relates to language diversity and can be effectively utilized in a critical approach to language education. He concludes that although world language educators have often anecdotally thought of the work they do as inherently interdisciplinary, the ability of language educators to explicitly articulate criteria that move beyond those currently in use in the profession will likely prompt more sophistication in this area—and there is much work to be done.

In Chapter 8, *Rethinking Our Focus on the Future: Reading Assessment in the Transdisciplinary Secondary English Classroom*, Wendy J. Glenn argues that assessments are tied needlessly to reading skills. She advocates for student choice in the English classroom where students are encouraged to develop meaningful questions and pursue answers across a variety of texts. She concludes that this approach will promote student engagement in reading and support their preparation for district and state exams—but most importantly, it will foster love for reading.

Following, Mileidis Gort presents *Transdisciplinary Approaches to Bilingual Student Assessment: Creating Authentic Reflections of Meaningful Learning Opportunities* in which she discusses the problems and short-comings related to monitoring bilingual student achievement and progress through current standardized testing practices. She offers a framework for assessing bilingual learners which adopts a multilingual, transdisciplinary perspective. She concludes that by addressing bilingual learners' unique characteristics, including systematic and multiple types of assessments of language proficiency and academic achievement, transdisciplinary approaches to bilingual student assessment are more likely to yield authentic reflections of bilingual learners' knowledge and understandings.

In Chapter 10, the first of two summative chapters, titled *Interdisciplinary Assessment: A System at the Heart of Teaching and Learning across Domains*, Jacqueline Kelleher speaks to issues of assessment broadly from a programmatic perspective. She offers clear, concise, and practical recommendations for assessment at a variety of levels. She concludes that effective assessment models which make goals, objectives, and anticipated outcomes readily understood lead to the development of greater collaboration, stronger programs, and enhanced opportunities for learning.

In our concluding chapter, *In Praise of Complexity* by Douglas Kaufman, David M. Moss, and Terry A. Osborn, we cite the diverse perspectives offered in this contributed volume and make specific recommendations for considering assessment beyond the boundaries of traditional disciplines.

Acknowledgments

We are grateful to the contributors and reviewers of this text. Naomi Silverman has been, as always, very supportive throughout all aspects of the long process of bringing this manuscript from merely an idea to reality. Our colleagues in the Department of Curriculum and Instruction at the Neag School of Education at the University of Connecticut have been very encouraging as well. Specifically, we want to thank Wendy Glenn and Tom Levine for their assistance in developing this manuscript. And finally, we thank our families for their patience and unwavering support during an often time-consuming process.

CHAPTER 1

The Promise of Interdisciplinary Assessment

DAVID M. MOSS, TERRY A. OSBORN, and DOUGLAS KAUFMAN

This is the age of assessment.

This authoritative message dictated to professional educators is abundantly clear, even to those who have historically shunned such utterances. It seems that somewhere along the way in recent years standardized testing came to be synonymous with assessment for many high ranking public officials—some well-meaning, some cynical and politically motivated—and they piled more and more standardized tests upon the desks of educators and their students. We assert that these tests, ostensibly designed to evaluate the academic competence of students and hold those who are failing our children accountable for their actions, rarely succeed in their intent.

There are a variety of reasons why we contend that current narrowly defined assessment practices are rarely worth the massive effort and cost. At present, the very nature of many standardized tests necessitate that the learning to be evaluated is narrow and often superficial. Thus, we evaluate the simple things—recall answers that can be summed up by a penciled dot on a bubble sheet or perhaps essays characterized by their number of paragraphs rather than by the quality of ideas. The limited assessment structures currently dominating public education have little room for evaluating anything but the finished products of students' academic endeavors. Rarely do we find any interest in analyzing students' progression of learning, their abilities to uncover and make sense of disparate information, to make multifaceted meaning from diverse perspectives, and use such knowledge to make constructive changes in their lives and in their world.

As colleagues, for many years we passively yearned for a time when assessment was characterized by broader, more inclusive notions. Then, in the spirit of scholar activism spurred on by the tenacity of what we considered overly prescriptive policies, we aimed to develop a manuscript which might serve as a catalyst to once again broaden the discourse and practice of assessment. We are not looking back. We don't aspire to return to a supposed simpler time in education, especially when research tells us how complex issues of assessment typically are. Moving forward is our principal aim. Perhaps the notion of moving beyond the current state of affairs is more appropriate given that this book stems conceptually from one that we published several years ago, titled *Beyond the Boundaries* (2003). Our deep concerns about the current nature of assessment policies and practices have compelled us to examine assessment by revisiting it within the context of another topic of interest: interdisciplinary studies.

In our previous book, we were motivated by a concern that the concept of interdisciplinarity, in terms of curriculum, was grounded in the tacit belief that the individual discipline was the sole authoritative origin for beginning a process of inquiry. We asserted that the creation of artificial boundaries around traditional disciplines often results in curriculum concerned exclusively on the learning (and quite frequently the subsequent forgetting) of discrete subject matter. We strived to establish a view of integrated learning, as underpinned by the recognition that knowledge itself is not bound by disciplines, and we furthered the concept of *transdisciplinary* learning. We defined the term "discipline" not as a set of content area facts, but as a lens through which we examine phenomena. Each discipline affords the learner different viewpoints and a potentially different set of learning tools as well as subject matter material to be explored. One of us argued:

> [T]ransdisciplinarity works to remove the notion that certain content matter is necessarily *owned* by any particular discipline, and we do not engage in transdisciplinary studies to meet outside requirements that identify exposure to specific content as the primary goal. Our goal is to find a problem or idea worth studying and bear the visions of multiple perspectives upon it in order to understand it more fully than if we were to observe it from a single vantage point. This understanding inevitably leads to content learning: in the process of using the disciplines in the same ways that a discipline expert would use them to view the world, students

and teachers learn the content that attracted subject-area scholars to the discipline in the first place. However, the larger payoff is that students know how to *use* the content to continue to grow.
(Kaufman *et al.*, 2003, p. 158)

This conceptualization has powerful implications for assessment. By redefining a discipline as a way of learning (influenced by the subject matter traditionally associated with it) we are, in effect, placing assessment at the center of the learning act rather than at the periphery, where it looks at products completed only after inquiry has ceased. We are now concerning ourselves with learning the viewpoints of the discipline, the attitudes of the discipline, the culture of the discipline—the *nature* of the discipline—as much as we are concerning ourselves with the subject matter traditionally bounded within. The discipline as a way of learning becomes an act of assessment in and of itself: we continually assess ourselves and others, from the genesis of one learning endeavor to the start of subsequent endeavors to which it gives rise, we assess the evolving answers to the questions we have posed, the new questions themselves, and we monitor our learning processes while they are current. We focus on how to use the discipline as much as on the learned particulars themselves, which are traditionally the only element being tested in today's climate.

Because of our nascent conception of transdisciplinary studies essentially eliminating many definitional barriers between learning and assessment, in this book we return to the disciplines as an organizational framework, asking leaders in particular fields to help us extend our examination of assessment, its current role in an interdisciplinary milieu and its potential for redefining and expanding the act of learning in formal schooling.

Given the high-stakes nature of standardized tests, often upon which student promotion is considered and/or local property values are established, there exists a moral imperative to act on behalf of our students and their communities. In short, we propose this age of assessment is undermining and perhaps even damaging public education, forcing schools to concern themselves only narrowly with what is learned and not at all with how and why it is learned. Such a model makes it easy to generate hollow numbers that we can eagerly watch rise and fall with annual reports, but it does little for promoting actual learning. In short, we are assessing the wrong things for the wrong reasons.

Our belief in the merit of this book lies in the reception our previous one received. It prompted lively discussions at scholarly conferences, and we were struck by how many attendees reiterated at least a rhetorical support for interdisciplinary curricula. Most practitioners, however, were candid in their comments, "How are we supposed to try something like this when these standardized tests are breathing down our necks?" If one looks to the literature on interdisciplinary curriculum, it is difficult indeed to find helpful guidance. Ackerman's criteria for assessing an interdisciplinary curriculum (1989), which include validity for, within, and beyond the disciplines, hold up quite well for evaluating the curriculum itself, but not necessarily for considering student performance or growth. If, as we agree with Ackerman, a good interdisciplinary unit has a "metaconceptual bonus" (p. 29)—an intellectual payoff that is greater than that of the sum of its parts—we argue that the vast majority of standardized exams are not nearly comprehensive or sophisticated enough to capture this holistic, multifaceted payoff and its ultimate inherent potential to jumpstart further learning.

So then, how do we assess? If we suggest that interdisciplinary curricula offer important, positive contributions to student learning, how do—and how should—teachers discover and document evidence that the interdisciplinary activities add any value to the students' learning experiences? When published national standards for the fields of mathematics, language arts, foreign language, science, and social studies mandate that the curriculum provides interdisciplinary connections (see Table 1.1), how do we know if students understand and benefit from those connections? How do we evaluate the capacity for new interdisciplinary understandings to stimulate further social and intellectual growth? These questions provided an impetus for the work.

We invited our contributors to take part in our ongoing interdisciplinary discussion. We chose colleagues and educators whom we recognize share our commitment to working across disciplinary divides, and who understood that theory decontextualized from the world of the working classroom has little relevance. Several of these chapters offer assistance that is *immediately* practical, suggesting topics, approaches, and techniques that might be applied in the classroom today. Other chapter discussions do not lend themselves to automatic classroom application; however, all concern themselves with the idea that theory and practice are inextricably intertwined and that educational reform—interdisciplinary and otherwise —relies on improved classroom practice.

As with our first book, we struggled with whether or not to cast these chapters through the eyes of those who define themselves so much through their individual disciplines. If, as we have speculated, any discipline is defined by boundaries that are arbitrary, are we condoning arbitrariness by having subject experts weigh in? Ultimately, we rejected that notion. Reminding ourselves of our definition of a discipline as a learning lens, we asked each contributor to cast her or his own lens on the topic of assessment in the interdisciplinary curriculum. Their beliefs and conclusions are not always in agreement, nor should they be. Instead we view the sum of their

TABLE 1.1 Outline of national standards which mandate interdisciplinary connections

Standards documents	Select examples of standards that support interdisciplinary learning
National Council for the Social Studies: *Curriculum Standards for Social Studies: Thematic Strands*	• "Social studies programs should include experiences that provide for the study of relationships among science, technology, and society" • "Social studies programs should include experiences that provide for the study of connections and interdependence"
National Council of Teachers of English/International Reading Association: *Standards for the English Language Arts*	• "Students read a wide range of print and non-print texts to build an understanding of texts, of themselves, and of the cultures of the United States and the world; to acquire new information; to respond to the needs and demands of society and the workplace; and for personal fulfillment"
National Research Council: *National Science Education Standards*	• "Connecting science to other school subjects, such as mathematics and social studies" • "Learning subject matter disciplines in the context of inquiry, technology, science in personal and social perspectives, and history and nature of science"
National Standards in Foreign Language Education Project: *Standards for Foreign Language Learning in the 21st Century*	• "Students reinforce and further their knowledge of other disciplines through the foreign language"
National Council of Teachers of Mathematics: *Principles and Standards for School Mathematics*	• "Instructional programs from pre-kindergarten through grade twelve should enable all students to recognize and apply mathematics in contexts outside of mathematics"

viewpoints as an opportunity to learn about assessment from a richer, more comprehensive, more *transdisciplinary* standpoint. As will be addressed in the summative chapter, these authors tender two key themes, the harsh reality of narrowly defined standardized testing predominant in schooling today along with how they embrace complexity of assessing beyond the boundaries of one's discipline.

Bibliography

Ackerman, D.B. (1989). Intellectual and practical criteria for successful curriculum integration. In H.H. Jacobs (ed.), *Interdisciplinary curriculum: Design and implementation* (pp. 25–37). Alexandria, VA: ASCD.

Kaufman, D.K., Moss, D.M., & Osborn, T.A. (eds.) (2003). *Beyond the boundaries: A transdisciplinary approach to learning and teaching.* Westport, CT: Praeger Publishers.

CHAPTER 2

Assessment is Not a Dirty Word

Measuring Knowledge, Attitudes, and Behaviors in Interdisciplinary Learning Environments

SCOTT W. BROWN

> An important purpose of assessment is not only to determine [how much and] what people know, but also to assess how, when, and whether they use what they know ... Assessment of cognitive structures and reasoning processes generally require more complex tasks that reveal information about thinking patterns, reasoning strategies, and growth in understanding over time.
>
> (Pellegrino *et al.*, 2001, pp. 62–3)

We live in a time when the word "assessment" is synonymous with "TEST" and it is regarded as a dirty word, a four letter word that connotes "high stakes testing," "teaching to the test," cramming, and cheating. There is much at stake regarding test results: graduation from high school, admission to college, merit pay for teachers, overhauling schools, and teacher certification programs. Real estate prices fluctuate when pass rates on state-wide assessments are reported by school districts and published in the local newspapers, as parents pay a premium to live in school districts with a history of high performance among their students.

As Linn (1986) stated twenty years ago, "the sharp criticisms of and serious concerns about the overuse and misuse of tests currently coexist with widespread demands for and increased reliance on tests" (p. 1153). Therefore, we should not be surprised about the importance placed on testing and assessment in American education, nor its controversial nature.

It is no wonder that following the publication of books such as *The Mismeasure of Man* (Gould, 1996) and *The Bell Curve* (Herrnstein & Murray, 1994), which are two popular readings on many college campuses, that assessment and test are considered dirty words by many educators. Many educators state that tests are driving the educational curriculum, and in many cases that is a very accurate observation, but an inappropriate use of a valuable component for education at all levels, including our public schools, business and industry, college campuses, and professional training. Imagine for a moment, what if there were no tests or assessments of what we have learned and what we can do as a result of courses or training completed? As you drive your car down the road, the other drivers have never been tested; as you buckle in to your seat ready to take off, the airline pilot has not been assessed in multiple situations; or when you go to see your physician, she prescribes a procedure or medication that has never been evaluated. I am sure that you certainly hope that each and every one of these people has been properly educated or trained, and also assessed in some manner. I know I do.

The goal of this chapter is not to convince you that "assessment" and "test" are not dirty words, though that would be great. The goal is to present a framework for measuring learning in interdisciplinary learning environments, within which educators at any level can conceptualize assessment, and its role and value in education.

After nearly twenty-five years of experience as an educational psychologist working to advance the field of educational psychology, teaching undergraduates, preparing Masters and doctoral students, working with colleagues, and developing learning and assessment environments for a wide range of learners and outcomes, there is one tenet I hold central: If it is worth spending time to teach something, or to build a learning environment in which students/participants may learn, *then* it is worth assessing whether or not learning has occurred. A second important tenet, and one of the major themes of this chapter, is that teaching and learning should be guided by the instructional design and curriculum goals, *not* the assessment. We should not teach to the test; we should teach to the curriculum! And if the curriculum is within an interdisciplinary learning environment (as most learning is), then we must move beyond the traditional forms of multiple choice tests to assessments that are sensitive to the goals and objectives of the curriculum, while maintaining the richness, both in breadth and depth, of the mixing of multiple content areas that are brought together to facilitate learning and transfer in an interdisciplinary world.

Assessments should inform the student about what he/she has learned, and what he/she has not. Assessments should inform the teacher so she knows what the student has learned and provide feedback regarding student performance on individual student performance as well as a group or class. This information at the individual level needs to be more than a grade, but suggestions about remedial activities, alternative strategies or enrichment opportunities, as appropriate, to maximize learning opportunities for all students. The teacher should also process feedback information about what worked and what needs changing regarding learning, the environment, and teaching performance. The question should be, if these curriculum goals are valuable and important to teach, have my students learned the necessary knowledge, attitudes and behaviors to demonstrate that they have learned, and learned to a high level? If not, what actions need to be taken to help the students and/or teacher? Assessments also provide feedback to the importance and value of the curriculum goals. In short, the role of assessment is two-fold, both formative and summative. It should provide feedback to students and teachers for educational adjustments during learning, and provide information for decisions about final performance, respectively (Anastasi, 1988).

Assessments Should Respond to Curriculum Goals

Testing needs to be more closely linked to instruction. Improving the link will require 'a combined enterprise representing test design based on knowledge of human learning and per performance, psychometric requirements and studies of test use.'
(Curtis & Glaser, 1983, p. 144)

Several years ago, I gave a lecture on educational psychology and the role of learning, at a major medical school in the United States. There are few domains that I can imagine where covering the entire curriculum is more critical than medicine. Medicine, as all physicians know, is an interdisciplinary field. The organs and systems are inter-related and they are impacted by environmental, physical, social, and emotional factors, such as pollen, a dog bite, work-related stress, high blood pressure, and family history. Each of these factors is an integral component of most medical school curriculum. As such, during my lecture, I made a point that medical school professors, as all professors, should be teaching to the curriculum, including these interdisciplinary elements. Further, I stated that the professors should be able to create their assessments before their first class, since the assessments should be based upon the curriculum and not just on what was taught. I made the point that they should be teaching to the curriculum and not the test, so that someone else should be able to create their test, maybe professionals with strong assessment and medical knowledge. After the lecture, many of the professors accosted me, they were shocked that I would suggest developing their tests before the course started and that I went so far as to state that someone else could develop their tests. After all, they were the professor and they knew what they had taught. My response was, "that is exactly the problem with most professor- and teacher-designed assessments."

So many teachers and professors teach very important and valuable information, but some of us drift from the curriculum that forms the instructional objectives (whether you are a supporter of Gronlund, 1995, Mager, 1984 or Gagne, 1965). We often do not construct assessments that are directly tied to the curriculum we are to teach; rather we test some portion of what we have taught. What would happen if the medical professor spent a lot of time on the heart but really didn't get a chance to spend any time on the kidneys? Do they still assess learning related to the understanding of the functioning of kidneys?

If we expect students to transfer their learning to other situations and we know that these other situations will be interdisciplinary in nature, as most of real life is, then we must teach them to do, learn, apply and transfer, and assess that as well. Unfortunately, we all too often develop assessments that are easier for us to administer and score, rather than an assessment that contains both the appropriate emphases on specific topics and skills, and that is related to what the final performance outcomes are. For example, while it may be appropriate to assess most beginning drivers of automobiles with a multiple choice examination focusing on shapes of signs, braking distances, and required actions when approaching a school bus, we would still want a performance assessment of driving skills in various traffic situations. In the same sense, an art student at a college would think it was an appropriate task to produce a drawing, painting or sculpture at the end of the semester, if that was the focus of the class, rather than a multiple choice exam of characteristics of famous styles and collections. The goal is to assess learning in the most appropriate manner based on the learning environment and performance expectations, both for the learning and later performance environments.

Knowledge Attitudes and Behaviors (KAB)

The knowledge, attitudes and behaviors approach (KAB) is based on instructional models within educational psychology that propose that educational change may be viewed through three dimensions of learning: cognitive, affective and performance (Bloom, 1976; Bloom et al., 1956). This pioneering work in identifying educational dimensions and a hierarchy of abilities within each dimension has been extended to examining constructivist approaches (as well as others) in a wide variety of interdisciplinary educational environments, ranging from disease prevention, to eating behaviors (Beavers *et al.*, 1982; Byrd-Bedbenner *et al.*, 1982). The KAB approached evolved from the cognitive, affective and performance dimensions of Bloom's work to the knowledge, attitudes, and behaviors assessment framework.

The KAB framework provides a three pronged assessment approach for interdisciplinary learning environments and outcomes, including disease prevention (Brown *et al.*, 1992; Lawless & Brown, 1997; Silver *et al.*, 1998), the training of educators (Brown, 1996; Holcomb *et al.*, 2004), the study of high school students engaged in simulations of international negotiations (Brown & King, 2000), and the impact of distance education programs (Harnar *et al.*, 2000). This approach provides a scaffold for teachers/instructors to answer three very important questions: "What do students know?" "How do they feel about the topic?" and "What do they do as a result of instruction?"

Within the KAB framework, knowledge refers to the cognitive dimensions of knowing, metacognition strategies and process, and networks of cognitive information (Alexander, 1992). It is declarative knowledge (i.e., knowing the capitol of Connecticut), procedural knowledge (i.e., knowing how to operate a word processor), and conditional knowledge (i.e., knowing when to take specific notes during a lecture) (see Alexander, 2003 and Alexander *et al.*, 1995, for a complete review of the knowledge domain). Knowledge refers to what we know, how we know it and how it is organized so that we may use it, whether facts, strategies or procedures. Knowledge is the most common attribute of learning assessed, but is only one of the components of learning if it is to be applied and/or transferred.

Attitudes, also known as dispositions, have multiple components. Attitudes are an important component in learning because of the role of beliefs and values in learning (Ajzen, 1993). If someone does not believe they can learn a specific topic or believes that they can learn the topic but does not value it, then the learning process may be impaired or incomplete. Self-efficacy and other context specific beliefs and values are often the focus of the attitude component of the KAB approach. As defined by Bandura (1997), self-efficacy refers to a person's belief that they can engage in a task and successfully accomplish the specific task. When a person does not believe that he or she can accomplish a specific task, they are less likely to engage in that task. For instance, when Melissa, a third-grade student, states "I am not good at math," it often is based on previous feedback she has received, often in the form of grades or the inability to complete the math task. Therefore, Melissa is less likely to work on her math homework because she does not believe she can be successful. Bandura (1997) details a number of effective methods for increasing a person's self-efficacy so that Melissa will work on her math homework and so she can achieve success. Changing Melissa's attitudes about math can get her engaged in math class and transfer to other settings as well, thereby directly influencing learning.

Behaviors require a person to perform a specific task or self-report previous performances. The assessment of behaviors does not include having a student describe how to perform a behavior; that is a knowledge issue. Rather behaviors must be directly observed, videotaped, self-reported, or the product of a behavior may be displayed. It is also important to note that in the assessment of behaviors, the student must be in an environment that is conducive to completing the behavior. For instance, a student would not be able to demonstrate the behaviors required to fold an origami paper crane if there was no paper available, even though the student has the knowledge and attitudes to support the folding of the crane.

The KAB approach enables instructors and researchers to examine the three dimensions of learning described by Bloom and his colleagues (Bloom, 1976; Bloom et al., 1956) and to diagnose specific dimensions and prescribe educational interventions specifically focused on one or more of the three dimensions when learning has not occurred, or has occurred incompletely (see Schrader and Lawless, 2004 for a further discussion of the KAB evaluation framework). Consider Matt's seat belt buckling behavior for example. When Matt does not exhibit the fastening of his seat belt when driving a car, it may not be because of Matt's lack of knowledge about the operation of a seat belt or his inability to perform the task.

It is important to note that in the assessment of behaviors the student must be in an environment that is conducive to completing the behavior. For instance, if there is no paper available, the student will not be able to fold the origami crane; even though the student has the knowledge and attitudes to support the folding of the crane, they were not able to demonstrate the behavior without the paper.

Although one of the easiest dimensions to assess, it is important to note that when Matt does not exhibit a specific behavior, such as fastening his seat belt when driving his car, it may not be because of Matt's lack of knowledge about the operation of a seat belt or his inability to perform the task. Matt may believe he is not at risk, because Matt considers himself a safe driver. The breakdown in learning will not be addressed in further focus on Matt's knowledge or behavior dimensions. Matt will need to change his attitude about seat belts so that he values that he is at risk, whether from his own driving or of the other drivers on the road. In this case the instruction would focus on attitudes valuing the safety provided by seat belts for Matt as a driver and his passengers. As demonstrated in Figure 2.1, when knowledge, attitudes and behaviors interact together, learning is

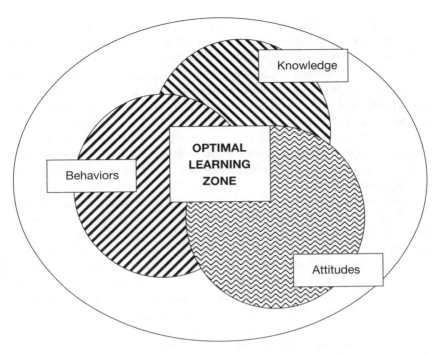

Figure 2.1 Knowledge, attitudes, and behaviors interacting to result in an optimal form of learning

optimized. The learner knows what to do and how to do it, has the values and belief systems in place to exhibit the learning, and the behavioral abilities to perform the task completely and accurately.

The KAB approach enables instructors and researchers to examine the three dimensions of learning described by Bloom and his colleagues (Bloom, 1976; Bloom *et al.*, 1956) and to diagnose specific dimensions and prescribe educational interventions specifically focused on one or more of the three dimensions when learning has not occurred, or has occurred incompletely. For further discussion of the KAB framework, see Schrader and Lawless (2004).

Assessing KABs in Interdisciplinary Environments—Several Examples

There are a couple of different approaches that could be taken at this point to discuss some of the issues of assessing outcomes of interdisciplinary programs with the KAB approach and how they play a critical role in education, learning, and performance. The approach selected in this chapter is that of examples: Examples of different projects that are interdisciplinary, varying from an educational program for disease prevention to assessing outcomes of middle and high school students engaged in an international negotiation simulation, to assessing the outcomes of a problem-based learning (PBL) environment for deaf students learning about science. Each case is unique in some aspects but they share the common requirement of assessing learning, whether by mandate of a granting agency, or demonstrating successful performance for course grades. Further, they all share a constructivist pedagogy embedded within a PBL environment, and they all embody the same assessment framework: Knowledge, Attitudes and Behaviors (KAB).

Lyme Disease Education—The United States Centers for Disease Control and Prevention (commonly known as CDC) is concerned about the level of incidence of Lyme disease, a disease transmitted by the bite of a tick. School aged-children are particularly at risk of contracting Lyme disease because they engaged in many of the activities that placed them in a high risk category. They play on the grass in sports and other recreation activities where ticks are known to be, they do not conduct "tick checks" and they know little about the preventive behaviors associated with the disease, nor their level of risk. The risk for children in the state of Connecticut is even more elevated because Connecticut has environmental conditions that are conducive to the transmission of Lyme disease. As a result, Connecticut has one of the highest incidents of Lyme disease in the country. The CDC hoped to reduce the incidence of Lyme disease in Connecticut's children through a comprehensive educational program that became known as the Lyme Disease Education Program (see www.ucc. uconn.edu/~wwwlyme). The challenge for this task was that reducing the incidence of Lyme disease in children was interdisciplinary in nature with aspects of social, environmental, and psychological variables.

Over a period of several years educational curriculum was developed consisting of videos (e.g., *Invasion of the Blood Suckers*, Brown, 1995; *Tick Invaders*, Brown, 1993), educational curriculum tied to middle and high school social studies and science curriculum, and educational games (Baird & Brown, 1993a; Baird & Brown, 1993b; DuBois & Brown, 1996; Lawless & Brown, 1994). At all levels, the educational intervention program were focused on increasing students' knowledge about Lyme disease, their understanding that they were at risk for contracting the disease (attitudes) and the production of prevention behaviors to reduce the incidence of Lyme disease. At the youngest grades this also included focusing on parent engagement in the education process.

The knowledge component of Lyme disease educational interventions consists of the origin of the disease, how it is transmitted, diagnosis of

Lyme disease and current treatments. Attitudes were addressed by focusing on risk factors and raising awareness so that individuals not only became aware of how they could contract the disease but that they were personally at risk of getting Lyme disease. Behaviors focused on conducting "tick checks" and how to correctly remove a tick from your skin if you found one on you.

To assess what knowledge the students had learned, multiple choice items about Lyme disease were developed with epidemiologists serving as subject matter experts. Attitudinal scales were developed focusing on student attitudes and values associated with Lyme disease prevention using a Likert scale (Strongly Disagree to Strongly Agree). Specifically, students were asked about their attitudes associated with disease prevention and the treatment for Lyme disease. Behaviors were assessed through self-reported behavior scales about specific actions taken, and activities completed (e.g., use of tick sprays, and protective clothing).

The results of the assessment of the Lyme Disease Education Project demonstrated significant and effective changes in knowledge, attitudes and behaviors (Brown *et al.*, 1992; Lawless *et al.*, 1997; Silver *et al.*, 1998). Over time however, it was noted that the behaviors reported began to regress to the baseline levels found prior to the implementation of the educational intervention. This information led to a revision to the overall implementation of the intervention.

Rather than teaching an isolated unit based on Lyme disease, inter-disciplinary materials were developed in social studies and science to show how diseases were transmitted and impacted the social structure and customs in history and current events. Students learned how diseases such as the Black Plague, small pox, AIDS, and Lyme disease have lead to scientific breakthroughs, and social changes, both historical and current. In turn, these changes influenced government funding for research, new vaccines, and the migration patterns of people away, among others. These revisions to the Lyme disease curricular materials curbed the regress of behavior scores and maintained student production of prevention behaviors.

Beyond the focus on knowledge, attitudes and behaviors in interdisci-plinary environments, this example also demonstrates the measurement of change over time. The KAB approach allowed the assessments to demon-strate immediate impact and also provide long-term measures of KAB maintenance.

The GlobalEd Project: International Negotiations—The GlobalEd project (www.globaled.uconn.edu) is a study of group decision making and nego-tiation skills among middle and high school students. Through a web-based simulation, GlobalEd enables students to grapple with the complexity of international negotiations as their class represents a country having to balance its social, economic, health, environmental and security concerns. As such, GlobalEd represents a true interdisciplinary learning environment.

Embedded in a realistic problem solving environment, where students make calculations about infant mortality rates, draft written documents, analyze data, assess the impact of global warming and evaluate the impact of trade agreements on their economy and national security (Brown & King, 2000).

The GlobalEd project requires students to work together and study their assigned country several weeks prior to the actual simulation. During this period, students learn about their country with the goal to act as if they were actually the government of the country, not as a group of Americans governing the country. The students learn about the people, the economy, the structure of the government, and the history and values of the people. They also learn about policies the country has regarding such issues as the environment, health care, economics, and defense. Students gain knowledge, adjust some of their attitudes about the interactions between the United States and other countries, specifically the new country they now represent, and they change some of their behaviors and actions as they make decisions about the types of interactions that they have with the other countries in the simulation. All interactions among the students in the different countries are web-based and recorded as part of the simulation, there are no face-to-face negotiations between countries, but a great deal of discussion within each country (each class).

GlobalEd uses technologies, such as email and synchronous and asynchronous discussion areas, to facilitate communication between groups of students at various school locations who represent different countries for a period of approximately six weeks. Students must interact with students from other schools using the technology tools provided in order to achieve the goals of the simulation, which are to draft and negotiate a multinational treaty with at least one other country. Students also learn to use the web resources for studying the history of their specific country, as well a gathering a variety of facts and opinions about their assigned country and the other countries in the simulation.

To study the impact GlobalEd had on students' academic outcomes, a KAB assessment of the intervention was developed using both quantitative and qualitative indices. The series of instruments are administered via the web, collecting demographic information, self-efficacy information related to the simulation, and their knowledge, attitudes and behaviors (KABs) regarding international politics, using computers, working in groups, and problem-solving. Self-report items on behaviors, such as the frequency of reading the newspaper and watching television for national and international news, were also collected. These KAB assessments cross disciplinary lines of science, economics, writing, social issues and current events. The KAB assessments are administered within two weeks prior to the start of the simulation and within two weeks following the end of the simulation to provide a pre- and post-testing set of scores across the KAB dimensions, assessing change.

Students' email communications are also collected and coded, then analyzed according to previous research on negotiation patterns (Boyer et al., 2005, 2006). These communication patterns tell researchers about patterns of communications and how they change over time as well as differences based on gender and age and experience. These negotiation patterns inform researchers and teachers about what a student knows, and their attitudes about school topics such as economics, environmental issues, arms control, and human rights, and behaviors such as watching the news, time spent on homework, and computer access and usage.

The findings of the GlobalEd Project indicate issues related to the knowledge of international relations, how to work in groups and student skills were assessed and statistically significant gains were demonstrated. Attitudes as measured by instruments focusing on self-efficacy for academic skills and the use of educational technology were demonstrated to significantly increase from pre- to post-testing. Self-reported behaviors were shown to increase related to reading newspapers, watching the news on television and skills working in groups to solve problems and make decisions (Boyer et al., 2004, 2005; Brown et al., 2003, 2004).

When using complex interdisciplinary learning environments, instructors should consider using a combination of qualitative and quantitative approaches to assessment. Through the use of a combination of approaches the instructor can triangulate findings as well as provide a richness of data demonstrating increased KABs across domains.

Classroom of the Sea—The Classroom of the Sea (COS) Project is an interdisciplinary learning environment designed to promote the growth of scientific knowledge, academic skills, and self-efficacy of deaf students (www.cos.uconn.edu). One of the unique characteristics of COS is that in this PBL environment in which students identify and address real problems of acoustics, marine life, changes in the ocean environment and the impact of various parts of the marine environment. Students travel out to sea on an actual research vessel (The *RV Connecticut*) multiple times a year to collect data, manipulate it, and share data and findings on the web for others to view. Many of the others who view this data are students at high schools across the USA, both hearing and deaf students, who are studying marine science.

The COS project developed a year-long instructional PBL module which focuses on the problems associated with the habitat for the harbor seal population found in the Long Island Sound. Harbor seals are indicators of environmental changes that may be occurring in Long Island Sound since they are sensitive to changes in their environment (e.g., water temperature, chemical pollution, noise, and human activity). Additionally, changes in their physical habitat, where they "haul out" for rest on rocks, beaches, and related areas, will also impact these mammals, and changes in the seals' food source can impact the size, fitness, and activities of the seal colonies. Social and economic issues are also part of this study as students learn about the impact of colonies of harbor seals on the fishing industry, and the impact decisions of construction and cabling across Long Island Sound will have on the configuration and location of the harbor seal colony. This integrated interdisciplinary learning environment incorporates many disciplines, such as biology, chemistry, and physics, as well as social studies, math, and English, enabling the students to prepare reports and study the seals from different points of view.

A major challenge, in working with deaf children within the discipline of science and related domains is how to communicate, through a sign language, system scientific concepts, and complex material. There are relatively few, widely accepted signs for specific scientific concepts such as gravity, electromagnetic, or photosynthesis. Many teachers and students develop a short hand for some of these complex concepts that are accepted across different teachers, or schools. Often teachers and students are forced to use finger spelling to convey these concepts, which leads to complications and delays in conveying a concept. Imagine if every time you wanted to talk about the concept of photosynthesis in a class, you had to spell it out, as p-h-o-t-o-s-y-n-t-h-e-s-i-s? This finger spelling process may lead to some concepts not being taught at all and less student learning.

The COS project team identified all science-related terms and expressions used in the curriculum and then compared them with nine published resources on signs. In the first analysis, only 40 percent of the 871 terms and expressions had established signs. The science teachers, scientists, and educational researchers are collaborating to examine how science literacy can be enhanced in light of this challenge. In some cases, signs for such terms as "compressional wave" can be invented and used in the classroom and environment. In other cases, it is best to sign the science conceptually using American Sign Language (ASL). A glossary for accepted scientific and marine science signs is located on www.cos.uconn.edu.

In collaborative knowledge building, teachers are encouraged to shift the focus of work from finding answers to improving theories (Bereiter & Scardamala, 2000). One of the advantages of the approach to improving theories is that it nurtures students to ask "knowledge-based" questions arising from their own puzzlement or perceived lack of understanding, rather than "text-based" textbook questions (Bereiter & Scardamala, 2000). According to Bereiter *et al.* (1997, as cited in Bereiter & Scardamala, 2000), the second advantage of shifting from finding answers to improving theories is that it engages students in a process much more like real science, where practitioners seldom expect to discover final answers but rather work to improve on existing knowledge.

The COS team designed PBL modules intended to meet the following objectives:

- construction of scientifically useful knowledge;
- development of scientific reasoning strategies;
- development of effective self-directed learning strategies;
- increase of motivation of learning; and
- more effective collaborative learning.

In order to assess the learning outcomes from this project, the KAB approach was employed for several reasons. First, there were no appropriate standardized assessments of science knowledge that were both acceptable to the science teachers of the deaf students and that were linked to state or national science standards, without relying heavily on skills of reading comprehension. It should be noted that reading comprehension is often found to be lower for deaf students (as measured by grade level) because of differences in syntax, the sentence structure of American Sign Language and a different early reading experience (Lang, 1994; Marschark *et al.*, 2002), not because of cognitive abilities. Second, the specific topics covered in the PBL environment were related to harbor seals and the environmental quality of Long Island Sound, which was not found to be assessed in a manner that was both reliable and valid. Finally, the teachers and researchers desired an assessment that would focus on the specific learning outcomes, as well as changes in attitudes about science that would result from this specific PBL experience.

Each trip out to sea, approximately 10 to 12 students complete a pre- and post-assessment of science attitudes, science behaviors, and science knowledge. Students write about their goals and objectives, as well as their accomplishments. Since many of our trips are web cast to other sites, we ask the students participating in the web casts to complete the same instruments.

Due to the many concerns discussed about the reading comprehension and language experiences with deaf students in assessing knowledge, concept maps were employed to provide an additional measure of student knowledge and understanding. Concept maps have been used in teaching and learning to both provide an effective schema for organizing complex information during the teaching process and assessing student understanding of content and the interrelatedness of complex ideas when assessing students. The students and teachers were trained in the use of concept maps prior to the formal assessments and all received the opportunity to either draw their concept maps of seals either freehand or using a computer program. Most opted to use the computer program Inspiration® to create their maps. A scoring system was developed accounting for the number of nodes, the direction of the arrows, and both correct and incorrect conceptions. The use of concept maps was found to be very effective in allowing the students to demonstrate a deeper and more thorough understanding of the seal concept without the limitations of writing syntax and sentence structure limitations that often results in lower assessments of the deep knowledge. Two sample concept maps created by high school students who had participated in COS for six months are provided in Figures 2.2 and 2.3.

Additionally, self-efficacy scales related to completion of science experiments, collecting and representing scientific data and communicating

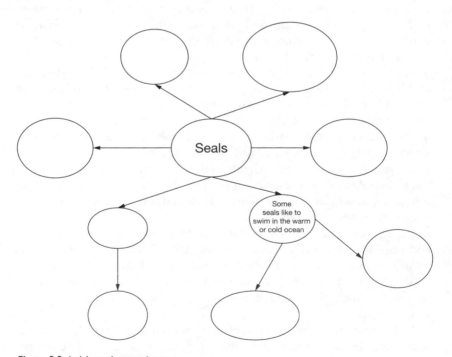

Figure 2.2 Judy's seal concept map

Erratum

We apologize for the omission of text in Figure 2.2 on p. 20. The correct figure appears below.

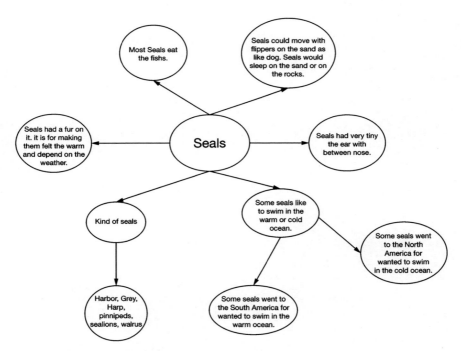

Figure 2.2 Judy's seal concept map

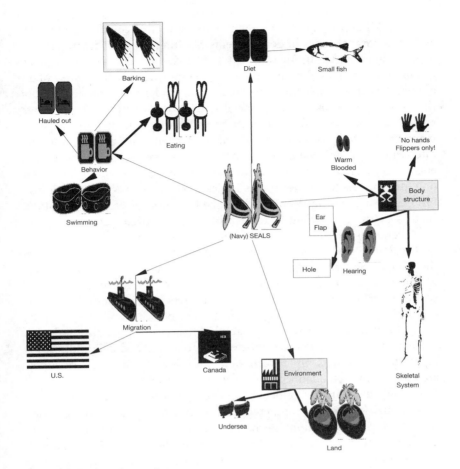

Figure 2.3 Kurt's seal concept map

scientific terms were also developed and administered within a longitudinal research model (multiple assessments throughout the year). Focus groups of students were also conducted several times during the year to assess changes in attitudes, the use of scientific signs, student expectations, learning outcomes, and the transfer of skills from science to other educational topics, providing both an attitude and behavior measure. Behaviors were further assessed through classroom and "field trips" observations using a live and recorded system for collecting the data. The behavioral observations demonstrated active learning and engagement by the students in collecting data, interpreting the data, predicting outcomes and implications, and general communications among the other students, the teachers and researchers, and the ship's crew (Brown *et al.*, 2002).

The KAB approach allowed for the assessment of cognitive, affective, and behavioral changes in deaf students resulting from the immersion in an interdisciplinary PBL environment. In this example, concept maps, focus groups, and behavioral observations were employed over the course of an academic year to assess program impact and student development across the domains of science, math, social studies, and writing. The findings are valuable not only for deaf or hard-of-hearing students, but also for mainstream students in terms of learning science in general, and the intertwining of multiple domains that one topic such as harbor seals can effectively integrate in motivating learning environments. For instance, not only did the results of the studies indicate increases in KABs, but it also resulted in a series of resources developed in support of deaf education, such as a glossary of scientific terms with a standardized system of signing and a series of interdisciplinary modules related to marine science topics.

The Husky Educational Technology Assessment Program—Schools in the United States are spending over $4 billion a year on technology (Archambault *et al.*, 2002). As a result of the vast amount of money being spent on technology, many educational leaders have expressed concerns on whether or not the technology is being effectively integrated to promote student learning. One issue is the fact that many educators have not been adequately trained. A study conducted by Moursund and Beilefeldt (1999) reported that less than fifty percent of public school teachers in their survey are sufficiently well qualified in educational technology use.

In 1999, the State of Connecticut made significant steps to improve the educational technology competency of its teachers by adopting a three-tiered model of educational technology competency. The three levels of competencies are grounded in the International Society for Technology in Education standards (ISTE, 2000). In addition, the competencies cut across the four strands addressed by the *The Connecticut Teacher Technology Standards* (2001): (1) Educational Technology Concepts and Operations; (2) Creating Learning Environments and Experiences; (3) Productivity and Professional Practice; and (4) Social, Legal, Ethical, and Human Issues. In order to improve the technology skills and competencies addressed in the three-tiered model, a professional development and assessment system was established. The Husky Educational Technology Assessment Program (HETAP) became the assessment component for measuring success at the three levels and became a mandatory component of assessment for all pre-service teachers at the University of Connecticut (http://teachtech. education.uconn.edu).

HETAP is a performance-based measure. According to both Airasian (2001) and Popham (2000), performance-based measures are assessments in which individuals carry out an activity or produce a product in order to demonstrate their knowledge. Performance-based assessments allow individuals to show what they can do in real life situations and may be better measures of what the person can and will actually do in specific environments (Wiggins, 1993). In HETAP, we encourage educators to demonstrate how they can apply educational technology to address and solve real problems, ones they may face on any given day. Additionally, performance-based assessments may be a more valid indicator of an individual's knowledge, attitudes, and behaviors. Performance-based assessment can provide impetus for improving instruction, and increase an individual's understanding of what they need to know and be able to do, as well as enhance transfer to a variety of settings.

HETAP has three components, each targeting a specific level of Connecticut's three-tier model. Each of these components differentially focuses on educators' use of educational technology to positively impact student learning. In Level I (LI), the educator demonstrates proficiency in the use of educational technology at a basic level, using personal productivity tools, operating the computer system, and responding to written prompts focusing on issues of professional development, ethical and social standards, and the use of educational technology with special populations of students. Specifically, LI measures skills in the area of word processing, database/spreadsheet, and presentation software programs. These components were chosen because they represented the tools used by the local educational agencies to construct and deliver instruction. In addition to demonstrating proficient use in these personal productivity areas, educators are also required to respond to a series of written prompts covering a wide array of topics from ethics to technology integration. The prompts are posted allowing educators to interact with one another during the assessment process, as they would in their own everyday practices. LI is completed by downloading a series of prompts and tasks anchored within a PBL environment, responding to the tasks and uploading their responses within a four-day period. Mirroring the use of this technology in the real world, educators may talk with one another, consult help files, etc., just as they would if they were working in their schools. Multiple parallel versions of the LI exist so that individuals will not retake the same version, and training will not teach to the test. All versions retain the same format, though the theme and actual tasks vary. To date, nearly 5,000 educators have successfully completed LI.

Level II (LII) requires the educator to have previously passed LI and is also embedded within a PBL environment. LII requires greater collaboration as the educators are assigned to discussion sections that are matched across the grade levels and content areas that they teach. The discussions allow for the educators to work independently or in groups to develop a lesson plan that is embedded within their own specific context to promote student learning using educational technology. LII allows four weeks to complete the process, which is culminated by the submission of a proposal that may take any one of several formats (e.g., Word, PowerPoint, Inspiration, or a combination of multiple formats). Each proposal must address all four of the strand standards.

Level III (LIII) is the highest level of the hierarchy and requires the educator to submit a portfolio of student work that they have facilitated and a written description of how the four strands have been addressed by the student and the educator. Educators must have successfully completed LII to engage in the LIII projects, which often take an entire academic year for the students and the educator to complete.

As the educator advances from LI to LII to LIII, the PBL context in which it is situated moves closer and closer to his/her own professional setting. For instance, in LI, the educator may be told that they are working with a group of teachers and students on the development of a school store and that they must edit a letter to parents, make changes to a school store budget and prepare a presentation to the school board. Whereas LIII is portfolio based, requiring a collection of specified components to be judged as successful. Moreover, the components of HETAP are designed to cross disciplines and grade levels. While LI emphasizes general educational technology skills and is a prerequisite to successfully completing the higher levels, LII and LIII cross disciplines and grade levels to focus on student learning using educational technology.

With the HETAP system, KABs are measured in ways that reflect the PBL and performance-based nature of the system's design. Knowledge is portrayed through the successful completion of the specific tasks. Attitudes are measured through the self-efficacy scales, and the changes from pre-assessment to post-assessment. Finally, behaviors are measured through the completion of the technology tasks. At lower levels of the assessment, knowledge and behaviors are linked together. As the educator progresses to higher levels of HETAP, the knowledge and behaviors begin to separate, as the focus of the assessment increasingly centers on what the educator has done to promote student learning in the classroom and becomes linked to the specific educational curriculum.

A score of 75 percent of all the possible points accrued across all four strands is required for successful completion of a HETAP assessment. Educators may take a specific level more than once without penalty. Professional development for educators preparing to complete HETAP is conducted by an independent group, to reduce conflicts of interest between training and assessment.

After completing the on-line sign form for the specific HETAP level to be taken, participants are brought directly to an on-line pre-efficacy survey.

At the completion of all requirements for that level, participants are required to complete an identical post-efficacy survey for pre- to post-comparisons. Scorers for each level use rubrics that were developed for both the personal productivity and written prompt components. These rubrics are available to the assessment participants before they submit their final work so that they may see how they will be assessed. Scores on submitted materials are based on an absent/present format. Points are awarded for correct application of the specified tasks. The written prompt rubric is based on a three point scale (Absent, Present, and Outstanding; 0, 1, and 2 points, respectively; allowing for participants to possibly exceed 100 percent).

Several studies examining the KABs of educators participating in HETAP have demonstrated the positive impact of participation in the assessment across all three dimensions of the KAB framework (Holcomb *et al.*, 2003a, 2003b, 2004). These findings have significant implications in performance-based technology assessment employing a problem-based learning environment. Studies such as these provide insight into educators and their ability to effectively utilize technology in an educational setting, as well as the seamless joining of professional development and assessment; it demonstrates the seamless distinction between learning and assessment using KABs (Holcomb, 2005). Learning occurs during the assessment process, just as assessment can occur during the learning process, with the ultimate goal of accurate assessments and optimal learning occurring simultaneously.

The Teachers for a New Era Project at UConn (TNE)—The TNE project at the University of Connecticut (www.tne.uconn.edu) is part of a consortia of eleven colleges and universities across the country that have been funded by the Carnegie Corporation, with additional funding from the Annenberg and Ford foundations, to develop model teacher education programs that result in demonstrable learning gains in the pupils of their teachers. The three design principles that each school must follow are: evidence-based decision making, using the research and data to make decisions; the engagement of professors in the arts and sciences to prepare teachers; and the development of an induction program, in which the preparation of teachers is based on a clinical practice model.

This challenge is being addressed at UConn by developing inter-disciplinary instruction, learning experiences and assessments of teacher education candidates similar to the knowledge, skills and dispositions approach used by the National Council for Accreditation of Teacher Education (NCATE, 2002). The instruction and assessments developed and employed focus on what teacher candidates, practicing teachers, and their students know, their attitudes, and specific behaviors they exhibit (KABs). These assessments cross discipline lines of university courses, K-12 schools, and as was just discussed in the HETAP, blend instruction and assessment seamlessly to promote learning in the teacher candidates and pupils they will teach in their classrooms.

At the University level, professors across a variety of disciplines (education and arts & sciences) work together constructing meaningful learning environments that are both engaging and deep in content. These are enacted both within the university class setting, as well as the clinical placements in the K-12 schools. These environments reflect the fact that student learning and teaching are interdisciplinary endeavors. As such, these learning environments are not only rich in a specific content discipline, but also provide our preservice teachers with multiple opportunities to explore pedagogy and methods across content areas and domains in true interdisciplinary settings. They require the preservice teacher to consider the social, academic, and health issues of student learning in our K-12 schools. They focus on the metacognitive processes necessary for effective integration of domains and transfer of skills across those domains such as writing, calculations, the scientific method, and the use of symmetry in music and art.

It is critical that as we measure our success in achieving the goal of preparing teachers who continually produce demonstrable learning gains in their students, that we assess both what the teachers and students know, what they value and how their self-efficacy, and what they actually do in the classrooms: KABs. Our faculty has received training on, and assistance in, the development of an array of assessment strategies to target these needs including concept maps, observations, writing prompts, and PBL assessment tasks. This approach has the benefit of not only promoting and assessing learning, but also provides an effective model for the preservice teachers to adopt when they have their own classrooms.

Summary

... testing should always be used in the interests of the children tested ...

(Scarr, 1981, p. 1159)

Assessment is not a dirty word, but test is a four letter word, one that can even be used in public ... sometimes. The words and concepts of assessment and test are here to stay and they must remain part of our educational vocabulary. As stated by the American Psychological Associations report on high stakes testing, "When tests are developed and used appropriately, they are among the most sound and objective knowledge and performance measures available. But appropriate development and use are critical" (APA, 2004).

As educators and researchers we must make sure that our assessments reflect our goals, intentions and values. These include:

1) that interdisciplinary learning is important and valued because it facilitates transfer for future applications and to a wide array of settings;
2) that learning takes at least three forms, knowledge, attitudes, and behaviors, they interact, and that each should be assessed to measure the impact of learning;
3) the whole is greater than the sum of the parts, and these parts come from the interdisciplinary nature of real world environments; and
4) effective assessments may employ both qualitative and quantitative methodology to best measure both the breadth and depth of learning and performance outcomes.

TABLE 2.1 Educational assessments that can be used as part of a knowledge, attitudes, and behaviors assessment approach for interdisciplinary learning environments

A sample of assessment techniques

Assessment	Format characteristics
Multiple choice items	One or more correct responses
Short answer	One or two words or short sentences
Worked problems	Details provided on how answer was derived
Essay	Holistic Rubrics
Performance-based	Simulations Laboratory experiments 2-way, or multi-point communications Projects
Observations	Observations during learning or performance. May be scored as observed or recorded (e.g., video) for later scoring and analyses
Interviews	Individuals Focus groups
Journaling	Self reflection about learning and performance, including analyses
Rating scales	Of learning activities Of outcome performance Of process May be self-report or by trained observers
Response scales	No correct response, but only one response per item (i.e., Likert scale—Strongly Disagree to Strongly Agree)
Concept maps	Representations of knowledge and understanding

The KAB framework is a theoretically grounded and empirically tested means for accomplishing this. However, the KAB framework is an approach, not a prescription. Within the KAB framework there is a wide variety of proven ways to measuring each dimension. As illustrated in Table 2.1, the options are diverse, but the selection of the options should be based on a direct link between the curricular goals and standards, the instructional interventions, and the intended outcomes. We should not be teaching to the test: We should be teaching to promote learning! How we choose to measure that learning will have a major impact on what we teach and how we teach, and how our students learn. So we must choose wisely. We must continue to assess our own assumptions about learning and assessments, and we must continue to move the fields of learning, instruction, and assessment forward with evidence and conceptual frameworks within which to interpret that evidence, so we can both teach effectively and assess wisely.

Author's Note

The author is very grateful to Kimberly Lawless for comments and suggestions on drafts of this chapter.

Bibliography

Ajzen, I. (1993). Attitude theory and the attitude-behavior relation. In D. Krebs & P. Schmidt (eds.), New directions in attitude measurement (pp. 41–57). New York: Walter de Gruyter.

Alexander, P.A. (1992). Domain knowledge: Evolving themes and emerging concerns. Educational Psychologist, 27 (1), 33–51.

Alexander, P.A. (2003). The development of expertise: The journey from acclimation to proficiency. Educational Researcher, 32 (8), 10–14.

Alexander, P.A., Jetton, T.L., & Kulikowich, J.M. (1995). Interrelationship of knowledge, interest, and recall: Assessing a model of domain learning. Journal of Educational Psychology, 87, 559–75.

American Psychological Association (2004). Public affairs: Appropriate use of high-stakes testing in our nation's schools. Retrieved March 24, 2005 from the American Psychological Association web site at: www.apa.org/pubinfo/testing.html.

Anastasi, A. (1988). Psychological testing (6th edition). New York: Macmillan.

Archambault, F.X., Kulikowich, J.M., Brown, S.W., & Rezendes, G. (2002, April). Developing performance assessments to measure teacher competency in the use of educational technology. Paper presented at the AERA conference, New Orleans, LA, April 2, 2002.

Airasian, P.W. (2001). Classroom assessment: Concepts and applications (4th edition). Boston, MA: McGraw-Hill.

Baird, K.E. & Brown, S.W. (1993a). What you should know about Lyme disease: Activity book. Storrs, CT: University of Connecticut.

Baird, K.E. & Brown, S.W. (1993b). What you should know about Lyme disease: Teachers Guide. Storrs, CT: University of Connecticut.

Bandura, A. (1997). Self-efficacy: The exercise of control. New York: W.H. Freeman & Company.

Beavers, I., Kelley, M., & Flenner, J. (1982). Nutrition knowledge, attitudes and food purchasing practices of parents. Home Economics Research Journal, 11 (2), 134–42.

Bereiter, C. & Scardamalia, M. (2000). Commentary on part I: Process and product in problem-based leaning (PBL) research. In Evensen, D.H. and Hmelo, C.E. (eds.), Problem-based learning (pp. 185–95). Mahwah, NJ: Lawrence Erlbaum Associates.

Bloom, B.S. (1976). Human characteristics and school learning. New York: McGraw Hill.

Bloom, B.S., Englehart, M.D., Frost, E.J., Hill, W.H. & Krathwol, D.R. (1956). Taxonomy of educational objectives. Handbook I: Cognitive domain. New York: David McKay.

Boyer, M.A., Brown, S.W., Butler, M., Florea, N., Hernandez, M. *et al.* (2004). Educating for global awareness: Implications for governance and generational change. *Global Change, Peace & Security, 16* (1).

Boyer, M.A., Florea, N., Butler, M., Brown, S.W., Meng, L. *et al.* (2005). Understanding security through the eyes of the young. In *The IPE Yearbook*, Lynne Reinner Press.

Boyer, M.A., Hudson, N., Niv-Solomon, A., Urlacher, B., Janik, L. *et al.* (2006). Gender, power, and negotiation: Some findings on the role of gender in conflict resolution. Paper presented at the annual meetings of the International Studies Association, San Diego, CA, March 2006.

Brown, S.W. (1993). *Tick invaders* (instructional video on Lyme disease for elementary school students). Atlanta, GA: U.S. Centers for Disease Control and Prevention.

Brown, S.W. (1995). *The curse of the blood suckers* (instructional video on Lyme disease for high school students). Atlanta, GA: U.S. Centers for Disease Control and Prevention.

Brown, S.W. (1996). The teacher education movement in the United States and the IBM program at the University of Connecticut. In S.W. Brown (ed.), *Trends and issues in education: Preparing for the next century* (pp. 1–24). Taipai, Taiwan: Tarnkang University Press.

Brown, S.W. & King, F.B. (2000). Constructivist pedagogy and how we learn: Educational psychology meets international studies. *International Studies Perspective, 1*, 245–54.

Brown, S.W., Cartter, M.L., Hadler, J.L., & Hooper, P.F. (1992). Lyme disease knowledge, attitudes, and behaviors, Connecticut, 1992. *Morbidity and Mortality Weekly Report*, July 17, *41* (28) 505–7.

Brown, S.W., Babb, I., Johnson, P.R., Scheifle, P.M., Lang, H. *et al.* (2002). Classroom of the sea: Problem-based learning for the deaf. Proceedings of the International Conference on Computers in Education, Auckland, New Zealand: IEEE Press.

Brown, S.W, Boyer, M.A., Johnson, P.R., Lima, C.O., Butler, M.J. *et al.* (2004). The GlobalEd project: Problem-solving and decision making in a web-based PBL. *Proceedings of Ed-Media 2004, the World Conference on Educational Multimedia, Hypermedia & Telecommunications*, pp. 1967–73, June 2004, Lugano, Switzerland. Available at: www.aace.org.

Brown, S.W., Boyer, M.A., Mayall, H.J., Johnson, P.R., Meng, L. *et al.* (2003). The GlobalEd project: Gender differences in a problem-based learning environment of international negotiations. *Instructional Science, 31* (4–5) 255–76.

Byrd-Bedbenner, C., O'Connell, L.H., & Shannon, B. (1982). Junior high home economics curriculum: Its effect on students' knowledge, attitude and behavior. *Home Economics Research Journal, 11* (2), 124–33.

Connecticut Teacher Technology Competencies 2001 (2001). Retrieved March 26, 2005. www.state.ct.us/sde/dtl/technology/CTTCt.pdf.

Curtis, M.E. & Glaser, R. (1983). Reading theory and the assessment of reading achievement. *Journal of Educational Measurement, 20*, 133–47.

DuBois, K. & Brown, S.W. (1996). *Biology curriculum enhancement project: Relevant Lyme disease issues (Teacher's guide)*. Published by the U.S. Centers for Disease Control and Prevention.

Gagne, R.M. (1965). *The conditions of learning*. New York: Holt, Rinehart & Winston.

Gould, S.J. (1996). *The mismeasure of man*. New York: Norton.

Greening, T. (1998). Building the constructivist toolbox: An exploration of cognitive technologies. *Educational Technology, 38* (2), 23–35.

Gronlund, N.E. (1995). *How to write and use instructional objectives* (5th edition). Upper Saddle River, NJ: Merrill/Prentice Hall.

Harnar, M., Brown, S.W. & Mayall, H.J. (2000). Measuring the effect of distance education on the learning experience: Teaching accounting via PictureTel©. *International Journal of Instructional Media, 27* (1) 37–50.

Herrnstein, R.J. & Murray, C. (1994). *The bell curve: Intelligence and class structure in American life*. New York: The Free Press.

Holcomb, L.B. (2005). Examining the impact of an educational technology assessment on pre- and in-service educators' attitudes and behaviors towards educational technology. Doctoral dissertation. University of Connecticut: Storrs, CT.

Holcomb, L.B., Brown, S.W., & Kulikowich, J.M. (2003a). Raising educational technology self-efficacy through assessment based on problem based learning. Paper presented at the NERA conference, Kerhonkson, NY. October 23, 2003.

Holcomb, L.B., Brown, S.W., Kulikowich, J.M., & Zheng, D. (2003b). Raising educational technology self-efficacy through assessment. Poster presented at the APS conference, Atlanta, GA, May 30, 2003.

Holcomb, L.B., Brown, S.W., Kulikowich, J.M., & Jordan, J.H. (2004). Assessing educational technology knowledge with a problem-based learning format: The Husky Educational Technology Assessment Project (HETAP). *Proceedings of Ed-Media 2004, the World Conference on Educational Multimedia, Hypermedia & Telecommunications* (pp. 2008–13), June 2004, Lugano Switzerland. www.aace.org

International Society for Technology in Education (ISTE). (2000). National Educational Technology Standards (NETS) for teachers. Retrieved March 12, 2005. Available at: http://cnets.iste.org/index3.html.

Lang, H.G. (1994). *Silence of the spheres: The deaf experience in the history of science.* Westport, CT: Bergin & Garvey.

Lawless, K.A. & Brown, S.W. (1994). *What should I know about Lyme Disease—teacher's guide: High school edition.* Washington, DC: U.S. Centers for Disease Control and Prevention.

Lawless, K.A. & Brown, S.W. (1997). Multimedia learning environments: Issues of learner control and navigation. *Instructional Science: Special Issue on Multimedia and Interactivity, 25* (2), 117–131.

Lawless, K.A., Brown, S.W., & Cartter, M.A. (1997). Applying educational psychology and instructional technology to health care issues: Combating Lyme disease. *International Journal of Instructional Media, 24* (4) 1–10.

Lawless, K.A., Brown, S.W., Mills, R.J., & Mayall, H.J. (2003). Knowledge, interest, recall and navigation: A look at hypertext processing. *Journal of Literacy Research, 25* (3) 911–34.

Linn, R. (1986). Educational testing and assessment: Research and policy issues. *American Psychologist, 41* (10), 1153–60.

Mager, R.F. (1984). *Preparing instructional objectives* (2nd edition). Belmont, CA: David S. Lake.

Marschark, M., Lang, H.G., & Albertini, J.A. (2002). *Educating deaf students: From research to practice.* New York: Oxford University Press.

Moursund, D. & Bielefeldt, T. (1999). *Will new teachers be prepared to teach in a digital age? A national survey on information technology in teacher education.* Eugene, OR: International Society for Technology in Education.

National Council for Accreditation of Teacher Education: Professional Standards (2002). Retrieved April 3, 2005. Available at: www.ncate.org/documents/unit_stnds_2002.pdf.

No Child Left Behind Act of 2001, Pub. L. No. 107–10, 115 Stat 1425 (2002). Retrieved March 15, 2005. Available at: www.ed.gov/offices/OESE/ecsa/.

Pellegrino, J.W., Chudowsky, N., & Glaser, R. (eds.) (2001). *Knowing what students know: The science and design of educational assessment.* Washington, DC: Board on Testing and Assessment, National Research Council, National Academy Press.

Popham, W.J. (2000). *Modern educational measurement. Practical guidelines for educational leaders.* Boston: Allyn & Bacon.

Scarr, S. (1981). Testing for children: Assessment and the many determinants of intellectual competence. *American Psychologist, 36,* 1159–66.

Schrader, P.G. & Lawless, K.A. (2004). The knowledge, attitudes & behaviors approach: How to evaluate performance and learning in complex environments. *Performance Improvement, 43* (9) 8–15.

Silver, B.A., Brown, S.W., & Lawless, K.A. (1998). Diagnosis—Lyme Disease: What does it mean for our children? *Connecticut Association for Supervision and Curriculum Development Journal,* 1998, 56–61.

Wiggins, G.P. (1993). *Assessing student performance: Exploring the purpose and limits of testing.* San Francisco, CA: Jossey-Bass.

CHAPTER 3

Assessment as Process

Transdisciplinary Self Evaluation from a Writer's Point of View

DOUGLAS KAUFMAN

The Disciplines as Verbs: Reading the World Multidimensionally

The power and purpose of an integrated curriculum lies in abandoning a traditional focus on discrete bits of subject matter that could just as easily be learned if the disciplines were not tied together in an artificial unit (Kaufman, 2003a). Previously, I have cited Meeth's conception of *transdisciplinarity* to define my own vision of an appropriately integrated curriculum:

> The highest level of integrated study is *transdisciplinary*, which is not of the disciplines at all. Transdisciplinary means beyond the disciplines. Whereas interdisciplinary programs start with the discipline, transdisciplinary programs start with the issue or problem and, through the process of problem solving, bring to bear the knowledge of those disciplines that contributes to a solution or resolution.
>
> (Meeth, 1978, p. 10)

In a successful transdisciplinary environment, the learner treats each of the various disciplines not simply as a place where specific subject matter is situated and organized in order to be learned, but as a way of reading the world from a unique perspective. When these different vantages conjoin in an exploration of any phenomenon, we begin to understand the phenomenon's rich complexity. Further, the subject matter at the center of a traditional curriculum is actually better learned when the discipline is treated as a way of seeing because the subject matter becomes a dynamic, authentic tool rather than decontextualized fodder to be memorized for regurgitation on a simple test. For instance, if someone wants to learn about insects in a transdisciplinary fashion, he or she may actually use—perhaps for the first time—the tools of the entomologist to examine the insect's physical construction, biological makeup, and scientific classification in the same ways a professional does. However, depending on the questions to be answered, the learner might also examine the insect from a historical perspective, searching for how the insect has been defined, viewed, and treated in the past; from an artistic perspective, perhaps drawing or painting it to get a deeper conception of its form; and maybe even from a *dancer's* perspective, closely examining its movements with a completely new eye in order to adequately translate them into a physical human composition. Each disciplinary eye reveals new features about the insect that would have otherwise never been recognized.

In essence, by initially defining the educative power of the discipline not by the specific subject matter situated within it, but by the way of reading the world to which it gives rise, the discipline becomes a verb—an *act of learning*. In this chapter, I draw on concepts developed within my own disciplines of writing and writing instruction to place assessment—and self-assessment, in particular—at the center of this act of learning. Many writing educators and theorists have adopted the term "process approach" to describe writing as a learning act. In their discussions of process, they identify assessment in much the way I argue transdisciplinary teachers must identify it: they refute the myth of assessment as the mere documentation of students' discrete subject matter retention and position it instead as an inevitable component of the ongoing creation of knowledge. When learning changes its identity from a product to an active process, the role of assessment becomes clear. Learners must now reflect on their prior knowledge and current work to set new goals and plans and to revise continually the direction that their inquiry takes.

A Very Brief Primer of Process Writing

Looking at writing as an act of learning is a relatively new endeavor in education. Until the early 1970s both the classroom teacher and the educational researcher focused primarily on the resulting product of composition

(Junger & Fleischmann, 2004; Perl, 1994; Tobin, 1994). Writing was examined for its form, its adherence to particular—and often arbitrary—rules of convention, and its imitation of themes defined by the teacher's expectations.

In 1971, however, Janet Emig published her landmark study, "The Composing Processes of Twelfth Graders," perhaps the first research to examine systematically the often convoluted and longitudinal act of composition-in-process. This work was followed by several published studies by Donald Graves and his colleagues, who looked at the processes of younger writers (Calkins, 1983; Graves, 1975, 1978, 1983).

The work of these researchers revealed that, when allowed to compose for themselves, students often adopt practices that are in many ways similar to those of experienced writers. They pre-write, playing with ideas and words before formal composition. They compose drafts to shape ideas. They discuss their ideas with others and receive feedback. They revise their drafts, often extensively. They edit to improve mechanical aspects of the text. They publish their work in a variety of venues. This research indicates that any writing act is not formulaic at all, but is situational: writers act in different ways based on a number of factors including the author's intention, assignment requirements, genre, background knowledge, time available to write, awareness of audience, etc. In essence, composition moves far beyond the simple documentation of previously wholly formed thoughts and is recognized as a complex act of learning in and of itself, in which the writer struggles to make and shape meaning during the entire writing process.

As the writer writes, she certainly creates a product, but because she regards writing as an extensive, experimental act of learning the benefits are two-fold: she not only learns about her subject as she experiments to create the product, she also learns how to write better in the long term because she writes more, and thinks more about her craft, in the ways that experienced writers do.

This conception has a profound effect on assessment. First, assessment must now recognize the act of learning as well as the resultant product. Second, the brunt of assessment now becomes the responsibility of the learner, who is the one *engaging* in the process. Although the teacher still has a clear role in evaluating students across a wide continuum of variables, self-assessment becomes a fundamental aspect of the learning process. In fact, we can no longer view assessment as a discrete entity: the acts of observing and reflection inherent in assessment during the process of creation blur the boundaries to such an extent that one can easily argue that assessment is, in fact, the learning process itself.

Creating a Continuous Cycle of Evaluation for the Transdisciplinary Curriculum

The philosophical underpinnings of this approach to writing translate directly to the larger construct of the transdisciplinary curriculum. We can extend the concept to regard *each* discipline as an act of learning—and each act of learning as an act of assessment—not simply as a repository for an end product. By using the crafts and tools of science, history, mathematics, dramatic or visual arts, and other disciplines in authentic situations to explore problems with the goal of solving them, the student learns the subject matter that reveals answers but also learns the nature of each discipline—its way of reading problems, its unique tools, its defining processes—in ways that strengthens his ability to understand and use the discipline in real world situations for a lifetime. In a previous publication (Kaufman, 2003a), I summed up the practical implications for this conception with a number of maxims to guide the creation of a transdisciplinary unit or curriculum:

1) Questions for study must be relevant to the learner. This relevance implies that the learner has some prior knowledge or experience with the subject encompassing the question, which provides a starting foundation for constructive learning. It also promotes motivation for exploration.

2) Because the focus of a transdisciplinary project is on discovering answers to questions about a particular theme or problem, these questions must be formed *before* specific subject matter is isolated for study. The initial focus is not on the subject matter, but on the questions to be addressed. Learning of subject matter comes from using the disciplines authentically, as lenses through which we examines the theme or problem.

3) Because each question requires a different approach to its solution, the learner will not necessarily utilize every discipline in any given unit of study. Only the disciplines that provide insight into the problems and questions at hand are included. This means that a transdisciplinary study is not always *interdisciplinary*: if only *one* discipline can conceivably help to answer the questions at hand, only one discipline will be used.

4) Reading the world through different disciplines clearly takes time to do right: transdisciplinary units are longer than the typical interdisciplinary unit. As writers know, time is an essential ingredient for deep examination, reflection, craftwork, and learning.

(Kaufman, 2003a, pp. 109–111)

Reflective assessment is prevalent in every aspect of transdisciplinary studies, so much so that we can chart assessment as a continual cycle that spirals through—and helps define—all learning activities. This cycle includes components of analyzing personal strengths and weaknesses; identifying questions to be studied; identifying a personal knowledge base that can serve as the foundation for examining the questions; figuring out an appropriate approach for addressing the questions; creating specific goals; creating specific plans to meet those goals; monitoring progress while in the act of learning; evaluating what you have learned; revising goals, plans, and actions according to what you have learned; evaluating how you learned what you have learned; and—as the cycle repeats—addressing new questions that have arisen out of the answers to the initial questions (Hansen, 1996, 1998, 2001; Kaufman, 2003a; Ogle, 1986).

In order to see how the continuous cycle of transdisciplinary assessment manifests itself in a learning event, let us create an exemplifying unit. First, I will outline some basic guiding steps that help to shape the creation of a transdisciplinary unit, as I have previously described them (Kaufman, 2003a):

- To begin, a student must have at least a burgeoning understanding of disciplines as lenses. They must know that members of different disciplines read the world differently. They need to reflect on how a writer sees the world; how a historian does; how a scientist, visual artist, mathematician, philosopher do. They must learn the unique features that help define each craft or discipline (a different matter than studying the subject matter within the discipline). They must assess the nature of each discipline in order to use it well.

- Next, a student needs to help develop a theme for study, which provides a focus for all subsequent investigation. To do so, they need to assess and articulate their interests and their knowledge. From this theme comes guiding questions that arise out of what a student genuinely wants to learn about a theme or problem. Importantly, in order to develop fruitful questions and eliminate superficial ones, students need to evaluate what they already know (or think they know) about the theme, then develop questions according to what they want to learn. This preliminary assessment activity is one of the marks of assessment as process: it begins at the beginning— students evaluate what they know, then figure out what they want to learn.

- Once participants formulate questions, they must then determine the best approach to answering them. To do so, participants must use their understanding of the different ways of seeing that each discipline affords. In essence, the students and teacher must assess which content areas will yield relevant answers to the questions posed. Not every content area will be relevant, and intensive assessment must determine which ones will and which ones won't.

- Once these components are in place, participants can now begin to develop specific curriculum activities that employ the unique tools and ways of seeing provided by each discipline. Once again, assessment is an integral part of this selection process as participants tap into prior knowledge and conceptions to create the most relevant learning situations.

In light of this basic framework, and the assessment that is obviously inherent to it, what follows is a description and discussion of several assessment processes and protocols one might use during the creation and implementation of a transdisciplinary unit.

Modes of Assessment in the Transdisciplinary Assessment Cycle

- Assess an area of interest.
- Analyze what you already know (or think you know) about it.
- Determine what more you want to know.
- Create guiding questions that arise out of this want.
- Determine which subject area, or areas, will help you answer the questions.
- Create specific goals and plans for answering the questions.
- Work toward answering the questions using your goals and plans.
- Consistently monitor and assess your progress toward meeting your goals—reevaluate and revise plans, as needed. This happens throughout the whole unit.
- Once a unit of study has been completed, formally evaluate work, expanding it beyond the traditional focus on the completed product. This evaluation focuses on at least three components:
  - The completed product that is traditionally evaluated, be it a project, a presentation, an examination, or something else. This product should be evaluated for both its power to document the learner's understanding and its power to teach others about the topic.
  - The quality of the process of creation. This, I suggest, is the most important element that is missing from almost every traditional mode of evaluation seen in schools. While it is very easy to create a rubric to assess the discrete physical product resulting at the end of a project, we ignore the messier, more complex work that

leads to the product. However, here we create a formal system to examine the actions we took to create the product.

— What was learned about the disciplines as ways of reading the world, ways of organizing and clarifying the matter of the world, and ways of defining the learner as an individual.

I devote the rest of this chapter to offering a template for creating a continual process of evaluation throughout the entire learning cycle. To do this, I take and adapt evaluation tools and concepts I have used in my own field of writing and literacy instruction. For the purposes of a clear example, I will adopt a transdisciplinary theme of study about Santa Fe, New Mexico. I'm using this theme because it is a personal topic of interest: Santa Fe is my hometown, but I have not lived there for several years and I find myself wanting to learn much more about many of the things I took for granted when I lived there. However, for our purposes, let's assume that a group of students and their teacher discover a common interest in the topic: in this case, a student has told classmates about a trip he took to Santa Fe for Las Fiestas, an annual celebration that has taken place since 1712. While he was there, the student saw Zozobra, or "Old Man Gloom," a 40-foot tall puppet that is burned at the beginning of Las Fiestas to symbolize the casting off of the year's accumulated cares and woes.

The conversation in the classroom quickly expands: a couple of other students have been to Santa Fe and begin to talk about what they saw. The teacher, listening in, recognizes a connection between this conversation and this term's curricular emphasis on exploration in the American West. She convenes a meeting of the entire class to suggest a transdisciplinary unit on Santa Fe and the Southwest. The students discuss the merits of this proposal and decide that this would be a worthy topic to explore.

The discussion that gave rise to this discovery is the unit's first element of assessment and it leads off the assessment cycle. What follows next is assessment that helps to define the concepts and subject matter to be studied.

K-W-H-L: A Classic Mode of Evaluation Adapted for the Transdisciplinary Curriculum

In 1986, Donna Ogle outlined a model for teaching and learning how to read expository texts. She called the model K-W-L because it asked the reader to engage in a three-step process of evaluation: (1) charting what the reader *knows* about the text topic at hand in order to activate prior knowledge, (2) formulating questions about what the reader *wants* to learn in order to organize subsequent study, and (3) documenting what the reader has *learned* after the reading has been concluded. Educators from other

TABLE 3.1 A chart that students would use to document their use of the KWHL steps

What do we know?	What do we want to learn?	How are we going to learn it?	What have we learned?

disciplines quickly recognized the more universal applications of this model as a general learning tool, and adopted and adapted it to organize and direct students' learning activities and reflections. In subsequent years, the basic model has been adapted in various ways to meet the particular needs of educators and learners. One of the common adaptations has been an extension of the model to K-W-H-L, with the H representing a further category: *how* are we going to learn what we want to learn? For the purposes of this discussion, this model is most applicable. A general chart that students would use to document their address of these steps appears in Table 3.1.

Assessing What the Learner Knows

This very simple model is immediately relevant to the transdisciplinary assessment cycle. To begin, the students, having already determined their theme of study, work together to document all they know, or think they know, about Santa Fe. (As the unit progresses, students will assess these "facts" about Santa Fe, revising their understandings as well as adding to it.) The assessment and documentation of prior knowledge creates a contextualizing landscape within which learners can place new concepts and information as they study their theme. Students begin to record their current conceptualizations: Santa Fe is in the Southwest. The Santa Fe Trail led to there. It's hot. Lots of shootouts happened there. I think Billy the Kid lived there . . .

Assessing What the Learner Wants to Learn

Next, students begin to create and organize a set of questions for study. The students do this *before* they determine which disciplines or subject areas they will incorporate into the unit. One can envision students coming up with an extensive list, which may look similar in theme to many other units of study:

- Where is Santa Fe?
- How would someone who has lived there his or her whole life define it?

- What is its population?
- What is its climate like?
- What is the geology like?
- What kinds of plants and animals live there?
- Who lives there? Are they different than people who live in other parts of the U.S.?
- How did it come to be?
- What influences shaped it?
- Is it famous for anything? Infamous? What famous people come from there?
- In what ways has it shaped the history of the United States?
- What are the problems that the city faces?

The list can continue indefinitely, and it will be important eventually to revise, consolidate, and eliminate some questions for the sake of focus and time constraints. At the same time, several questions might contain sub-questions. A question like, "Is it famous or infamous for anything?" might reveal several sub-questions about famous literature, technological innovations, cultures, art, weather, etc.

Assessing How the Learner will Learn

In this phase, learners relate the questions at hand to their knowledge about the respective disciplines and the viewpoints they can bring to the exploration. Looking at the above questions, we might reasonably expect that the learners would assess the relative merits of each of the potential disciplines and decide that the disciplines of geography, history, English (including biography, literature, and historical texts), science (including geology, climatology, and botany), and the social sciences (including political science and sociology) are applicable.

However, because of the transdisciplinary focus on process as well as product, this phase also requires examination of another aspect of the learning cycle: knowledge about the disciplines to be used. Within the "H" column here, another "K" appears: "What do I know about each of the disciplinary lenses I may use to examine the theme and its components?" Students and teacher discuss the nature of the disciplines as tools and weigh them against the theme's questions. This allows the teacher to monitor students' potential to actually use the disciplines. If assessment reveals important gaps in their understanding or experience, the class must spend time investigating key aspects of the disciplines that will help them address their mission. The equation becomes more complex and infinitely more interesting.

Goal-setting and Plan-making as Assessment

Another reflective, organizational activity that leads to a clear conception of *how* the learner will learn is goal-setting and plan-making, which deserves its own section. Goal-setting is an integral component of the assessment cycle—one that asks the learner to project into the future. This requires a deep analysis of what that future might look like and how the learner will get there. I conceive of goal-setting as:

> . . . a conscious projection of future accomplishments . . . a space on a spiraling continuum of reflection where a learner charts a new course of purposeful activity or changes a current course. Goal-setting draws on learners' previous knowledge, their understanding of personal talents and limitations, and their ability to conceive of a course of action that leads to new knowledge, ability, and growth.
>
> (Kaufman, 2003b, pp. 17–18)

Hansen (1998) has proposed that all good evaluators ask themselves at least five questions: (1) What do I do well? (2) What is the most recent thing I've learned to do? (3) What do I want to learn next in order to grow? (4) What will I do to accomplish this? and (5) What might I use for documentation? (p. 39) Embedded in questions 3 and 4 is the component of goal-setting.

I have frequently worked with classroom students on goal-setting, and together we have created numerous models to organize goals and plans so that we can more easily recognize them, monitor them, and revise them as the learning process commences. Table 3.2 shows a possible "Goal

TABLE 3.2 A goal organizer adapted from an elementary school classroom

GOALS OR QUESTIONS

PLAN	DISCIPLINES USED

DOCUMENTATION OF ACHIEVEMENT

WHERE DO I GO FROM HERE? (New goals and questions arising from discoveries)

Organizer" for an integrated unit, which I have adapted from one created in an elementary school classroom where I worked (Kaufman, 2003b).

In trying to answer the question "How will I learn it?" students use this organizer to shape the activities that lead to the attainment of their larger intentions, and it serves as a map for all subsequent activity. The learners draw off of the questions they have posed to create encompassing goals or, if appropriate, simply use the questions themselves as starting points. After writing one goal or question at the top of the chart, participants discuss a procedural plan to achieve the goal or find answers to the questions. As they create the plan, they assess which disciplinary lenses will help them attain their goal. Documenting these goals, plans, and lenses in a physical, graphic form allows learners to examine them more efficiently and with clearer eyes, to evaluate any strengths and difficulties in the questions and plans, and to revise accordingly (in much the way a writer works when she examines a draft on a page).

In our own unit on Santa Fe, some of the questions may be answered easily or may be perused in more depth, depending on how participants interpret them. Answering a seemingly simple question like "Where is Santa Fe?" might involve a brief plan to use the geographer's tools of maps, atlases or current satellite technology involving GPS to determine its specific latitude and longitude and identify its placement in relation to other points of interest. However, learners might also extend the concept to determine the significance of its location: why it is where it is. Suddenly, topographic maps might prove significant. Students may want to examine current and historical watersheds, indigenous crops as influenced by location, the extended geographical properties that make the town accessible, and its relationship to other towns and outposts that made communication and trade possible. Throughout, students continue to shape their plan of action and clarify the disciplinary lenses, procedures, and tools that will lead to the most significant answers. This once simple question now may need to utilize the disciplines of geography, satellite technology, agricultural science, limnology, and many others.

Often, even the simplest question might take a much richer and more complex shape during this process, and several of the questions might either begin to blend together or take the form of sub-questions that reside under a larger question or theme. Concurrently, participants usually recognize the vast scope of their lists and begin to narrow their primary questions to ensure investigative depth rather than shallow breadth. In the case of our unit, the students may discover enough meat to chew on in a question like the one above or choose to focus on a few more obviously rich questions, such as "Who lives there? Are they different than people who live in other parts of the U.S.?" or "In what ways has it shaped the history of the United States?"

These determinations are one of the reasons that this element of the assessment cycle is valuable: it helps the learners to shape and revise their original list of questions in order to narrow their focus, clarify their relevance, and eliminate redundancy.

In this framework, students must draw on their prior knowledge to analyze goals and map out plans to find the answers to their personally relevant questions. They, not the teacher, have these primary responsibilities. For learners who have never been challenged in this way, these charges will initially prove difficult. However, it is, in fact, our responsibility to *create* difficulties where students actually engage in appropriate struggle. As we do, we scaffold students' learning, providing just enough help so that the struggle compels students forward rather than holds them back.

At this point, transdisciplinary learners have developed questions, developed goals and plans for answering those questions, and determined which disciplinary lenses will help them accomplish their goals. The products created from this assessment work serve as a map for all subsequent activity, guiding the general direction of learners. However, as we shall see, the specific direction is not set in stone, and the map is always open to revision as assessment continues and the learners make new discoveries.

Documenting and Assessing Learning

The last responsibility in a typical K-W-H-L assessment cycle is to document the attainment of answers and goals. As learners conduct their exploration, guided by their plans, they are required to provide explicit evidence of their learning. This requirement forces them to assess their learning continually, while they are in the midst of learning, conscientiously collecting evidence that can be used to support their position that they have met goals. This process is akin to the writer continually evaluating her words to identify the successful attainment of her intentions, then revising where intention has not been met or where new discoveries have been made.

Finally, assessment as an ongoing process ensures that new answers will always lead to new questions. As students learn more about their topic, theme, or problem, new questions multiply. Students document the questions that arise. In doing so, they create a potential starting point for further learning, perhaps through another curriculum unit, perhaps through independent study. Here, their work reveals the cyclical nature of learning as new questions inevitably arise out of the documentation of new discoveries.

Monitoring Learning

One of the many important products that continual self-evaluation elicits is the transdisciplinary learner's newfound understanding of the strengths and inadequacies of her learning process. As she examines both her questions and the way she seeks to answer those questions, she discovers false starts, and dead-end streets.

Commensurately, she continues to assesses the adequacy of her tools and approaches. Physically documenting her plans and approaches on her Goals Organizer helps her to answer fundamental questions: "What is working? What is not? What have I learned so far? What do I still need to learn? How can I revise my plans and actions to learn what I need to learn?" A sound transdisciplinary unit contains formal sessions where learners review their goals, plans, and approaches in order to revise them. Again, the activities of the transdisciplinary learner begin to mirror those of the writer who deeply examines his or her drafts to determine what is extraneous, what is missing, what is poorly worded, what is disorganized, what is redundant, and what leads the reader into peripheral or irrelevant territory. In the case of our Santa Fe unit, the group might discover that the tools they are using are inadequate and that they will require tools from different disciplines. They may discover that some of the approaches they are using (maybe maps *and* GPS) are redundant or a waste time. They may discover that the lens of a particular discipline leads them off track—allowing them to play with interesting tools and technology but really not helping them to answer the specific questions at hand. They may even discover that a particular question has become irrelevant—that they need to move on to other questions or create new ones. In all cases, formal evaluation leads to action that shapes the learning event and opens the learner up to clearer directions and new possibilities.

Product-Process Evaluations: Completing the Cycle and Beginning a New One

At the end of any integrated unit there are resulting products that document learning. They may be projects, demonstrations, or written reports, among other possibilities. In a traditional assessment process, this is the evidence that the teacher ultimately evaluates, uses to determine student success, and grades. In a transdisciplinary curriculum, however, the success of the learning process is equally important to the resultant product, and the assessment system must reflect this.

In the literacy courses I teach I often offer the story of two students. One, Kayla, was a brilliant writer who consistently produced excellent pieces in writer's workshop, almost always revolving around her obsession with horses. While the writing was magnificent, I rarely saw her challenge herself or push her writing in new directions. On the other hand, I also taught an extremely reluctant writer, A.J., who rarely wrote in class. However, he had recently been reading poetry by Shel Silverstein and other humorous poets and one day, to my surprise, he said he wanted to try to write a poem. As he struggled with his first piece he was forced to explore the conventions of poetry. He examined the work of his favorite poets, tried drafting some rhymes, grew frustrated, conferred with me, read some more, tried some free verse, and returned to rhyme.

In the end his final product was competent, but certainly nothing close to the natural brilliance I saw in Kayla's writing. However, when A.J. formally reflected on his work, he was able to document tremendous growth in his understanding of poetry. He discussed his new conceptions of poetic forms, his struggles to master them, and his realization of what he still needed to learn. He revealed a newfound enthusiasm for writing.

The question I ask my college students after telling this story is, "Who do I grade higher, Kayla or A.J.?" My answer is that they both received A's. A lower grade for A.J. would devalue the exact growth for which I had been hoping. If growth in learning and in the ability to translate that learning to an improved product is an academic goal, then we must grade that goal accordingly. At the same time, we cannot penalize a student for her facility in creating a good product without first clarifying expectations for further growth. In this case, if Kayla was stuck in a creative rut and had discontinued growing as a writer, it was my obligation to raise the bar and scaffold her work toward higher and more diverse goals. I valued the fine product through the final grade, but now needed to clarify new expectations. If this kind of work is done consistently, students understand and learn how to push themselves further independently.

Writers place great value on process: on the ability to work independently, on finding appropriate resources, on conferring with knowledgeable others, on crafting and revising products until they teach others as well as they teach themselves. So do students working in a transdisciplinary setting. They now need assessment tools that allow them to examine process as well as product. In my role as a teacher of writing, I use a form at the end of projects that allows both the writer and the teacher to examine the writer's work in a more multifaceted way. I adapted the form from one used by Linda Rief, a highly acclaimed middle school language arts teacher (Kaufman, 2000, 2001; Rief, 1992, 1999, 2007). It compels writers to examine their work from conception to final product in such a way that they can use their discoveries to influence subsequent writing. On the first page of the form the writer examines her process deeply and then documents it by answering a series of questions that ask about her process of creation, her problem solving, her collaboration with others, how she revised her work-in-process, what she learned through writing that will help her in the future, and what surprised her.

To adapt this form to the transdisciplinary unit is easy; the fundamental goals of each learning situation are the same: for learners to become more reflective, more independent, more well-informed craftspeople who can create products through which they can learn and teach more. Adaptation simply requires a reshaping of the questions to address the focused qualities and goals of the specific endeavor. For the purposes of our unit consider, some of these:

- What was your process of discovery? How, specifically, did you go about finding answers to your questions?
- How did you decide which disciplinary lens or lenses to use?
- How did you solve problems that arose during your inquiry?
- How did you work together with other members of your team (or with people whom you used as resources)? What roles did you find each of you playing? Why did you adopt those specific roles?
- How and why did you revise your inquiry approach as the unit went on?
- What did you learn by conducting this investigation that will help you investigate, teach, or learn in the future?
- In the specific, what did you learn about the nature of the discipline or disciplines that you used to find your answers?
- What surprised you?
- What else should we know about your inquiry and learning that we would not know by experiencing just the products that arose from it?

Each of these questions compels the learner to reflect consciously on his or her actions and the thinking behind it—the *craft* and the *process*. My writing students offer extensive narratives on these questions, which are often longer than their actual pieces. By doing so, they map for themselves a clearer understanding of their work as writers. So it is for the transdisciplinary learner.

The above list can be revised at the participants' discretion as long as the questions result in a deep reflection on the learner's part about the crafts of exploration and discovery. End-of-project assessment becomes an essential part of the learning process, not simply a judgment passed down after the fact, which has little relevance to future work. The transdisciplinary student learns and grows as much from reflection about process as she does from the original act of creation, itself.

The second page of the form looks like a simple rubric, as seen in Table 3.3.

Here, students reflect in a way that allows them to project into the future and to visualize potential goals for subsequent writing or activity. I require them, first, to examine their crafting process, about which they wrote on the first page, and to document for themselves two or three aspects of their process that they believe were successful. I want these documented very briefly, in bulleted form. They serve as a checklist of accomplishments to refer to during subsequent projects. These are the foundations of future learning.

The learners then documents two or three aspects of their processes that they would like to improve. For a writer, this may include taking more time to revise, conferring more with outside readers, taking risks by writing in discomfiting genres, etc. For the transdisciplinary learner, it may include improving another specific disciplinary skill. In all cases, the learners' answers serve as the beginning of new process goals that will enhance their craft in the future.

The assessment process is then repeated as the learners move away from craft in order to examine the product of their craft. This is the material that usually receives the sole attention of the teacher. Within this transdisciplinary construct, the learner also has a clear hand in the assessment. For students to reflect competently on their own work it often requires rigorous training on how craftspeople view their products in order to improve them. Many students feel uncomfortable doing this, and some initially write, "If I didn't think it was perfect, I wouldn't have handed it in to you!" Response to this requires careful work over time by the teacher, first, to prove to the

TABLE 3.3 A chart to be utilized to evaluate process and product

	Student comments	Student grade	Teacher grade	Teacher comments
P R O C E S S	What I did well/improved			
	What I need to work on			
P R O D U C T	What I did well/improved			
	What I need to work on			

learners that they won't be penalized for identifying weaknesses in their work and, second, to teach them that no learning endeavor has yet resulted in perfection. We teach, instead, that true education is defined by the learner's ability to improve continuously by mastering self-evaluation and using the resultant learning to act. The learners here attempt to identify two or three specific aspects of their products that work particularly well. This may be a section of vivid description, well organized information, an artifact that allows the audience to make easy meaning, etc. Again, the students carefully review their work and identify two or three aspects that they feel still need careful attention and improvement. This is a requirement: I expect that they will be able to find at least gentle dissatisfaction with some aspects of their work. I want the objects of this dissatisfaction to be explicit in their minds so that they can consciously address similar issues in future work.

The Teacher's Assessment

All this work is the responsibility of the learner, which is as it should be. Self-assessment—too often devalued in most educational models—is at the heart of the transdisciplinary learning process. However, the teacher also has a responsibility to evaluate in ways that help the learner move forward. In my writing course, I conduct the same evaluative process as the writer does, using their forms to document my comments. My own approach is systematic and designed to temper any prejudicial views I might hold. First, before I read any of their reflections about their process, I read the completed project and evaluate it, documenting the specific aspects of it that (1) struck me as particularly enlightening and (2) prevented me, as a learner, from making full meaning or gaining full satisfaction from it. This is the teacher's traditional role: assessing product; however, my stance as a *learner*, rather than academic judge, forces me to search for the writer's intentions within the product.

Next, I read their reflections about their process without looking at the second sheet that contains their evaluations. This offers me insight into both the learner's creation and thinking processes that extend beyond the observations I have been recording during classes. It also allows me to comment on what appears to be working well and make suggestions for improving processes. I then assign two grades: one for process and one for product.

It is only then that I view the second page and compare my evaluations and grades to the ones that they have given to themselves. If grades are roughly equal but they have graded themselves slightly higher, I calculate an average from the four grades and assign that as the final grade. If our grades are roughly equal, but mine are slightly higher, I will average out my two grades for a final grade. If our grades differ significantly (by close to a full letter or more), the learner and I sit down for a conference to discuss the discrepancy. I must provide the writer with explicit evidence supporting my grade, and she must do the same. If the learner doesn't have a rejoinder that addresses my concerns, the grade will remain closer to my grade. However, the learner often articulates clear evidence that compels me to raise the grade. And, more often than one might expect, I must convince a student that her grade should be much higher than she has offered herself. Again, I offer specific evidence as to *why* so that the learner can use the information for future reference. In all cases I try to create an arena where the writer must think carefully and craft a response that documents her learning and growth. That is paramount.

Conclusion

Transdisciplinary studies looks at the world through multiple perspectives, and its assessments must do the same things, evaluating both achievement and growth through a deep examination of both process and product in regard to the use of each disciplinary lens utilized. Reflecting on the richness of this conception, I think about the profound damage our current national assessment trends inflict on our schools. I have argued that the ubiquity of high-stakes standardized testing nationally stifles transdisciplinarity:

> The problem is this: in order to standardize a test for use with a large population, one must tightly narrow the boundaries of the knowledge, skills, abilities, and potentials being assessed. With millions of students being tested one can't consider the complete value of the student as a learner and doer. It would be too costly, labor intensive, and time consuming. In assessing writing, for example, one can't focus on more complicated matters like the multifaceted qualities of written expression that make it intriguing to a reader or the ability to craft a powerful argument over time (and time is the one of the most important conditions for the professional writer). Instead, we are forced to quantify the value of a single small product—produced in a very artificial situation—using a very narrow set of criteria.
>
> (Kaufman *et al.*, 2003, p. 161)

But the power of transdisciplinary studies lies in its diametric opposition to this simplistic assessment construct. The boundaries of transdisciplinary studies swell to encompass multitudinous perspectives, activities, and challenges, and the assessment that is integral to the mission—is, in fact, one of its defining features—must follow suit. The assessment must be as complex as the actions it examines or else we have no transdisciplinarity at all.

Evaluation is not a mere afterthought but resides at the center of the curriculum. It is the reflective aspect of the larger act, from which it is impossible to be extracted or separated. When done completely and well, it enhances content knowledge by putting it in its proper place among the larger acts of process—the continually spiraling acts of searching, thinking, and learning that define young students as independent agents who can assume powerful roles in a democratic society. Previously, I wrote:

> We want to be able to evaluate students—and have students be able to evaluate themselves—as to their abilities and their potential to find information and knowledge, make sense of it, use it in real-life situations, and create their own knowledge. We want them to see evaluation as an affirmation of *value* and to be able to create goals and plans to increase value. Evaluation becomes less an abstract judgment of product at a narrow point in time and more of a useful tool for educational and social growth.
>
> (Kaufman *et al.*, 2003, p. 162)

If the purpose for transdisciplinary studies is, as I argue, to engender a more holistic, useful concept of the world through a richer, more multifaceted exploration of it, then assessment is at the heart of the exploration—is, in fact, an exploration itself. The search for the answers to profound questions and our definition of assessment become, in effect, one and the same. The continual, cyclical process of assessment defines transdisciplinary studies.

Bibliography

Calkins, L.M. (1983). *Lessons from a child: On the teaching and learning of writing*. Portsmouth, NH: Heinemann.

Calkins, L.M. (1994). *The art of teaching writing* (2nd edition). Portsmouth, NH: Heinemann.

Emig, J. (1971). The composing processes of twelfth graders. Urbana, IL: National Council of Teachers of English

Graves, D.H. (1975). An examination of the writing processes of seven-year-old children. *Research in the Teaching of English, 9* (3), 227–41.

Graves, D.H. (1978). *Balance the basics: Let them write*. New York: Ford Foundation.

Graves, D.H. (1983). *Writing: teachers and children at work*. Portsmouth, NH: Heinemann.

Hansen, J. (1996). Evaluation: The center of writing instruction. *The Reading Teacher, 50* (3), 188–195.

Hansen, J. (1998). *When learners evaluate*. Portsmouth, NH: Heinemann.

Hansen, J. (2001). *When writers read* (2nd edition). Portsmouth, NH: Heinemann.

Junger, J. & Fleischman, S. (2004). Is process writing the "write stuff"? *Educational Leadership, 62* (2), 90–1.

Kaufman, D. (2000). *Conferences & conversations: Listening to the literate classroom*. Portsmouth, NH: Heinemann.

Kaufman, D. (2001). Organizing and managing the language arts workshop: A matter of motion. *Language Arts, 79* (2), 114–123.

Kaufman, D. (2003a). Reading the world and writing to learn: Lessons from writers about creating transdisciplinary inquiry. In D. Kaufman, D.M. Moss, & T.A. Osborn (eds.), *Beyond the boundaries: A transdisciplinary approach to learning and teaching* (pp. 97–115). Westport, CT: Praeger.

Kaufman, D. (2003b). Setting literacy goals: Shawna as president, Shawna as poet. *Thinking Classroom/Peremena, 4* (4), 17–24.

Kaufman, D., Osborn, T.A., & Moss, D.M. (2003). Where do we go when we step beyond the boundaries? In D. Kaufman, D.M. Moss, & T.A. Osborn (eds.), *Beyond the boundaries: A transdisciplinary approach to learning and teaching* (pp. 155–166). Westport, CT: Praeger.

Meeth, L.R. (1978). Interdisciplinary studies: A matter of definition. *Change, 10* (10), 6–9.

Ogle, D. (1986). K-W-L: A teaching model that develops active reading of expository text. *The Reading Teacher, 39,* 564–70.

Perl, S. (1994). Writing process: A shining moment. In S. Perl (ed.), *Landmark essays on writing process* (pp. xi–xx). Davis, CA: Hermagoras.

Rief, L. (1992). *Seeking diversity: Language arts with adolescents.* Portsmouth, NH: Heinemann.

Rief, L. (1999). *Vision and voice: Extending the literacy spectrum.* Portsmouth, NH: Heinemann.

Rief, L. (2007). *Inside the writer's-reader's notebook: A workshop essential.* Portsmouth, NH: Heinemann.

Tobin, L. (1994). Introduction: How the writing process was born—and other conversion narratives. In L. Tobin & T. Newkirk (eds.), *Taking stock: The writing process movement in the '90s.* Portsmouth, NH: Boynton/Cook.

CHAPTER 4

Beyond Trivial Science

Assessing Understandings of the Nature of Science

DAVID M. MOSS, JOHN SETTLAGE, and
CATHERINE KOEHLER

Content continues its reign of supremacy in science education. For nearly a century, science teaching has involved the conveyance, memorization, and recitation of an ever-expanding body of specialized knowledge. In classrooms, students parrot such phrases as "mitochondria are the powerhouse of the cell" while cramming to recall the formula for photosynthesis. Yet when one considers the many global challenges we face in an age of dwindling natural resources and rapidly advancing technologies, such learning seems trivial. At several intervals over the previous century, reform-minded efforts attempted to break the content barrier with a so called process-oriented approach to learning science. An unanticipated and adverse outcome of such efforts was the emergence of a false dichotomy between these two aims. That is, science often came to be taught in such a way that the process of engaging in scientific activities became an isolated curricular objective, distinct from the resulting knowledge.

When science is taught as absolute content versus process students are rarely afforded access to the very essence of the field itself. Science is a dynamic human construct, and there is no procedural scientific method which results unerringly in new knowledge. In a very real sense, science is more about questions than answers. Underpinned by empirical evidence, scientific knowledge evolves as we pursue more sophisticated questions. Indeed, when science is viewed as a culture with its own artifacts and customs, then teaching science ought to involve guiding students in becoming competent and willing participants in that culture (Aikenhead, 1996, 2000). The two-dimensional oscillation between content and process often neglects authentic science by failing to account for the crucial Nature of Science dimension.

A revitalized vision for science teaching and learning has taken hold in recent decades. The notion of *scientific literacy* is widely supported by scholars as the conceptual foundation upon which our current reform efforts should be built. Literacy in science is operationally defined as having an informed perspective on scientific issues facing society (e.g., cloning, stem cell research, and global warming) but perhaps more importantly characterized by a willingness to participate in the democratic social discourse underpinning such issues. Thus, content becomes the landscape upon which the notions of discovery, logical thinking, creativity, and ethical issues are explored. When science education is viewed through this lens, the Nature of Science becomes paramount to the learning and teaching of science. Science content is not necessarily marginalized; to the contrary, we are able to make strategic decisions about the importance or value of various science topics to be included in the curriculum. With scientific literacy as an educational goal we can sidestep the unreasonable desire to cover all content in favor of exploring the Nature of Science within the context of learning relevant and timely content. Regarding content in this way is our best prospect of achieving our aim of promoting a scientifically literate society.

Given the prevalence of accountability in educational environments, assessment serves as the driving force for making decisions. Everything from professional development to curriculum adoption to classroom activities is shaped by the authority of assessments. When policy dictates very narrow views of what counts as evidence of learning, then decisions are often made based upon budgetary considerations (e.g., assessing the greatest number of students with the least amount of expense) which is largely to the detriment of an accurate and comprehensive account of learning required for promoting scientific literacy. The challenge becomes how to accommodate both the desire for furthering scientific literacy while simultaneously responding to the urgent call for accountability measures.

Assessment throughout multiple domains, or interdisciplinary assessment, is offered as a means to bridge the gap between accurate and efficient accountability without an exclusive focus on content mastery. Advancing a more comprehensive approach to assessment in science, this chapter discusses the Nature of Science and scientific literacy, and offers an assessment framework that transcends content and process, and perhaps even the traditional boundaries of why we have historically taught science itself.

Pragmatically, we step away from the absurd notion that we can teach everything our students will ever need to know in science. The implication of such a stance forces us to address the normative issues underpinning the value or worth of which science content is taught. Time and time again, highly specialized content area professionals have lobbied hard for their content to be "in," making a case that their content is so critical to the present day curriculum. The result is inevitably a collection of curriculum goals in which science is reduced to a laundry list of disconnected nuggets of knowledge. Without a process by which we can make informed decisions regarding our science curriculum, coupled with a lack of an understanding that we cannot do it all, we are doomed to endure an overstuffed program of study for our children.

Since the disputes between competing factions, historically between content and process and more recently between scientific literacy and accountability measures, have generated more flash than substance, we offer a different approach. In an effort to describe how decision-makers could achieve a balance among competing forces, we propose two conceptual frameworks for sorting through all of the science curriculum options. In our view, these frameworks suspend the knee-jerk autonomous response of privileging one camp over the other. Instead, it is the novelty of this framework which we feel can contribute to a healthful consideration of what it is students should be expected to learn within science as well as how we might then go about assessing their understandings.

We propose utilizing the Nature of Science as a filter to limit and strengthen targeted science learning. Nature of Science represents the core or very essence of science itself and serves as our curricularhub—moving beyond individual content strands as represented by various specialties. This very notion of the Nature of Science transcends traditional curricular boundaries, and although that is an exciting prospect for breaking the content mold, it may be too broad a conceptual filter by which we realistically consider curriculum and assessment. To operationally define the facets of science which may best promote literacy in the field, we propose the two concepts of *Science for Democratic Participation* and *Science for Promoting Quality of Life* as an overarching framework for shaping science curriculum and assessment. At this point, we delve into the ideas of the Nature of Science in an effort to provide a conceptual foundation upon which we will later examine the possibilities offered by using democratic participation and quality of life as frameworks for organizing science education.

The Nature of Science

Perhaps not surprisingly, attempts to define the Nature of Science, the very essence of science itself, has been fraught with controversy. Even the phrase

Nature of Science contributes to the problem as it invokes both a multifaceted epistemology while at the same time implying there is one core set of principles describing all that science is and everything that scientists do (Lederman, 1992; Lederman & Zeidler, 1987). Pragmatically, researchers and educators who deal with Nature of Science issues have now begun to operationally define Nature of Science for research and curriculum purposes. This important step will break a decade's long cycle in which our discourse was bogged down in illuminating the finer points of the Nature of Science, with little recognition of the consensus which exists regarding the principal tenets.

In recent years, the science education community has come to agree that scientific practice does not necessarily involve seeking one right answer, but seeks to learn all we can. Some commonly agreed upon Nature of Science tenets which are consistent with a postmodern view are: (1) science fosters awareness of the physical world, (2) science describes order in the world by theories that are simple and comprehensive, (3) science is dynamic, (4) scientific knowledge is tentative, and that (5) there is no one scientific method.

Understanding and assessing ones' conceptions of the Nature of Science has been a long time goal of many science education researchers (Cooley & Klopfer, 1961; Cotham & Smith, 1981; Kimball, 1968; Meichtry, 1993; Rubba & Anderson, 1978). One of the most widely used assessment tools in Nature of Science research was developed in 1961 by Cooley and Klopfer (1961) at Harvard University, the Test on Understanding Science (*TOUS*). This bubble sheet, paper and pencil test was given to students, science teachers, and research scientists for the purpose of testing their general knowledge about the scientific enterprise, scientists, and the methods in which scientists conduct their research (Cooley & Klopfer, 1963a, 1963b). The *TOUS* contains sixty questions and where the examinees are asked to determine which one of the four multiple choice statements best answers the question at hand. This instrument elicits three subscales which construct an overall score, e.g. (1) understandings about the scientific enterprise, (2) the scientists, (3) methods and aims of science.

There has been much criticism of the *TOUS* instrument. Researchers have argued that content validity of the instrument is an issue. Some also suggest that many of the items reflect a negative viewpoint of science (Aikenhead, 1973). The *TOUS* questionnaire requires that the reader have a high reading ability and this may inhibit the comprehension of the questions for high school students. When the instrument was used with this population, it was concluded that high school students had inadequate understandings of the scientific enterprise and scientists (Aikenhead, 1973; Cooley & Klopfer, 1963a, 1963b; Lederman, 1992).

Another widely used instrument to determine ones' conceptions of scientific knowledge was developed by Kimball in 1968, the Nature of Science Scale (NOSS). This model measured eight assertions which Kimball hypothesized as important characteristics of science: (1) curiosity, (2) process-orientation, (3) comprehensiveness and simplicity, (4) no one scientific method, (5) the values of science, (6) human endeavor, (7) dynamic, and (8) tentativeness. The NOSS was a series of twenty-nine statements that used a Likert-type three-point scale. Respondents who agreed with the statements would score two points, those with a neutral response to the statements scored one point and those that disagreed with the statement scored a zero. Although not prescribed for use in uncovering students' conceptions of Nature of Science, it was used to determine philosophers', science teachers', and scientists' conceptions of Nature of Science.

Rubba (1977) developed the Nature of Scientific Knowledge Scale (NSKS) to measure secondary students' understanding. It is comprised of forty-eight statements using a five point Likert-type scale and was modeled after the nine factors of Nature of Science as prescribed by Sholwalter (Meichtry, 1993). Rubba and Anderson (1978) further consolidated the instrument to elicit six subscales of Nature of Science, e.g. (1) amoral, (2) creative, (3) developmental, (4) parsimonious, (5) testable, and (6) unified.

These instruments, the TOUS, NOSS and NSKS, have been used to assess pre-college students' conceptions of Nature of Science and are sensitive to multiple characteristics of Nature of Science constructs. Overwhelmingly, researchers who used these instruments have concluded that students hold inadequate conceptions of the tentativeness of scientific knowledge and Nature of Science (Cooley & Klopfer, 1963; Kimball, 1968; Rubba & Anderson, 1978). Do these research instruments adequately measure students' conceptions of Nature of Science? Are these collective results due to the inadequacy of measurement instruments or do students really possess inaccurate conceptions of the Nature of Science?

Criticism regarding the validity of these research instruments has been discussed in many science education research forums (Aikenhead, 1973, 1988). Some argued that there is an implicit researcher bias associated with the questions used in these paper and pencil instruments because it forces participants to select their answers from the choices posed to them (Lederman et al., 2002). Others argued that the statements and multiple choice answers reflect the philosophical position of the researcher (Ryan & Aikenhead, 1992). Aikenhead (1988) suggests that Likert-type responses yield the least accurate and most ambiguous results and advocates interviewing students to investigate the sources of their beliefs. Lederman and O'Malley (1990) concur with Aikenhead and advocate for the use of a follow-up interview to dissolve possible researcher misinterpretation of standardized paper and pencil instruments. Their research initiated the wave of qualitative investigations in the area of exploring Nature of Science understandings.

A significant attempt to bring a qualitative perspective to Nature of Science research, steering clear of the critiques of forced-choice assessment tools, was an instrument developed by Lederman and O'Malley (1990) called the Views of the Nature of Science (*VNOS-A*). To investigate students' conceptions of Nature of Science and the source of their beliefs, Lederman and O'Malley used a seven item, open-ended questionnaire followed by a post-questionnaire interview. Lederman and O'Malley claimed that:

> The implications for the use of paper and pencil tests to assess students' beliefs about science are clear. The responses given by students using this data collection format are vague and are often misinterpreted by researchers. The use of the interview to gather and clarify data about students' beliefs appears to be essential if one is to avoid the pitfalls of misinterpretation.
>
> (Lederman and O'Malley, 1990, p. 235)

The open-ended questions in the *VNOS-A* required participants to answer in a narrative format without forcing them to choose a response. To avoid misinterpreting participants' responses, a semi-structured interview was developed to try to unpack their deeper understanding of Nature of Science. Without the interviews, students' responses could be misinterpreted (Lederman *et al.*, 2002). Embellishing the positive assets of *VNOS-A* by adding questions to elicit the social and cultural context of science and the existence of a universal scientific method, the questionnaire evolved into a comprehensive instrument that targets multiple tenets of the Nature of Science. This newly evolved *VNOS-C* (Lederman *et al.*, 2002) attempts to assess certain non-controversial tenets of the Nature of Science as defined by Lederman *et al.* (2002), e.g. (1) science knowledge is tentative, (2) empirical, (3) theory-laden, (4) partly the purpose of human inference, (5) imagination, (6) creative, and (7) socially and culturally embedded as well as investigates students' conceptions about the distinction between observation and inference, the lack of one method for doing science, and relationship between laws and theories. Research has departed from a purely quantitative approach to assessing understandings (e.g., earlier standardized instruments such at *TOUS*, *NOSS* and *NSKS*) to more qualitative assessments. In these approaches, the researcher tries to disclose the participants' deeper understanding of the Nature of Science (Moss *et al.*, 2001).

Much of the past research has focused in the development of an instrument to assess students' and teachers' conceptions of Nature of Science. This line of research has seemed to run its course, and the next logical and compelling strand of research needs to focus on more pragmatic issues of Nature of Science instruction. In his 1992 article titled, "Students' and Teachers' Conceptions of the Nature of Science: A Review of the Research," Lederman describes four lines of research, distinct yet related, that has driven the Nature of Science research for the past decade. These lines of research include: (a) assessment of student conceptions of Nature of Science, (b) development, use, and curricula designed to "improve" students' conceptions of Nature of Science, (c) assessment of, and attempts to improve, teachers' conceptions of Nature of Science, and (d) identification of the relationship among teachers' conceptions, classroom practice, and students' conceptions of Nature of Science. How science instruction is actually conducted in the schools is of particular interest to most science educators. Along the line of research into the classroom practice of Nature of Science, a model for teaching the Nature of Science was developed by Koehler and Moss (2005) (Figure 4.1).

This model strives to dissolve the dichotomy inherent in science teaching, e.g. content versus process. It was designed to operationally define the Nature of Science and to demonstrate that to effectively facilitate Nature of Science instruction one must consider the relationship between inquiry, content, and process. When applying this model to facilitate curriculum reform, there are several assumptions that first need to be considered. First, teachers must have their own working definition of Nature of Science.

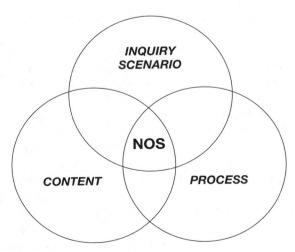

Figure 4.1 Model for teaching the Nature of Science

As prescribed in this model, Nature of Science includes the notions that science is: (1) creative and imaginative, (2) tentative, (3) dynamic, (4) parsimonious, (5) empirically based, (6) theory-laden, (7) interpretative (humanistic), (8) demands evidence, (9) cultural and social, and (10) not restricted to one method of investigation. These tenets, and perhaps others, must be understood within the context of the scientific enterprise.

The second assumption is that teachers must possess adequate content knowledge in one of the areas of science (Earth/space, Life, Physical). Abd-El-Khalick (2001) reported that preservice teachers have articulated as reasons for their lack of attention to the Nature of Science in their lesson planning and classroom practices barriers such as lack of scientific content knowledge/confidence and pedagogical practice. We believe a strong background in a scientific discipline can help facilitate understandings of the Nature of Science for students by affording teachers the opportunity to strategically select among the vast landscape of content and delve into meaningful discourse with their students regarding issues underpinning the topic at hand.

Third, educators should understand that each component of the model has equal importance. A logical starting point to consider instruction is the top element of the model: The inquiry scenario. Although historically content has been the driving force behind science curriculum, this model emphasizes an inquiry scenario or question, that is socially or environ-mentally relevant to students' lives, should drive instruction. Since the goal of science education reform is to promote scientific literacy, ideally this model should engage students in the process of critical thinking as applied to socially relevant issues.

An additional element in the model is content. Content is an essential component to support the inquiry scenario. Since one assumption is that the teacher has a solid content knowledge in at least one of the science areas, it places the teachers as the facilitator of student learning. As students work through the challenge of the inquiry scenario, the teacher acts as a resource and guide to foster students' learning.

The third element of the model is science process, sometimes referred to as skills. The process of "doing science," that is the skills to conduct science, directly supports the content and the inquiry scenario. Science process focuses on problem solving and decision making, experimentation, and the use of mathematics as it applies to science. It is important to note that "doing science" does not translate into understanding science. The Nature of Science must be explicit in our teaching, at all levels, in order to facilitate learning in this area (Abd-El-Khalick *et al.*, 1998; Moss *et al.*, 2001) and it is the teachers' responsibility to make the Nature of Science explicit in the science classroom.

Teachers will face challenges as they move from a content driven curriculum to one that place inquiry and the Nature of Science at the forefront of science teaching and learning. One challenge in facilitating this model for teachers is developing the inquiry scenario itself. Many have reported that it is difficult to shift the paradigm of a content driven curriculum toward one that requires students to take responsibility of their own learning by introducing an inquiry scenario as a means to promote engagement. They have articulated that it takes too much time to initiate inquiry lessons as their curricula require a heavy emphasis on content. Of course, this heavy emphasis on content is directly tied to an over emphasis on the assessment of content. Thus, at this point in the chapter, we turn our attention directly to assessment. We will explore how assessment may serve to emancipate science education from a content driven model and offer an alternative given our aims for a scientifically literate society.

Purposes of Assessment

We readily inquire, "Does he know Greek or Latin?" "Can he write poetry and prose?" But what matters most is what we put last: "Has he become better and wiser?" We ought to find out not who understands most, but who understands best (Montaigne, 1991, p. 15).

Science assessment is something we routinely engage in. If we want to know whether the car we are driving is moving at an appropriate speed, we glance at the dashboard display. When we are considering whether to commit to a plunge into the ocean, we check the temperature of water by dipping in a toe. Our standard for these two scenarios are speed and temperature; whether the standard is met, is readily and plainly evident. However, when such technical approaches to testing are turned toward educational purposes, the process becomes much less benign.

Looking across a century of educational assessment we learn assessments were developed for the purpose of creating greater social efficiency. This translated into using IQ scores to determine individual capabilities and then provide instruction according to each person's supposed innate potential, characteristics which were thought to be fixed in one's genetic structure (Shepard, 2001). Today, the inherent biases of standardized tests, including the content of the items and the differential performance of different cultural groups (Meier, 2002), would suggest standardized testing may have progressed in efficiency but not with regard to effectiveness. When test results are used for sorting students (e.g., into special programs or particular courses), purportedly to make the most economical use of limited educational resources, then it should be no surprise to hear of the misuses of test data. Until we re-conceptualize the purposes with which assessment data are gathered and used, we are unlikely to use assessments as a mechanism for equitably supporting student learning (Kornhaber, 2004).

Sad as it might sound, the suggestion that assessments be used to improve science teaching and learning is compellingly stated (e.g., Harlen, 1994), yet only rarely implemented. We suspect part of the problem is not from having a lack of alternative assessment methods; if anything the opposite is the case. Various forms of drawing and illustrating have been suggested as tools for tapping into students' understandings (White & Gunstone, 1992). The compilation of student work into a portfolio has been similarly advanced as a way to use assessments in the service of enhancing learning (Wiggins, 1998). But as much as we are drawn to these assessment approaches because they offer so many more options than filling in a bubble sheet, we contend these alternatives are severely limited—unless the purposes of science education are advanced beyond regurgitating a great deal of information. In this regard, we subscribe to Montaigne's appeal to focus upon substantive understandings rather than abundant knowledge.

A More Complete View of Science

The American Association for the Advancement of Science (1989, 1993) and the National Research Council (1996) have endeavored to define the knowledge and skills students should develop during their years in K-12 education. The developers of these documents have not only expanded the target audience to include all students, not just those destined for scientific careers (Rudolph, 2002), but they went beyond providing lists of terms and definitions students are supposed to master. As noted earlier, a topic of considerable discussion among science educators for quite some time (Shulman & Tamir, 1973), has been the idea of the Nature of Science.

To appropriately assess a student's science abilities requires examining more than content or process knowledge, but also their abilities to appropriately apply the process of inquiry (Hein & Lee, 1999). When students are assessed for their inquiry skills there are several essential elements. One element of inquiry is the students' skill at managing research questions, including their ability to transform generalized notions into investigable questions. Another element of inquiry is students' ability to evaluate the alignment between evidence and the attendant explanations. Assessing these features of student understandings is central to a contemporary view of scientific literacy (Donovan & Bransford, 2005).

We fully support moving science assessment beyond content mastery, and applaud efforts to more closely define what is meant by "inquiry" which in turn provides guidance about assessing inquiry (Olson & Loucks-Horsley, 2000). But efforts to develop appropriate assessments of students' abilities to perform inquiry have not been accompanied by a similar emphasis upon assessing their capabilities within the Nature of Science domain. This is not to suggest other science educators and policy-makers are unaware of this need e.g., "the teacher must be knowledgeable about the Nature of Science, including both the products—the powerful ideas of science—and the values, beliefs, and practices of the scientific community that guide the generation and evaluation of these powerful ideas" (Donovan & Bransford, 2005, p. 479), but we continue to be struck by the lack of mention, let alone recommendations, about assessing the Nature of Science as part of routine science instruction. We have explored assessing the Nature of Science as part of research protocols in the previous section, because examples of the Nature of Science assessment in day-to-day teaching are essentially absent.

We view this as a serious omission. First, by neglecting to give sufficient attention to the Nature of Science, students develop incomplete, and hence inaccurate, perceptions of the scientific enterprise. In addition, it seems possible that our collective neglect of Nature of Science may contribute to the long-standing tendency of science seeming to be the purview of white males. Although not naïve enough to expect that giving due attention to the Nature of Science will overthrow years of gender-bias in scientific careers nor spontaneously close the achievement gaps between White students and their Black and Latino peers, we hold onto the hope for Nature of Science instruction, and assessment, to become part of the solution.

A Real World Example

During a unit on Air and Weather being taught to third graders, an assessment was created to determine the extent to which students had grasped the key content as well as means for evaluating the effectiveness of the science instruction. One component of this assessment is provided here in Figure 4.2. When this item was administered, the students were shown the actual equipment represented in the illustration and asked to individually respond in writing in the space provided on the test.

To respond to this question, a third grader would need to be capable of several tasks, not the least of which is being able to read the test question. In terms of its readability, this item falls somewhere in the second grade reading level. Yet, there is a considerable amount of thought demanded with this assessment. The student must recognize that he or she is being asked to make a prediction (selecting between two alternatives) and then provide a written justification for his or her choice. Before we present samples of actual student responses, think about how you might explain

Here is a picture of a cup and a bowl. The cup is holding a ball of paper. The bowl is almost full of water. If you turn the cup upside down the paper won't fall out.

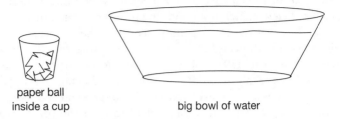

paper ball
inside a cup   big bowl of water

Your teacher takes the cup and turns it upside down. Then she pushes the cup down into the bowl. What do you think would happen? (circle your answer and then finish the sentence).

The paper would get wet because ...   The paper would stay dry because ...

Figure 4.2 Assessment item used for a third grade unit about air and water

in writing why the paper would remain dry even as the cup it was in was submerged below the water's surface.

Were we to evaluate the responses (Figure 4.3) in order to determine who was right and who was wrong, we might regard all of these responses as incorrect. Student A was incorrect in predicting the paper would become wet. Student B, who recognized the paper would stay dry, doesn't completely explain why the water doesn't rise inside the cup. And Student C, even though she selected the correct prediction, failed to describe the role of air in preventing the water from reaching the paper.

Student A

Paper would get wet—Because of the water in the bowl.

Student B

Paper would stay dry—Because water and air cannot be in the same place at the same time.

Student C

Paper stays dry—Because the cup is blocking the paper so it will not get wet.

Figure 4.3 Selected students' responses to the assessment item

However, were we to use this assessment in a formative fashion, that is to say as a glimpse into the ongoing development of students' understandings, we are privy to important information. For example, even though Student A made an incorrect prediction, there is little to dispute about her explanation; indeed, if the paper did get wet it would likely be because of the water in the bowl. Student B's response is made all the more interesting because the idea he is advocating was not formally presented to the class. Following this assessment, the class could build upon this idea and generate a working model which stated that water and air cannot simultaneously occupy the same space. They might use this mental model to explain how pushing air through a tube would displace any water that was present. This might be a key step along the way of learning the accepted scientific notion of air pressure. Viewed in this formative light, his response and explanation seems appropriate, if not technically correct. Finally, Student C's answer indicates that the assessment item may not have provided sufficient specificity. Again, we won't dispute the truth in what the student wrote, in this case the cup kept the water from reaching the paper. Perhaps if the teacher and the assessment item had more specifically prompted the student to invoke the role of air in the situation, we may have obtained a better indication of what she knew in relation to our aim for this assessment.

In retrospect, this assessment could have been improved if it had made an effort to address students' conceptions of the Nature of Science. This could be accomplished in several ways. For one, the students could not only be asked to predict and describe their thought processes, but be subsequently given the materials so they could test the accuracy of their predictions. Especially if the initial prediction proved incorrect, the student would have the opportunity to show his or her ability to match evidence with explanation as he or she tried to describe what happened. An only slightly more complex assessment would have the students use a cup that had a removable stopper plugging its base. Trying to explain why the water rises when the stopper is removed would create another occasion to invoke the role of air as well as applying understandings to a novel situation. Finally, asking students to directly relate the concept of air pressure to key aspects of weather, a common curricular element in third grade, would further serve to bring in a Nature of Science perspective. Looking years ahead, we anticipate these students to be able to make sense of carbon sequestration strategies, principles of atmospheric chemistry, and other scientific ideas underpinning global change—we believe such understandings are built upon a solid foundation fostered in the earliest years of formal schooling. Consider for a moment several of the Nature of Science tenets presented earlier, and one can immediately see the connections: (1) science fosters awareness of the physical world, (2) science describes order in the world by theories that are simple and comprehensive, (3) science is dynamic, (4) scientific knowledge is tentative, and that (5) there is no one scientific method. It is less obvious how addressing these same ambitions might be met using a more traditional, multiple-choice item; the implication is that our desire for a clear sense of students' science learning necessitates using a greater variety of assessment tools to be beyond measuring recall of content. Treating assessments as a mechanism to inform instructional decision-making is not an insignificant shift in thinking. Formative assessment is regarded as a powerful pedagogical technique that has far-reaching effects on student learning. Black and William (1998) report how formative assessment contributes to substantial improvements in students' learning, and these advances have been documented for students with and without diagnosed learning disabilities (Fuchs *et al.*, 1997).

We have found that when culturally appropriate instructional strategies are applied, students from a wide range of language backgrounds can successfully demonstrate their understandings on this type of assessment item (Settlage *et al.*, 2005). What seems increasingly necessary and important in order for science educators to approach their goal of scientific literacy is to combine a more accurate and all-encompassing perspective about science with a view of assessment of which testing is only a subset (Doran *et al.*, 1994). By this we want to pull Nature of Science from the margins of the science assessment discussion. Simultaneously, we wish to reinforce a more inclusive perspective about who should be targeted within science instruction. We view these two desires as complementary: both would benefit by using a cultural perspective of science. Treating science as culture and making such a perspective explicit to all students promises to give students from a greater variety of cultural heritages (Parsons, 2000) and language backgrounds (Lee, 2003) access to scientific literacy.

In the final section of this chapter, we will discuss the hierarchy of assessment, and outline our vision for reform in this area.

Interdisciplinary Assessment and Science Education

We have argued that the teaching and learning of the Nature of Science should be at the very heart of science education. Moving beyond an almost exclusively content-driven focus for education in the sciences, we have offered a conceptual framework which demonstrates the relationship between content, process, and inquiry. Historically, these three notions have existed in tension with each other, often placing a strain on the progress of reform. Beyond what is typically thought of as an interdisciplinary point of view, and consistent with a transdisciplinary perspective (see Moss, 2003), we view the Nature of Science as the very core, or essence of science, and thus a unifying element in this branch of learning. Although the Nature of Science should serve as a principal facet of assessment in science, we must also consider broader concepts within the rhetoric of reform if we are to ensure that assessment serves as a catalyst for achieving our aims for even teaching science in the first place.

As briefly discussed earlier within this chapter, the notion of scientific literacy is widely maintained by scholars as the foundation upon which our current reform efforts should be built, and our ultimate aim for science education. And although operationally defined as having an informed perspective on scientific issues facing individuals and society, it is also characterized by a willingness to engage in social discourse necessary for a free and open society. To further clarify this understanding, we purport the following two notions as essential for literacy in science:

Science for Democratic Participation
Science for Promoting Quality of Life.

The ideas encompassed by these statements are transdisciplinary by their very nature and offer a framework by which assessment can further be considered. When preparing students for participation in public discourse, what are the various learning and curricular considerations? We argue that science curriculum must be timely and relevant to the pressing issues of the moment, while at the same time considering what challenges society might face in the long term. Issues relating to biotechnology and the human genome, sustainability, energy, and even terrorism will be publicly debated over the next generation and beyond. Yet, supplanting the current curriculum with an entirely new set of topics, as relevant as they might be, may not most effectively serve our students. Since the very Nature of Science describes the scientific enterprise as one of an ongoing innovation of ideas which builds upon our previous knowledge in a dynamic way, science curriculum can certainly take its cues from this reality. This recognition of a continuum of knowledge in science embraces the notion that ideas are not static, and can serve as a lens, or perhaps filter, by which we can make strategic decisions about what to teach. That is, as we look forward to what we expect students will need to know to fulfill their democratic responsibilities, we must consider the scientific foundation upon which their opinions and beliefs will ultimately be built. Thus, we have given meaning to our extensive knowledge base in science in relation to preparing engaged and informed citizens.

The second notion of science and promoting a superior quality of life can be considered in the same light as the first. Here, issues of human health and technology may serve as the cornerstones for curriculum, yet there exists the same relationship between all we have learned and what we still need to know. Perhaps one slight contextual difference here might be the very personal nature of decisions individuals will need to make. Issues of extending life through technological means have been at the forefront of public debate within the past few years, and although discussed publicly, individual decisions will likely remain private. Regardless, the need of a high quality education in science will be necessary to facilitate an informed decision making process. The Nature of Science is such that the cut and dry notions of right and wrong are replaced with complex nuances of perspectives backed by varying degrees of evidence. Considering the assessment example cited earlier in this chapter where we advocated students have additional opportunities to weigh evidence, we see how a Nature of Science aspect to assessment can serve students beyond the unit theme, and provide a foundation for rational thinking.

Together, the ideals of science for democracy and quality of life allow us to consider the relationship across what might be considered a hierarchy of concepts common to the lexicon of science education. Given today's political reality of accountability in education, assessment can serve to unify, not to polarize aspects of the profession. Content, process, and inquiry all help define the Nature of Science, while science literacy (as defined by quality of life issues and the need for public discourse in a democracy) provides much needed clarity to the enduring aim for science education. And yet, even given this comprehensive and transdisciplinary framework for considering the teaching and learning of science, it is still up to professionals at all levels to make the normative decisions necessary in deciding what we ought to be teaching our children. We are fearful, as history has demonstrated time and time again, that the lure of trying to introduce children to every little trivial bit of science knowledge will result in the reality that the coverage of content mentality will remain king.

Concluding Remarks

We close this chapter with a final recommendation for considering education in science beyond a solely content driven, single discipline approach, with the anticipation that the aspects of the Nature of Science discussed throughout this chapter will emerge as an alternative.

Although explicitly stated earlier, it bears revisiting. Content has a critical role in science education. Previous reform efforts have failed because they, perhaps inadvertently, set up false dichotomies between content and other key aspects of science. Various content strands are often considered in isolation from each other, which is to be expected given the way scientists themselves have historically approached the profession. However, given the recent understandings of the interconnectedness of disciplines in science, a fresh approach of the consideration of content is warranted. In *Project 2061: Science for All Americans* (AAAS, 1989) the authors discuss broad themes which pervade science. They note that these are "ideas that transcend disciplinary boundaries," (p. 123). These themes, sometimes known as unifying concepts or big ideas, include systems, models (both physical and conceptual), constancy, patterns of change, evolution, and scale. The *National Science Education Standards* (NRC, 1996) propose similar unifying concepts, and acknowledge that these concepts could serve as a focus for instruction at any grade level. Beyond a focus for instruction, we argue they can serve to promote a transdisciplinary perspective in and beyond science. For example, when one considers the topic of human evolution as a central curriculum theme, facets of biology and geology are explicitly represented along with issues which may typically be considered within the domain of social studies, such as settlement patterns. Evolution becomes a window into the Nature of Science, and day-to-day content consistent with this theme should be chosen and assessed which facilitates science understandings across the disciplines and not merely as discon-nected nuggets of information.

Within this chapter, we have endeavored to illustrate how content is merely a facet, albeit an important one, of the Nature of Science. Content should not be thought of as disconnected trivial facts, but as elements of unifying concepts, or big ideas, in science. Moving beyond the traditional disciplines of science, content becomes a rich landscape for exploration in science education. Yet, difficult decisions must still be made with regard to what students need to know and be able to do so that they may fully participate in the very serious issues facing individuals and society in these formative years of the new millennium.

Assessment is often referred to as "high stakes," implying that much is on the line with regard to how students test in science. We concur with the high-stakes nature of science education, but not with regard to content driven, one-time standardized exams—but with the prospect of letting down yet another generation of citizens who must learn to navigate an ever complex world of challenges and opportunities.

Bibliography

Abd-El-Khalick, F. (2001). Embedding nature of science instruction in preservice elementary science courses: Abandoning scientism, but . . . *Journal of Science Teacher Education, 12* (3), 215–33.

Abd-El-Khalick, F., Bell, R.L., & Lederman, N.G. (1998). The nature of science and instructional practice: Making the unnatural natural. *Science Education, 82,* 417–36.

Aikenhead, G.S. (1973). The measurement of high school students' knowledge about science and scientists. *Science Education, 57* (4), 539–49.

Aikenhead, G.S. (1988). An analysis of four ways of assessing students' beliefs about STS topics. *Journal of Research in Science Teaching, 25* (8), 607–27.

Aikenhead, G. (1996). Science education: Border crossing into the subculture of science. *Studies in Science Education, 27,* 1–52.

Aikenhead, G. (2000). Renegotiating the culture of school science. In R. Millar, J. Leach & J. Osborne (eds.), *Improving science education: The contribution of research* (pp. 245–64). Philadelphia, PA: Open University Press.

American Association for the Advancement of Science (1989). *Science for all Americans.* New York: Oxford Press.

American Association for the Advancement of Science (1993). *Benchmarks for science literacy.* New York: Oxford Press.

Black, P. & William, D. (1998). Inside the black box: Raising standards through classroom assessment. *Phi Delta Kappan, 80* (2), 139–44.

Brickhouse, N.W. (1990). Teachers' beliefs about the nature of science and their relationship to classroom practice. *Journal of Teacher Education, 41,* 53–62.

Cooley, W.W. and Klopfer, L. (1961). *Manual for the test on understanding science.* Princeton, NJ: Educational Testing Science.

Cooley, W.W. & Klopfer, L. (1963a). The history of science cases for high schools in the development of student understanding of science and scientists. *Journal of Research in Science Teaching,* 1, 33–47.

Cooley, W.W. & Klopfer, L. (1963b). The evaluation of specific educational innovations. *Journal of Research in Science Teaching,* 1, 73–80.

Cothham J.C. & Smith, E.L. (1981). Development and validation of the conceptions of scientific theories test. *Journal of Research in Science Teaching, 18* (5), 387–96.

Donovan, M.S. & Bransford, J.D. (2005). *How students learn: History, mathematics, and science in the classroom.* Washington, DC: National Academy Press.

Doran, R.L., Lawrenz, F., & Helgeson, S. (1994). Research on assessment in science. In D.L. Gabel (ed.), *Handbook of research on science teaching and learning* (pp. 388–442). New York: Macmillan.

Fuchs, L.S., Fuchs, D., Karns, K., Hamlett, C.L., Katzaroff, M. *et al.* (1997). Effects of task-focused goals on low-achieving students with and without learning disabilities. *American Educational Research Journal, 34,* 513–43.

Harlen, W. (1994). *The teaching of science.* London: David Fulton Publishers.

Hein, G.E. & Lee, S. (1999). Assessment of science inquiry. In National Science Foundation (ed.), *Inquiry: Thoughts, views and strategies for the K-5 classroom* (pp. 99–107). Arlington, VA: National Science Foundation.

Kimball, M.E. (1968). Understanding the nature of science: A comparison of scientists and science teachers. *Journal of Research in Science Teaching,* 5, 110–20.

Koehler, C. & Moss, D.M. (2005) Does the history of science help promote nature of science understandings for preservice teachers? Only time will tell. *Proceedings from National Association for Research in Science Teaching,* Dallas, TX, 2005.

Kornhaber, M.L. (2004). Appropriate and inappropriate forms of testing, assessment, and accountability. *Educational Policy, 18,* 45–70.

Lederman, N.G. (1992). Students' and teachers' conceptions of the nature of science: A review of the research literature. *Journal of Research in Science Teaching, 29* (4), 331–59.

Lederman, N.G. & Zeidler, D.L. (1987). Science teachers' conceptions of the nature of science: Do they really influence teaching behavior? *Science Education, 71,* 721–34.

Lederman, N.G. & O'Malley, M. (1990). Students' perceptions of tentativeness in science: Development, use and sources of change. *Science Education, 74* (2), 225–39.

Lederman, N.G., Abd-El-Khalick, F., Bell, R.L., & Schwartz, R.S. (2002). Views of the nature of science questionnaire: Toward valid and meaningful assessment of learners' conceptions of the nature of science. *Journal of Research in Science Teaching, 39* (6) 497–521.

Lee, O. (2003). Equity for linguistically and culturally diverse students in science education. *Teachers College Record, 105,* 465–89.

Meichtry, Y.J. (1993). The impact of science curricula on student views about the nature of science. *Journal of Research in Science Teaching, 30* (5), 429–33.

Meier, D. (2002). *In schools we trust: Creating communities of learning in an era of testing and standardization.* Boston, MA: Beacon Press.

Montaigne, M. (1991). *The complete essays* (M.A. Screech, trans.). New York: Penguin Books. (Original work published 1580).

Moss, D.M. (2003). The end of science . . . and where other disciplines begin: Exploring the nature of science. In D.K. Kaufman, D.M. Moss, & T.A. Osborn (eds.), *Beyond the boundaries: A transdisciplinary approach to learning and teaching* (pp. 47–67). Westport, CT: Praeger Publishers.

Moss, D.M., Abrams, E.D. & Robb, J. (2001). Examining student conceptions of the nature of science. *International Journal of Science Education, 8,* 771–90.

National Research Council (1995). *National Science Education Standards.* Washington, DC: National Academy Press.

Olson, S. & Loucks-Horsley, S. (2000). *Inquiry and the National Science Education Standards: A guide for teaching and learning.* Washington, DC: National Academy Press.

Parsons, E.C. (2000). Culturalizing science instruction: What is it, what does it look like, and why do we need it. *Journal of Science Teacher Education, 11,* 207–19.

Rubba, P. (1977). The development, field testing, and validation of an instrument to assess secondary student's understanding of the nature of scientific knowledge. Unpublished doctoral dissertation, Indiana University, Bloomington.

Rubba, P.A. & Andersen, H.O. (1978). Development of an instrument to assess secondary school students' understanding of the nature of science knowledge. *Science Education, 62* (4), 449–58.

Rudolph, J.L. (2002). *Scientists in the classroom: The cold war reconstruction of American science education.* New York: Palgrave.

Ryan, A.G. & Aikenhead, G.S. (1992). Students' preconceptions about the epistemology of science. *Science Education, 76* (6), 559–80.

Settlage, J., Madsen, A. & Rustad, K. (2005). Inquiry science, sheltered instruction, and English language learners: Conflicting pedagogies in highly diverse classrooms. *Issues in Teacher Education, 14* (1), 39–57.

Shepard, L.A. (2001). The role of classroom assessment in teaching and learning. In V. Richardson (ed.), *Handbook of research on teaching* (4th edition) (pp. 1066–1101). Washington, DC: American Educational Research Association.

Shulman, L.S. & Tamir, P. (1973). Research on teaching in the natural sciences. In R.M.W. Travers (ed.), *Handbook of research on teaching* (pp. 1098–1148). Chicago, IL: Rand-McNally.

White, R. & Gunstone, R. (1992). *Probing understanding.* Philadelphia, PA: Falmer Press.

Wiggins, G. (1998). *Educative assessment: Designing assessments to inform and improve student performance.* San Francisco, CA: Jossey-Bass.

CHAPTER 5

Re-Solving the Tension Between Interdisciplinarity and Assessment

The Case of Mathematics

JEAN MCGIVNEY-BURELLE, KATHERINE MCGIVNEY,
and JANE M. WILBURNE

As noted in the introductory chapter, numerous well-known and respected discipline-based professional organizations in the U.S. have published position statements and standards documents advocating for an interdisciplinary approach to teaching and learning at the K-16 level (Klein, 1997; National Council for the Social Studies [NCSS], 1994; National Council of Teachers of Mathematics [NCTM], 1989, 2000; National Council of Teachers of English [NCTE], 1996; National Research Council [NRC], 1986, 1989; National Science Foundation [NSF], 1996; National Science Teachers Association [NSTA], 2003; Rutherford & Ahlgren, 1990). Echoed in these papers is the observation that life does not recognize the discrete categories of knowledge we call disciplines and accordingly, in order to prepare students to tackle the significant social problems we face today, problems which cannot be solved by a single disciplinary approach, students must begin to develop interdisciplinary perspectives. As a result of these calls for change, teachers across all grade levels and specialties have been called upon to be pedagogically bold and cross the arguably artificial boundaries of traditional academic disciplines to collaborate and engage students in solving real-world problems so that everyone may work toward a new, more comprehensive point of view than can be achieved by the perspective of any one field (DeZure, 1999).

In tandem with the shift toward interdisciplinary curricula in K-16 classrooms have been politically-charged pronouncements for holding schools and teachers more accountable for student achievement as measured by their performance on high stakes standardized tests (e.g., No Child Left Behind [NCLB], 2001). In line with NCLB, school improvement is measured by adequate yearly progress, a performance objective based on the minimum percentage of students who must attain the specified proficiency level. NCLB provides sanctions for schools that do not improve, including permitting students to transfer to a higher performing school in the district, providing free private tutoring, replacing school staff, and, after five years of school failure, letting the state assume control of the school. This represents the first time that the future of individual public schools rests on student achievement on standardized tests—tests which frequently draw distinct disciplinary lines and emphasize recall of facts over critical thinking and complex problem solving. As a result, school administrators and teachers are highly motivated to make changes in curricula, teaching, and assessment that will optimize students' testing success.

The simultaneous moves towards interdisciplinary curricula and supporting pedagogy on the one hand and accountability and evaluation through high stakes standardized testing on the other seem incongruous, at best. If classroom teachers are to embrace the notions and practices of interdisciplinarity in this climate they must be convinced their students' achievement within the disciplines will not suffer in doing so. In light of this, teachers need to develop and use tools that demonstrate evidence of their students' understanding of the discipline-based skills, concepts, and processes that play an essential role in interdisciplinary activity. This raises several questions, chief among them, "What types of activities and assessments can be used to gauge students' understanding of disciplinary ideas which are embedded in interdisciplinary study?" In this chapter, we explore this question in the context of mathematics. In doing so, we will describe a potential role for mathematics in interdisciplinary activity as well as strategies for assessing students' understanding of mathematics in interdisciplinary activity.

Interdisciplinarity: Benefits and Challenges

The question of whether to teach disciplines in a discrete manner versus implementing an interdisciplinary curriculum remains at the center of the debate on how to improve teaching and learning in schools (Klein, 1998; Tchudi & Lafer, 1996). Clearly, the traditional disciplines of mathematics, English, history, science and the like divide knowledge into organized and helpful hierarchies of skills, concepts, procedures, theories, and ways of knowing that bring order to our understanding and structure to our schools. At the same time, this discipline-defined model of curriculum and instruction may prevent students from developing the interdisciplinary perspective required to tackle complex, real-world problems that are rarely aligned with individual disciplines. As evidenced by Meier *et al.* (1996), students taught within the lecture-based disciplinary system typically are not able to solve problems that require them to make connections and use relationships between concepts and content.

Klein (1990) defines *interdisciplinarity* as the synthesis of two or more disciplines such that a new level of discourse and assimilation of knowledge is achieved. In practice, the process of interdisciplinary instruction often begins with a topic, theme, problem, or project that requires active student participation and knowledge of multiple disciplines in order to reach a resolution (Dabbagh *et al.*, 2000; Gordon *et al.*, 2001; Sage, 2000; Tchudi & Lafer, 1996). The emphasis is on becoming more knowledgeable about a variety of disciplines, making connections within and among disciplines, seeing problems from multiple perspectives, appreciating diversity, and developing an ability to solve complex problems.

In contrast to the study of segmented disciplines, interdisciplinary study is said to have numerous and far-reaching benefits for students and teachers. Namely, interdisciplinary curriculum has the potential to resolve the artificial fragmentation of knowledge that students and faculty criticize (Korey, 2002); to motivate students by engaging them in investigating meaningful and relevant issues or problems; to improve students' ability to think critically and navigate with ease between different fields of study (Davis, 1995; Klein, 1998; Newell, 1994; Rhodes, 2001) and to draw faculty from seemingly disparate disciplines closer together and improve cross-disciplinary communication (Austin & Baldwin, 1991; Davis, 1995, Rhodes 2001).

Prospective employers have weighed in on the issue of the benefits of interdisciplinary work in schools as well, suggesting that chief among the "new basics" required to keep the U.S. workforce competitive are employees' ability to work collaboratively to solve ill-defined problems, adapt to change, communicate effectively, perceive patterns, absorb new ideas, and apply reasoning skills (Meier *et al.*, 1996; Ward & Lee, 2000). In essence, as noted by Korey (2002) success in the twenty-first century demands "an acrobatic intellect capable of constant readjustment" and, she adds, interdisciplinary approaches have the potential to "exercise the mental muscles needed for this kind of thinking" (p. 2). Learning theorists provide more support for interdisciplinarity by suggesting it addresses new understandings of how people learn (i.e., constructivist epistemology) and lends itself to more effective teaching practices.

While the benefits of interdisciplinary curricula are obvious, Grossman *et al.* (2000) have noted the difficulty of implementing and sustaining interdisciplinary interventions over the long haul. Beyond the ever-present logistical problems of not having the time and resources needed to develop, test, and refine authentic interdisciplinary materials, lie more complex challenges involving long-standing traditions of subject-area departments and the epistemological and pedagogical beliefs of the specialists working within them. As noted by Grossman and Stodolsky (1995) subject area departments provide a milieu for the development of a host of attitudes and beliefs about schooling and its purposes and as one ascends the academic latter these disciplinary affiliations become more and more powerful (Becher, 1989). This is particularly true in the discipline of mathematics.

The Case of Mathematics

Over the last decade, mathematics teachers at all levels have been under increasing pressure by industry, professional organizations, accrediting bureaus, university administrators, and outside funding agencies to develop meaningful interdisciplinary programs and courses. In response to this, interdisciplinary initiatives *within* the field of mathematics have increased significantly. For example, mathematics programs that emphasize connections, context, and modeling have sprung up across the U.S. including *Connected Mathematics Program* (Michigan State University) at the middle school level and *Interactive Mathematics Program* (Key Curriculum Press), *Mathematics: Modeling Our World* (Consortium for Mathematics and Its Applications), and *Contemporary Mathematics in Context* (Core-Plus Mathematics Project) at the high school level. These programs emphasize connections among mathematical ideas (rather than among different disciplines), having students construct new concepts and knowledge based on prior knowledge, and applications of mathematics in real-world contexts. At the university level, the Mathematics Association of America [MAA] (2004) recently published the Committee on the Undergraduate Program in Mathematics [CUPM] Guide which contains six general recommendations for all university mathematics departments. Namely, every course should:

1. Strive to present key ideas and concepts from a variety of perspectives.
2. Employ a broad range of examples and applications to motivate and illustrate the material.
3. Promote awareness of connections to other subjects (both in and out of the mathematical sciences) and strengthen each student's ability to apply the course material to these subjects.

4. Introduce contemporary topics from the mathematical sciences and their applications.
5. Enhance student perceptions of the vitality in the modern world.
6. Further, mathematical sciences departments should encourage and support faculty collaboration with colleagues from other departments to modify and develop mathematics courses, create joint or cooperative majors, devise undergraduate research projects, and possibly team teach courses or units within courses.

Despite these recommendations, researchers have noted considerable resistance on the part of high school mathematics teachers and university mathematicians to adopt interdisciplinary models of curriculum and instruction. In interviews with high school mathematics teachers, Woodbury (1998) found that the notion of pursuing interdisciplinary teaching of a core curriculum did not seem fruitful for many of the participants. Not only did these teachers lack any mental images of how an effective interdisciplinary curriculum might operate, but they were also incapable of identifying any examples of meaningful interdisciplinary thinking. Even when some teachers could provide examples, they articulated reservations of this approach, suggesting that a curriculum with an interdisciplinary focus would weaken the integrity of the mathematics curriculum (Woodbury, 1998). Korey (2002) found similar beliefs regarding interdisciplinary study among university faculty. For example, Korey (2002) cited one professor who suggested that interdisciplinary study was more appropriate for graduate study since students have to "get through this essential material before [students] even have anything to think *with*" (p. 2).

The resistance of K-16 mathematics educators to embrace interdisciplinarity may be attributed to several reasons. First, traditional approaches to teaching mathematics emphasize isolated facts and formulaic procedures over broad concepts and generalizable ideas. Typically, students are expected to memorize collections of definitions, formulas, algorithms, and theorems in order to complete a set of routine exercises or to solve decontextualized problems. Second, mathematics teachers and mathematicians often view the pairing of mathematics with a discipline, outside the scientific domain, as watered down, believing that serious mathematics cannot be taught within the structure of a humanities course. The "mathematicians' culture" may also contribute to the lack of interdisciplinary cooperation on the part of university mathematicians. In a study by the American Mathematical Society [AMS], conversations with chairs and deans of research mathematics departments over a seven year period revealed a consistent and common theme, namely the tendency of mathematicians to eschew interactions with other departments or with faculty outside mathematics (Ewing, 1999). Taken together, these issues, along with long-standing traditions of separate terminologies, distinct epistemologies, and different methods of proof and verification provide significant roadblocks to successfully incorporating mathematics with other disciplines in interdisciplinary study.

In order for mathematics teachers at all levels to embrace inter-disciplinary work they must understand, as DeZure (1999) noted, that "interdisciplinarity is not a rejection of the disciplines . . . (rather) it is firmly rooted in them" (p. 1). As Newell (1998) points out, while students clearly need the "depth and focus of disciplinary ways of knowing," they also need "interdisciplinarity to broaden the context and establish links to other ways of constructing knowledge."

On a practical level, mathematics teachers also need evidence that interdisciplinary ways of knowing do not come at the expense of developing a deep understanding of the disciplines. While there is a dearth of sound research studies examining this issue, there is at least some evidence that it may be possible to effectively merge interdisciplinary teaching and assessing and accountability within the disciplines. (See Gardner's *Project Zero*.) As noted by Bailey (2003), schools that implemented standards-based interdisciplinary curriculum at the elementary, middle and secondary levels reported positive effects on student achievement in a variety of subject areas (Cordogan & Stanciak, 2000; Kling & Zimmer, 1999; McKinnon, 1997). Further, at the college level, Korey (2002) found in an interdisciplinary mathematics and humanities course that "for students in all majors the mathematics and humanities courses were more effective in sustaining and increasing desirable attitudes about mathematics than was the standard first-year calculus course or the lively advanced applications courses" (p. 4).

Reasoning: The Role of Mathematics in Interdisciplinary Activity

So what role can mathematics play in interdisciplinary study? As noted by Krahn (1999), "mathematics is not tethered to a specific set of courses or subjects, rather mathematics is a process" (p. 1) and therefore, "the focus in mathematics classrooms should be more on the process of reasoning than on the foundation of knowledge and information." What is mathematical reasoning? The National Council of Teachers of Mathematics [NCTM] (2000) describes reasoning as the process of "developing ideas, exploring phenomena, justifying results, and using mathematical conjectures in all content areas" whereby students come to expect that "mathematics makes sense" (p. 56). Reasoning-in-action involves recognizing patterns in real-world situations, determining the reason for the patterns, and then conjecturing and proving that the pattern always holds.

Approximately 50 years prior to the NCTM Standards (2000), eminent mathematician and mathematics educator G. Polya (1952) coined the term *plausible reasoning* and described it as understanding new concepts from examples, trying out special cases, and searching for similar solution patterns. In the passage below he elaborates on the role of plausible reasoning in mathematics and reveals an arguably interdisciplinary perspective on how reasoning is used across a variety of academic fields.

> Why should a mathematician care for plausible reasoning? His science is the only one that can rely on demonstrative reasoning alone. The physicist needs inductive evidence, the lawyer has to rely on circumstantial evidence, the historian on documentary evidence, the economist on statistical evidence. These kinds of evidence may carry strong conviction, attain a high level of plausibility, and justly so, but can never attain the force of a strict demonstration . . . Perhaps it is silly to discuss plausible grounds in mathematical matters. *Yet I do not think so.* Mathematics has two faces. Presented in finished form, mathematics appears as a purely demonstrative science, but mathematics in the making is sort of an experimental science. A correctly written mathematical paper is supposed to contain strict demonstrations only, but the creative work of the mathematician resembles the creative work of the naturalist: observation, analogy, and conjectural generalizations, or mere guesses, if you prefer to say so, play an essential role in both.
> (Polya, 1952, p. 739)

In a similar way, Krahn (1999) describes the *art of reasoning* in interdisciplinary activity as a recursive process of inductive and deductive thinking. According to Krahn, mathematics teachers foster mathematical reasoning by creating learning opportunities where students move first from "puzzling" data to a suggested meaning (i.e., inductive reasoning) and then move from the suggested meaning back to the data (i.e., deductive reasoning). Krahn describes this process as a "double movement" whereby students first leave the environment typically associated with mathematics and enter other academic disciplines linked by problems and concepts after which they return to mathematics to refine their ideas. In particular, the first move requires students to gather data, reflect on this information, and develop insights from interdisciplinary perspectives. The second move then returns students back to traditional mathematics where they may reexamine the data using established principles and procedures so they may develop more powerful analyses. The return trip to the traditional mathematics environment becomes the starting point for another excursion into interdisciplinary activities and so on. As Krahn notes, "this double movement of induction-deduction; expanding-contracting; generalization-specialization; interdisciplinary-disciplinary; reflects the process we want our students to assimilate. It is the coordinated movement between discipline-specific and interdisciplinary associations that promote effective education."

Assessing Mathematical Reasoning in the Context of Interdisciplinary Activity

Knowing how to simplify algebraic expressions, write and solve equations, graph, interpret, integrate and differentiate functions, and prove theorems are among the mathematical skills required of students in most high school and university mathematics' courses. These skills typically rely on students' memorization facts and ability to mimic rote procedures. While the content may be sophisticated and the skills complex, there is limited transfer of these skills when students are faced with real world problems. Moreover, today's businesses and industries are equipped with high-tech software programs and computer systems which eliminate the need for most of the skills which are the focus of most traditional high school and college mathematics courses. Simply put, the content and pedagogy of most traditional mathematics courses rarely compel students to engage in opportunities to use higher level reasoning skills and to make sophisticated mathematical connections. In a similar way the assessment of these skills is often based on artificial contexts and rigid separation of concepts. Using assessments that focus on discrete content only reinforces memorization of definitions and applications of rote procedures rather than focus on students' reasoning.

Polya's view of plausible reasoning and Krahn's notion of the art of reasoning in interdisciplinary activity stand in stark contrast to traditional mathematics instruction and, consequently, demand new approaches to assessment which are aligned to interdisciplinary curriculum. In this dynamic approach to teaching and learning, assessment *for* learning, rather than assessment *of* learning, is the focus. The emphasis is on assessing the *process* rather than the *product* of instruction. With this process-oriented interdisciplinary view of mathematics, students' reasoning and thinking is as important as the actual mastery of the discipline content.

Assessing students' reasoning skills in the context of interdisciplinary activity requires more than evaluating their performance on tests and quizzes. As noted by NCTM (1999) assessments of students' mathematical understanding must provide a rich variety of problem situations; give students opportunities to investigate problems in many ways; question and listen to students; and look for evidence from multiple sources (NCTM, 1999). In developing reasoning skills students are expected to make, explain and verify conjectures, defend their ideas, and continue to refine their thinking as new information from across the disciplines becomes available. In particular, mathematics assessments in interdisciplinary contexts should focus more on the process of gathering and interpreting data from across the disciplines and using this information to develop mathematical models that help to represent and illuminate the phenomena under investigation. In this way, interdisciplinarity lends itself to more authentic on-going assessments such as classroom discussion, observations, lab reports, performance assessments, and presentations that simulate authentic, real world experiences, and are more relevant to students.

Students' reasoning and understanding can be exhibited in these assessments if students are required to describe and explain their processes and procedures. Writing assignments, for example, provide a unique window into students' thoughts and the ways in which they navigate through the solution to a problem. Writing a report or research summary requires students to gather and organize information, clarify their thinking, and make appropriate interdisciplinary connections. Student presentations and class discussions on approaches to solving real-world problems can help teachers determine the nature and quality of students' reasoning and provide information for instruction. Embedding assessments throughout interdisciplinary activity which require students to set goals, monitor their work, and evaluate their efforts prepares them to develop the ability to analyze their own thinking, have clear self-insight, and follow through on projects. (See NCTM's (1999) *Mathematics Assessment: A Practical Handbook* for a detailed description of these assessment tools.)

Why Is It So Cold in Caracas?: An Interdisciplinary Activity Investigating the Relationship between Latitude and Temperature

So what might the teaching and assessing of mathematics in the context of interdisciplinary study look like? We offer, as an example, a brief overview of one interdisciplinary activity we've used in a variety of forms with students ranging from middle school through freshmen year of college and in a variety of settings including in a traditional algebra course as well as an interdisciplinary team-taught mathematics/social studies/science course. Here we focus on how this lesson is typically approached in a high-school mathematics classroom.

The mathematical objectives of the activity are clear—students are expected to be able to collect data, create a scatter plot of the data, find a best-fit model for the data set, interpret correlation coefficients, identify outliers of data sets, and use the model to answer questions. Variations of these skills can be found in any national or state-level curriculum standards or recommendations for students enrolled in middle school, high school and even college level mathematics. While many of these skills can be (and often are) taught and assessed in a context-free environment, we have found that by taking simple steps to embed these skills in the context of interdisciplinary activity, students appear to draw more heavily upon their prior knowledge to guide their work; come to a better understanding of how seemingly disparate disciplines can inform one another and allow us to solve problems; apply sophisticated reasoning skills to make sense of problems; and demonstrate and communicate their understanding of mathematics in deeper and more meaningful ways.

At the heart of the activity lies a simply stated yet open-ended question: "What is the nature of the relationship between latitude and temperature?" The lesson begins by engaging students in a conversation about their understanding of this relationship. Students at all levels bring a good deal of informal knowledge of latitude and temperature to the activity and generally offer responses akin to, "As latitude increases, temperature decreases" or "As latitude decreases, temperature increases." To get students to dig a bit deeper in thinking about this question we often inject into this conversation a follow-up question regarding whether students believe their statements about latitude and temperature are *always* true. While some students quickly concur, others reserve their judgment. When pressed further, few students are able to offer counterexamples to these statements and rarely can any students offer plausible reasons for why counterexamples may exist.

The lesson typically proceeds with students working in pairs to collect temperature and latitude data of 10–15 major cities in the Northern Hemisphere using the website www.worldclimate.com. Using available technology (e.g., graphing calculator) students create scatter plots of their data (latitude vs. temperature) and find mathematical models that best fit the data set. In the case of algebra, students generate and graph lines of best fit and then compare them with the original scatter plot of the data. For example, one pair's data set and line of best fit is shown in Figure 5.1.

Invariably, students' data sets include outliers—that is, ordered pairs of data that stray away from the graph of the best-fit line. In the model above, Miami, Florida and Caracas, Venezuela may be considered outliers. Using the best-fit linear model students can calculate the predicted temperature for Caracas to be 76.8° and see that it overshoots its actual temperature

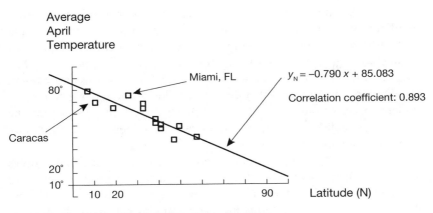

Figure 5.1 Example of outliers in Northern Hemisphere data

(70.3°); that is, it is cooler in Caracas than the students found using their model. At this point we typically return to the question, "Is it always true that as latitude increases temperature decreases?" Armed with their data students are much more likely to respond, "No" but they still are able to offer little in the way of explanation.

Next, students are encouraged to do some investigative work using the internet to offer probable reasons for the outliers. Often, as in the case above, students come to see the role that geography, and in particular, altitude plays in temperature. That is, the fact that Caracas sits at an altitude of 800 meters (about ½ mile) explains why its actual temperature is less than other cities at higher latitude and that Miami's sea-level location results in an actual temperature warmer than cities at lower latitudes. Other types of outliers present an excellent opportunity for the class to discuss several plausible geographic explanations, for example, the influence of the Gulf Stream and the impact of large populations on temperatures. Through this activity students come to understand that outliers can indicate faulty data or areas where a certain theory—in this case, the inverse linear relationship between latitude and temperature—that might not be valid. Students also must decide whether they should keep these data points or reject these data points to obtain more robust models.

The students' work in this lab is similar to Krahn's description of the *art of reasoning* in interdisciplinary activity via a series of double movements— that is, students move first from "puzzling" their latitude and temperature data to arrive at a best fit linear model (i.e., inductive reasoning) and then move from the model back to the data (i.e., deductive reasoning) to understand the outliers and make adjustments to their model. In this case, students leave the environment of mathematics and enter the disciplines of social studies or science after which they return to mathematics to refine their ideas. In the first move students gather data, reflect on this information, and develop insights from other disciplines. The second move then returns students back to traditional mathematics where they may reexamine the data using established principles and procedures so they may develop more powerful analyses.

Throughout this activity students are expected to keep detailed notes in their mathematics notebooks. At the end of the project students are expected to make short formal technology-rich presentations (e.g., PowerPoint presentation with internet links and graphing calculator displays) to share their work with the class. In these discussions each pair of students must demonstrate their understanding of the mathematics skills, concepts, and processes inherent in the activity but they also reveal their level of interdisciplinary reasoning and communication skills as they describe their data sets, best-fit models, outliers and explanations for each outlier. Students are evaluated by both their peers and instructors using a rubric that assesses students' understanding of mathematics, their interdisciplinary reasoning skills, and their ability to clearly communicate their ideas.

Clearly, the mathematics skills and processes addressed in this lab could easily be presented and assessed in a context-free, discipline-based manner. So one might ask, what is the benefit for students in using this approach? To begin, students have the opportunity to experience first-hand the messy work of applied mathematicians engaged in gathering data, finding models and revising them when new information becomes available. In this approach, students benefit from new perspectives gained by opening other disciplinary doors and taking a look at mathematics problems with a new lens. Students studying mathematics in an interdisciplinary setting have the opportunity to make sense of mathematics in context, that is, to attach real-world meaning to seemingly abstract concepts. Further, students get to hone their reasoning and communication skills as they attempt to share their work with their peers. The benefits for mathematics teachers are equally compelling. With little effort mathematics teachers can embed the requisite concepts and skills in their curriculum into problems that are more engaging and challenging for students. Moreover, in a team-teaching environment mathematics teachers can benefit from working with and learning from colleagues in the social studies who may be more knowledgeable about the complex role that geography plays in the relationship between latitude and temperature.

Summary

Today's challenge is to prepare students to know and understand mathematics and to be able to apply this knowledge within other areas of mathematics as well as in other disciplines. Students need to develop the mathematical power necessary to stretch their basic understanding, make cross-curricular connections, use inductive and deductive reasoning, and solve real-life problems. Applying mathematics in an interdisciplinary setting provides opportunities for true learning and understanding to take place. An interdisciplinary focus enables students to engage in data collection, apply current technologies, use oral and written communication skills, and apply mathematics to real-world problems. They allow students to employ problem-solving skills, formulate their conceptual understanding, and engage in critical thinking.

An interdisciplinary approach to instruction requires changes to the way we assess students' mathematical understanding. Alternative assessments that focus on the process of students' mathematical reasoning rather than the product of instruction give a more accurate picture of the nature of students' mathematical reasoning and more accurately reflect the kinds of skills needed by today's workforce. Making these shifts in assessment practices may enable assessment to advance education in a way that is more interdisciplinary and not merely to "record its status" (Mathematical Science Education Board, 1993, p.1).

Bibliography

Austin, A. & Baldwin, R. (1991). *Faculty collaboration: Enhancing the quality of scholarship and teaching.* ASHE-ERIC Higher Education Report No. 7, Washington, DC: The George Washington School of Education and Human Development.

Bailey, L. (2003). Meeting standards without sacrificing quality curriculum in the middle school. *Research in Middle Level Education, 26* (2), 1–10.

Becher, T. (1989). *Academic tribes and territories: Intellectual enquiry and the cultures of disciplines.* Bristol, PA: Society for Research into Higher Education and Open University Press.

Cordogan, S. & Stanciak, L. (2000). *An examination of the effects of an interdisciplinary curriculum program on behavior and academic performance in a suburban high school. (A compilation from the first three years of a four-year study).* Paper presented at the annual meeting of the American Educational Research Association, New Orleans, LA.

Dabbagh, N., Jonassen, D., & Yueh, H. (2000). Assessing a problem-based learning approach to an introductory instructional design course: A case study. *Performance Improvement Quarterly, 13* (3), 60–83.

Davis, J.R. (1995). *Interdisciplinary courses and team teaching.* Westport, CT: Oryx Press.

Dewey, J. (1991). *How we think.* Buffalo, NY: Prometheus Bros. (Originally published in 1910.)

DeZure, D. (1999–2000). *Interdisciplinary teaching and learning.* Available at: http://oira.syr.edu/cstl2/Home/Teaching%20Support/Resources/Subscriptions/POD/V10/V10N3.HTM.

Ewing, J. (ed.) (1999). *Towards excellence: Leading a mathematics department in the 21st century.* Providence, RI: American Mathematical Society.

Ganter, S.L. & Kinder, J.S. (eds.) (2000). Targeting institutional change: Quality undergraduate science education for all students. (Conference Executive Summary), *Targeting Curricular*

Change: Reform in Undergraduate Education in Science, Math, Engineering, and Technology (pp. 1–17). Washington, DC: American Association of Higher Education.

Gordon, P., Rogers, A., & Comfort, M. (2001). A taste of problem-based learning increases achievement of urban minority middle-school students. *Educational Horizons, 79* (4), 171–5.

Grossman, P. & Stodolsky, S. (1995). Content as context: The role of school subjects in secondary school teaching. *Educational Researcher, 24* (8), 5–11.

Grossman, P., Wineburg, S., & Beers, S. (2000). When theory meets practice in the world of school. In S. Wineburg & P. Grossman (eds.), *Interdisciplinary curriculum: Challenges to implementation.* New York, NY: Teachers College Press.

Haynes, C. (ed.) (2002). *Innovations in interdisciplinary teaching.* Westport, CT: Oryx Press.

Hoy, R. (2004). New math for biology is the old new math. *Cell Biology Education, 3* (Summer), 90–2.

Jacobs, H. (1989). *Interdisciplinary curriculum: Design and implementation.* Alexandria, VA: ASCD.

Klein, J. (1990). *Interdisciplinarity: History, theory and practice.* Detroit, MI: Wayne State University Press.

Kling, D. & Zimmer, K. (1999). *Weaving curriculum strands together: Data driven results on the implementation of an interdisciplinary/integrated model for high school reform.* ERIC document 429–457.

Korey, J. (2002). Successful interdisciplinary teaching. Paper presented at the 2nd International Conference on Teaching of Mathematics, Hersonissos, Crete.

Krahn, G. (1999). Interdisciplinary culture—A result not a goal. (1999) *Proceedings of the interdisciplinary workshop on core mathematics: Considering change in the first two years of undergraduate mathematics.* West Point, NY. Available at: www.dean.usma.edu/math/activities/ilap/workshops/1999/files/krahn.pdf.

Lederman, N. & Niles, M. (1998). 5 Apples + 4 oranges=? *School Science and Mathematics, 98* (6).

McGraw, S. (ed.) (2003). *Integrated mathematics: Choices and challenges.* Reston, VA: NCTM.

McKinnon, D. (1997). Curriculum innovation involving subject integration, field-based learning environments, and information technology: A longitudinal case study of student attitudes, motivation, and performance. Paper presented at the annual meeting of the American Educational Research Association. Chicago, IL, March, 1997.

Mathematical Sciences Education Board (1993). *Measuring what counts. A conceptual guide for mathematics assessment.* Washington, DC: National Academy Press.

Meier, S.L., Hovde, R.L., & Meier, R.L. (1996). Problem solving: Teachers perceptions, content area models and interdisciplinary connections. *School Science and Mathematics, 96* (5), 230–237.

Miller, K., Metheny, D., & Davidson, D. (1997). Issues in integrating mathematics and science. *Science Educator, 6* (1), 16–21.

Moore, D. & Cobb, G. (2000). Statistics and mathematics: Tension and cooperation. *American Mathematical Monthly,* 615–30.

National Council for the Social Studies (1994). *Expectations of excellence: Curriculum standards for social studies.* Silver Springs, MD: NCSS.

National Council of Teachers of English (1996). *Standards for the English language arts.* Urbana, IL: NCTE.

National Council of Teachers of Mathematics (2000). *Principles and standards for school mathematics.* Reston, VA: NCTM.

National Research Council (1989). Everybody counts: A report to the nation on the future of mathematics education. Washington, DC: National Academies Press.

National Research Council (1996). *National science education standards.* Washington, DC: National Academies Press.

National Science Foundation (1996). *Shaping the future: New expectations for undergraduate education in science, mathematics, engineering, and technology* (NSF96–139). Arlington, VA: NSF.

National Science Teachers Association (2003). *Standards for science teacher preparation.* Arlington, VA: National Science Teachers Association.

Newell, W. (1994). Designing interdisciplinary courses. In J. Klein & W. Doty (eds.), *Interdisciplinary Studies Today* (pp. 35–51). San Francisco, CA: Jossey-Bass.

Newell, W. (1998). Professionalizing interdisciplinarity. In W. Newell (ed.), *Interdisciplinarity: Essays from the literature* (pp. 529–563). New York: College Board.

Newman, M. (2004). Coauthorship networks and patterns of scientific collaboration. *Proceedings of the National Academy of Sciences of the United States of America*, 101, suppl. 1.

Nissani, M. (1997). Ten cheers for interdisciplinarity: The case for interdisciplinary knowledge and research. *Social Science Journal*, *34* (2), 201–16.

Polya, G. (1952). On plausible reasoning. In *Proceedings of the International Congress of Mathematicians—1950*, *1*, *739*. Providence, RI: American Mathematical Society.

Polya, G. (1954). *Mathematics and plausible reasoning*. Princeton, NJ: Princeton University Press.

Rhodes, F. (2001). *The creation of the future*. Ithaca, NY and London: Cornell University Press.

Rutherford, F.J. & Ahlgren, A. (1990). *Science for all Americans*. Oxford: Oxford University Press.

Sage, S. (2000). A natural fit: Problem-based learning and technology standards. *Learning and Leading with Technology*, *28* (1), 6–12.

Tchudi, S. & Lafer, S. (1996). *The interdisciplinary teacher's handbook: Integrated teaching across the curriculum*. Portsmouth, NH: Boynton/Cook.

Ward, J. & Lee, C. (2002). A review of problem-based learning. *Journal of Family and Consumer Sciences Education*, 20(1), 16–26.

Wiggins, G. & McTighe, J. (1998). *Understanding by design*. Alexandria, VA: ASCD.

Wineburg, S., Grossman, P., & Goodlad, J. (2000). *Interdisciplinary curriculum: Challenges to implementation*. New York, NY: Teachers College Press.

Woodbury, S. (1998). Rhetoric, reality and possibilities: Interdisciplinary teaching and secondary mathematics. *School Science and Mathematics*, *98* (6).

CHAPTER 6

Hello Dolly!

Interdisciplinary Curriculum, Authentic Assessment, and Citizenship

ALAN S. MARCUS

> The students hesitated in initiating eye contact with me the day I played the song Hello Dolly from the musical of the same name. Although they were accustomed to my requests for them to sing (I often asked them to sing the popular music to which they listened), without speaking, they sent a clear message: "Sorry, Mr. Marcus, this crosses the line." A proper decorum of visual and verbal communication was quickly re-established when I explained that there would be no singing, but instead a debate about a female named Dolly . . . Dolly the cloned sheep.

Hello Dolly was part of an interdisciplinary unit merging social studies and biology around the common theme of cloning and genetics that was derived from questions about the value of cloning to society. This chapter, using the Dolly unit as one model, proposes that citizenship education is at the core of social studies and of education more generally, and that the creation of interdisciplinary curriculum with authentic assessment is best suited to support the goals of citizenship education. First, I provide some contextual background through an examination of current issues in social studies curriculum and assessment. What follows is an exploration of how interdisciplinary curriculum, specifically one that utilizes authentic assessment, can be employed to promote citizenship education. Citizenship education is not the only purpose of social studies or schooling, and I do not suggest that all curricula should be interdisciplinary. However, I propose that by creating a series of interdisciplinary units relying primarily on authentic assessment, schools can more successfully achieve the goals of citizenship education.

Two specific secondary school examples are presented as models of interdisciplinary curriculum: the first is the unit on cloning and genetics already mentioned, and the second is an elective social studies course titled: *20/20 Visions of the Future: Anticipating the Year 2020*. The discussion in this chapter focuses on the secondary social studies classroom, which is traditionally taught in an isolated disciplinary setting.

Current Issues and Dilemmas

"[S]ocial studies educators have spent a century arguing over what the field 'is' and never reached consensus" (Thornton, 2005, p. 10), and thus "the very lack of agreement regarding the purposes of the field, perhaps more than any other characteristic, has become the hallmark of social studies" (Ross & Marker, 2005, p. 142). The issues and dilemmas influencing social studies curricula and teaching might be broadly categorized into questions about why social studies should be taught, what content should be taught, and how that content should be taught. Although this chapter does not present extensive debates about these issues, a brief discussion is relevant to the larger dialogue about interdisciplinary curricula and assessment.[1]

What *is* social studies? What is the purpose of social studies education? There is broad consensus among educators and social scientists that a primary goal of social studies education, and of education more broadly, is to develop good citizens (Barton & Levstik, 2004; Ross, 1997; Thornton, 2005; VanSledright & Grant, 1994; Wraga, 1993). This rationale is reinforced in national standards and state curriculum frameworks (California Department of Education Curriculum Framework; Center for Civic Education; Connecticut Department of Education Curriculum Framework; National Council for the Social Studies Standards, 1994) and is also supported by the general public (Barton & Levstik, 2004). However, what does it mean to be a good citizen, and what does constructive citizenship education entail? Is it to instill patriotism or build nationalism? Do we educate citizens to sustain and maintain democracy? Is it to create critical thinkers, good map readers, public servants, or even loyal capitalist consumers? Perhaps we teach social studies to create citizens who understand today's world by examining the past. These are just some of the questions asked and ideas debated by lawmakers, professional historians and other social scientists, teachers, curriculum developers, and teacher educators.

Traditionally, social studies includes the sometimes overlapping and amalgamated, and at other times contradictory and disconnected, purposes of citizenship education including a general knowledge of historical facts, critical thinking, and the promotion of patriotism, among others (Barton & Levstik, 2004; Nash *et al.*, 1997; Ross, 1997). More recently, many who teach social studies and develop social studies curricula have advocated the development of a more enriched historical understanding and a multicultural perspective as critical components of a social studies education and citizenship (Banks, 1994; National Council for the Social Studies Standards, 1994; National History Standards, 1994; Seixas, 1996; Wineburg, 2001). These added dimensions of social studies education have created new challenges for the assessment of student understanding as teachers strive to develop new assessment techniques to reliably measure these nontraditional goals.

As the debates about reasons to teach social studies rage, there are parallel discussions about what to teach and how to teach it. Do we attempt to cover all of global and United States history or study less material, but study it in more depth (breadth vs. depth)? Should economics or geography be required courses? Should social studies teachers focus on a more traditional historical narrative emphasizing our country's European roots or present alternative points of view and include the voices of underrepresented groups? Does knowing history mean learning facts or promoting deeper historical thinking? These disputes are not quite as dichotomous or as easily categorizable as I present them here, but illustrate the difficulty in designing a social studies curriculum, particularly given these issues as political lightning rods.

The contentious nature of current issues in the teaching of social studies is not new, but continues to challenge teachers, and ultimately, their students. The "social studies wars" (Evans, 2004) show no sign of abating and may, along with other conditions of schooling, act as barriers to interdisciplinary work involving social studies.

Barriers to Interdisciplinary Work with Social Studies

Social studies is naturally interdisciplinary, easily connected to and overlapping with science, language arts, fine arts, and other subjects.[2] Yet social studies is rarely taught in an interdisciplinary manner in secondary schools where the curriculum is most often organized by academic disciplines. Barriers to interdisciplinary teaching are prevalent in schools, and it is important to recognize their potential impact on interdisciplinary curricula. There are at least two groupings of barriers: those resulting from the structure of schools, curricula, and government oversight, and those that are a consequence of intra-discipline issues. These barriers are not mutually exclusive.

Teachers advocating interdisciplinary teaching and learning struggle against the structure of schools and curricula. At the secondary level, social studies continues to be taught predominately in an isolated class period as students wander from one subject to another in a disconnected daze. *No Child Left Behind* further emphasizes the isolation of subjects by asking states to demonstrate improvement in student learning that is discipline-based. States organize curriculum frameworks by discipline and administer standardized exams that focus on subject matter and distract students from meaningful interdisciplinary learning. These standardized measurements, most of which use multiple-choice questions, discourage the type of authentic learning and assessment that I argue is critical to successful citizenship education. They focus on knowing facts, thus emphasizing rote memorization rather than more meaningful critical thinking.

Many of the current issues and dilemmas in social studies education discussed earlier—breadth versus depth, competing narratives of history, and the role of critical thinking—directly affect teachers' abilities to develop and implement interdisciplinary curricula. Teachers may become so caught-up in the intra-discipline tumult that they become entrenched in a way of thinking or grow to be utterly confused.

Although these issues may distract teachers from the ability or desire to enact interdisciplinary lessons, there are possible alternatives to assist teachers in maneuvering around these barriers. Cuban (2001) calls the types of barriers presented here dilemmas. Problems, Cuban proposes, are solvable, but dilemmas require management because ultimately they cannot be solved, and they involve multiple competing values. One such way to manage these social studies dilemmas may be through interdisciplinary curriculum design that values authentic assessment and the student experience.

Against this backdrop it may seem that all of the intra-disciplinary issues in social studies education generate enough of a challenge without the complication of an interdisciplinary agenda. Yet one point that it seems almost all social studies stakeholders can agree upon is that citizen education is central to the mission of schooling and particularly of social studies (Barton & Levstik, 2004; Thornton, 2005). Although there are various conceptions of what it means to be a good citizen and thus how to mold or encourage superb citizens, I seize onto the notion that citizenship education is a core component of K-12 education, and that interdisciplinary curricula offers one potentially productive means to support this goal.

Interdisciplinary Curriculum, Authentic Assessment, and Citizenship

Building on the notion that citizenship education is one of the most important and most agreed upon purposes of social studies education, this section provides a framework for citizenship education and its import-ance, and a rationale for why interdisciplinary curriculum, combined with authentic assessment, can buoy the goals of citizenship education.

Citizenship Education

Citizenship education has been a central goal of the social studies and education more generally for nearly one hundred years (Ross, 1997) and continues to be social studies' primary rationale (Barton & Levstik, 2004; VanSledright & Grant, 1994) with "democratic citizenship and citizenship education [as] arguably, the two principal and most historically dominant concepts in the entire field of social education" (Vinson, 2001, p. 400). National and state standards also support citizenship education as an important goal. Table 6.1 illustrates how citizenship education is incorp-orated into national social studies and civics standards and state curricular standards with California and Connecticut as examples.[3]

One of the most common underlying purposes of citizenship education is to promote and maintain our democracy; however, there are many competing ideas about what type of citizen best fosters democracy (Evans, 1997; Ross, 1997; Westheimer & Kahne, 2004). While most concur that the promotion of democracy is an important mission (Westheimer & Kahne, 2004), over the past century various constituencies have promoted citizen-ship education to be about knowing historical facts—what Hirsch (1988) calls cultural literacy, understanding the functions of our government, patriotism, character education, community involvement, other civic par-ticipation such as voting and jury duty, critical thinking about problems in society, and promoting justice, among others (Barton & Levstik, 2004; Nash *et al.*, 1997; VanSledright & Grant, 1994, p. 305; Westheimer & Kahne, 2004).

Among all of these models of citizenship, Westheimer and Kahne (2004) help us to sort through the citizenship muck by presenting and discuss-ing three "visions" (p. 239) of citizenship that are derived from the current debate as to what kind of citizen is required to support an effective demo-cratic society: (1) the personally responsible citizen, (2) the participatory citizen, and/or (3) the justice-oriented citizen. Table 6.2 provides a brief description of each type of citizen.

I agree with Westheimer and Kahne's proposition that the personably responsible model is not enough and is "an inadequate response to the challenges of educating a democratic citizenry" (Westheimer & Kahne, 2004, p. 243). Personal responsibility is certainly a desirable trait in citizens and community members, but it is not unique to or adequate for a democratic society. After all, these same traits could apply in a dictatorship or other non-democratic forms of government (Barton & Levstik, 2004).

TABLE 6.1 Citizenship and national/state curriculum framework excerpts

National Council for the Social Studies	An understanding of civic ideals and practices of citizenship is critical to full participation in society and is a central purpose of the social studies.
	Social studies programs should include experiences that provide for the study of the ideals, principles, and practices of citizenship in a democratic republic.
National Civics Standards	*9–12 Content Standards*
	What are Civic Life, Politics, and Government?
	What is civic life? What is politics? What is government? Why are government and politics necessary? What purposes should government serve?
	What are the Roles of the Citizen in American Democracy? What is citizenship?
	What are the rights of citizens?
	What are the responsibilities of citizens?
	What civic dispositions or traits of private and public character are important to the preservation and improvement of American constitutional democracy?
	How can citizens take part in civic life?
State of Connecticut Curriculum Frameworks	Student will . . . demonstrate an understanding of how ideals, principles and practices of citizenship have emerged over time and across cultures.
	Students will demonstrate knowledge of the rights and responsibilities of citizens to participate in and shape public policy, and contribute to the maintenance of our democratic way of life.
State of California Curriculum Frameworks	Students evaluate and take and defend positions on the scope and limits of rights and obligations as democratic citizens, the relationships among them, and how they are secured.

TABLE 6.2 Three visions of citizens (Westheimer & Kahne, 2004)

Type of citizen	Characteristics
The personally responsible citizen	Acts responsibly—obeys laws, gives blood.
	Programs seek to build character by emphasizing honesty, integrity, self-discipline, and hard work.
The participatory citizen	Actively participates in civic affairs at local, state, and national levels.
	Programs teach how government and community-based organizations work and train to participate.
The justice-oriented citizen	Believes in the importance of pursuing social injustice.
	Programs analyze and understand the interplay of social, economic, and political forces and create social change.

That is not to say that personal responsibility is not important, but it should be only one layer of citizenship education.

I propose then, that truly successful citizenship education does not ignore the importance of personally responsible behaviors such as obeying laws, but focuses primarily on citizens who actively participate in civic affairs, understand how our democratic society functions, can critically think about social issues and problems, and take action when necessary. In other words, I support the notion that citizens are personally responsible in the sense that they are upstanding members of the community, but, emphasize the centrality and significance of citizens who participate and are justice-oriented. The purpose of schooling should be to expose students to these various conceptions of citizenship and scaffold the connection between active citizenship and democracy all the while emphasizing the value of the democratic way of life.

Although a potential tension exists between the personally responsible citizen, who may be patriotic and loyal, and the justice-oriented citizen who is often critical of society and the government, I believe these categories are not mutually exclusive. Personally responsible citizens can still obey the law and exhibit patriotism (though not blind patriotism) while at the same time critically examining society. In fact, one could argue that true loyalty to the government and society means maintaining a democracy that includes freedom of speech and the free flow of ideas. As soon as blind patriotism (e.g., McCarthyism) becomes dominant, we are no longer citizens promoting the democratic way of life. Citizens should be personally responsible for sustaining democracy, not any one political party or any one form of patriotism. After all, healthy critique is an important way to initiate reform and improvement.

In advocating the scaffolding of both the participatory and justice-oriented citizen, I must recognize that Westheimer & Kahne (2004) perceptively propose that participatory and justice-oriented citizenship signify potentially different beliefs and imply important implications for pedagogy and curriculum. However, they also state that while school programs do not necessarily meet the aims of more than one type of citizen, it is possible for educational programs to "further both goals [for the participatory and justice-oriented citizen]" (p. 241). This is not to declare that school activities designed to develop citizenship address both types of citizens at the same time (though many may do just that), but that any citizenship program or set of activities seeks to cultivate both types of citizens over the course of a student's K-12 education.

Although "conceptions of democracy and citizenship have been and will likely always be debate" (Westheimer & Kahne, 2004, p. 238), my aim here is not to extensively deliberate theoretical models for citizenship education, but to draw on established scholarship as a model for what citizenship education could be, and as I propose, should be, as enhanced by inter-disciplinary curriculum and authentic assessment.

Interdisciplinary Curriculum and Citizenship Education

While the brunt of the responsibility for citizenship education has tradi-tionally rested with the social studies, citizenship education is a goal of education more generally, and should be shared more broadly through interdisciplinary curriculum. I am not advocating for a complete restruc-turing of state or district curriculum, but for schools to develop a series of interdisciplinary units to be infused during the school year and/or to cultivate elective courses. Developing a series of units and elective courses is more manageable and realistic than a complete restructuring, allowing for each school to draw on the expertise of its faculty and to meet the needs of the community and students, and is thus more flexible and adaptable.

How does interdisciplinary curriculum support the development of the participatory and justice-oriented citizen? This idea is not entirely new as "educational theory and practice have long embraced interdisciplinary studies as a powerful means of educating students for enlightened demo-cratic citizenship" (Wraga, 1993, p. 211). Central to the importance of interdisciplinary teaching is that citizenship in a democracy is complicated. In order to participate and be focused on justice, citizens need to be able to draw on knowledge from multiple disciplines and utilize skills devel-oped through multiple disciplines. "[T]he interdisciplinary imperative for citizenship education stems from the reality that in order to understand and to act upon complex societal issues effectively, citizens must be able to integrate knowledge from a variety of subjects" (Wraga, 1993, p. 201).

A significant difficulty is that few specific disciplines within social studies (e.g., history, geography, and economics) have citizenship education at the core of their purpose (Evans, 1997). The same holds true for non-social studies disciplines such as biology, mathematics, literature, and world languages. While it may be possible to extrapolate the necessary know-ledge and skills one subject at a time, a more efficient and perhaps effective model is to use interdisciplinary units to realize citizenship education. The supremacy of discipline-based education "flies in the face of efforts to educate an enlightened citizenry for a democratic society" (Wraga, 1993, p. 202).

Finally, as Wraga (1993) concludes, "[c]ivic competence involves, among other things, the ability to identify a pressing social problem, to examine it in its widest dimensions and implications, and to act upon it accordingly" (p. 201). Yet, the problems and dilemmas confronted by citizens which may require participation and justice seeking are rarely bound by discipline.

These problems and dilemmas are interdisciplinary in the knowledge required to understand them and in the skills necessary to manage them.

Interdisciplinary units, while still drawing from the knowledge base in each discipline, can potentially offer activities that are more realistic and similar to a citizen's societal existence. These units may create opportunities for inquiry into real-world dilemmas in a more holistic manner. One reason for this is that interdisciplinary units are more likely to be issue-based or theme-based. Interdisciplinary units can also be designed specifically with citizenship education goals at their core. Students will still be exposed to the workings of each discipline through the traditional curriculum but will be able to better connect their knowledge and skills from each discipline and apply them to citizenship. Interdisciplinary units are essential; however, in order to fully take advantage of their potential, these units should rely heavily on authentic assessments, as discussed next.

Authentic Assessment and Citizenship Education

The goal of citizenship education through interdisciplinary curriculum is enhanced through the use of authentic means of assessing student learning. The purpose of assessment should not be just to assign grades, but to measure how well we are achieving our learning objectives, which then provides a tactic to improve our teaching and thus student learning.

One of the most common and traditional forms of assessment in social studies is the multiple choice exam. Unfortunately, these exams emphasize memorization of information and passive learning over the skills, ways of thinking, and types of activities necessary for successful citizenship education as defined above. In order to meet the objectives of developing citizens we can no longer rely so heavily on the types of lessons and objectives that are best measured through multiple choice exams or other assessments that tend to stress the importance of memorization and fail to engage students. Knowing basic facts does support a deeper under-standing of social studies and other subjects and can be an important part of learning; however, it does not develop the ways of thinking and types of skills essential for participatory and justice-oriented citizenship.

More recently, many teachers and teacher educators advocate alternative types of assessment including *authentic assessment* that "conveys the idea that assessment should engage students in applying knowledge and skills in the same way they are used in the real world" (Drake & Nelson, 2005) and that shows students have the "ability to do things that are valued in the adult world" (Brandt, 1996, p. 5). In the real world lives of students, their experiences are not sorted by discipline. Outside of school, adolescents do not experience math at 9 a.m., French at 10 a.m., and physical education at 3 p.m. A student's world *is* interdisciplinary. Interdisciplinary curricula may be a more authentic way to learn, and authentic assessment engages students in activities that mirror their real-world experiences and are, therefore, interdisciplinary. Thus, authentic assessment and interdisciplinary curricula complement and support one another in bridging students' real life experiences and schooling.

For example, instead of responding to multiple choice questions and answering an essay question, students might write a letter to the editor of the local paper or interpret a political cartoon; instead of, or in addition to, reading a textbook about history, students might analyze and interpret primary source documents, visit historic sites, and generate their own solutions to past social problems. I distinguish between authentic assessment as defined above and performance assessment which asks students to create a product to demonstrate knowledge. All authentic assessments are also a type of performance assessment, but not all performance assessments are necessarily authentic. Authentic assessments "simulate or replicate authentic, messy, real-world challenges, contexts, and constraints faced by adult professionals, consumers, or citizens" (Wiggins, 1998, p. x).

The knowledge and skills students will need to make decisions as citizens can be fostered through authentic assessment. According to Gardner, students "lack the capacity to take knowledge learned in one setting and apply it appropriately in a different setting. Study after study has found that, by and large, even the best students in the best schools can't do that" (Gardner as quoted in Brandt, 1996, p. 4). Using authentic assessment with interdisciplinary units may aid students in bridging the gap between discipline-based course work and real-life settings in which their citizenship flourishes or flounders. In fact, one study, as reported by Ross (2001), indicated that students who were assessed through more authentic learning experiences such as mock trials and student government "had greater civic knowledge and engagement outside the classroom than other students" (p. 395). He concludes that:

> we should not be content to merely teach the principles of democracy and then wait for our students to translate those principles into action. This great leap forward, from understanding democratic principles to active engagement as a democratic citizen and ultimately to the creation of a truly democratic society requires all of us to start making connections that are generally not made.
> (Ross, 2001, p. 396)

Curriculum that is interdisciplinary and relies heavily on authentic assessment may provide the stimulation needed for students to become educated citizens and participate meaningfully in a democratic society.

Models of Interdisciplinary Units and Authentic Assessment: Dolly and Visions of the Future

What might interdisciplinary units employing authentic assessment and supporting citizenship education look like? What follows are two examples that serve as models of the type of interdisciplinary curriculum using authentic assessment that I believe is possible and necessary.

Dolly the Cloned Sheep

Kennedy High School,[4] located just outside of downtown Atlanta, GA, is a math/science magnet school. During my seven-year tenure at the school, I was asked to teach a unique course for the magnet program from a social science perspective. The course was titled *Topics and Issues in Medicine*— a pre-pre-med class—and it covered a history of medicine, public policy and health care, issues in the medical profession (types of careers, medical insurance, etc.), and bioethics. During the initial year of the course, Julie Heath, a biology teacher and the Science Department Chair, and I chaperoned a field trip to Boston together. During our four-day trip we discovered that we both taught about genetics and cloning from very different perspectives but with similar goals for student understanding. Our idea for an interdisciplinary unit was born and we implemented it the following school year.

The cloning unit's underpinning was the question of the impact and value of cloning to society. Rather than starting from the disciplinary perspectives, we focused on what is important to know and understand and avoided what Kaufman (2003) calls the "cute" interdisciplinary unit (p. 98). We were not familiar with any particular theoretical model for creating our interdisciplinary unit in this manner, but it so happened that Ms. Heath and I desired similar goals for our students: to understand the science behind genetics and cloning and analyze/debate the potential impact—positive and negative—on various segments of society. Our central question asked how cloning impacted society, ultimately considering whether or not cloning should be allowed. If so, what should be cloned and by whom? Rather than considering separate disciplinary perspectives on the topic, we believed that the science and ethics of cloning were intertwined, perhaps like the double helix of DNA we studied during the unit. Although there were days when Ms. Heath taught how cloning could be achieved, using the case of the cloned sheep Dolly[5] as an example, and there were days when I led discussions and activities around the impact of cloning on society, we did not view these as "biology days" and "social studies days." Understanding the science was critical to discussing the ethical implications, and no study of science is complete without exploring the potential societal impact. If the class were still taught today, we might include discussions about President Bush's policies on embryo research policy, the California ballot initiative to provide money to fund embryo research, or even the recent Star Wars films "Attack of the Clones" and "Revenge of the Sith." In both films cloned humans play a key role.

The cloning unit was divided into two segments. In various years the first part lasted roughly three to eight days within a daily block schedule with 94 minutes periods. During part one, our classes met together. Part two of the unit had each class retreating back to their own classroom space where the unit was connected to other parts of the curriculum in each course. In the medical issues class, the cloning unit was one of five or six units[6] within the larger issue of bioethics.

Dolly Assessment

The unit's assessments were also split into two segments. We conducted formative assessment during the joint sessions while a summative assessment took place once the classes were re-divided. The students participated in two types of formative authentic assessment. The first was an exercise where students were paired into married couples who could choose the characteristics of their cloned child with each characteristic costing a set sum. Couples were constrained by a small monetary allowance and the costs associated with the characteristics and chose from among physical characteristics (blue eyes, athletic), types of intelligence, various genetic defects (or lack thereof), etc. Students worked with their partner to choose their child's characteristics and participated in small-group and whole-class discussion about their decision making process and about cloning more broadly, including issues of values and government policy. As scaffolding prior to the activity, students read and discussed several articles about the science and ethics of cloning. The goals of this assessment were for students to understand how limited resources impact medical decisions, evaluate the value of genetic traits and the ethical and moral implications associated with cloning, re-evaluate prior assumptions and points of view through exposure to multiple perspectives, and analyze the past, present, and future role of government policy in the cloning debate. This interdisciplinary assessment asked students to build on their knowledge of the science of genetics and cloning and consider some of the policy and moral issues with which scientists and elected officials grapple. It also provided multiple perspectives from the fields of science and social studies as well as from individual students. By engaging students in an authentic learning and assessment activity students role-played how the issue of cloning could play out in the real world. Ms. Heath and I did not grade the students based on which characteristics they chose but examined how well they defended their choices and how these decisions were framed through science and policy lenses.

The second authentic assessment consisted of a debate about the value of cloning to society and whether or not cloning animals and humans should be legal. Issues that were addressed in various years by students included the role of the government in society and in relation to science, the origin of people's morals and values, the role of religion in public policy, and the impact of limited resources in society. The goals of this assessment were for students to develop well-supported claims about whether cloning should be legal, analyze the impact of religion, limited resources, scientific data, and other factors in policy decisions, and evaluate the scientific perspectives on cloning. The assessment asked students to draw from their own knowledge in conjunction with multiple disciplinary perspectives, and assessed students based on their ability to intelligently participate in an activity that might mirror public discussions of important policy issues related to scientific advances.

The summative assessment was not authentic and consisted of different versions of an exam in both classes with multiple-choice questions focused on the science of cloning and genetics and essays concentrated on the ethical and societal questions. Upon reflection, a more authentic summative assessment could have added even more value to the unit, particularly in terms of citizenship education.

Table 6.3 illustrates the way the unit's topic and assessments connect to participatory and justice-oriented citizenship.

TABLE 6.3 Two types of citizens and bioethics unit

Type of citizen	Characteristics	Issues addressed during unit that connect to type of citizen	Specific assessment used
The participatory citizen	Actively participates in civic affairs at local, state, and national levels. Programs teach how government and community-based organizations work and train to participate.	• The role of government in society and in relation to science • Understanding limited resources • Considering multiple perspectives	• Debate about whether cloning should be legal
The justice oriented citizen	Believes in the importance of pursuing social injustice. Programs analyze and understand the interplay of social, economic, and political forces and create social change.	• What is a public good? • Role of religion in public policy • Understanding limited resources and their allocation • Making decisions about government policy	• Couple choosing cloned child • Debate about whether cloning should be legal

Although this unit did not have the explicit goal of citizenship education, it encouraged the skills and behavior commensurate with the participatory and justice-oriented citizen with an emphasis on the justice-oriented citizen. The next model provides an alternate case that reflects on a year-long class rather than a single unit.

20/20 Visions of the Future: Anticipating the Year 2020

Thanks primarily to a very supportive principal, dedicated students, and some persistence, *20/20 Visions of the Future: Anticipating the Year 2020* was created as a social studies elective at Kennedy High School. The course was guided by the teacher, but was also heavily reliant on the students to develop the course's core curriculum and determine its goals. The class, based on a project at Tufts University, the Education for Public Inquiry and International Citizenship (EPIIC)[7] project, was designed to spend the year exploring a theme in-depth and to organize a regional symposium for high school students. Students also visited EPIIC to participate in a workshop with other high school students. Each participating school represented a country or non-governmental organization and took part in a role-playing simulation around issues of global importance. Each year during the five-year tenure of the course, I chose a theme, often in conjunction with Tufts' EPIIC theme, and asked the students to determine our primary focus of study within that theme.

Here I will focus on year two of the class, 20/20 Visions of the Future. Twenty-four students participated in the year-long course. Several of these students were veterans of the previous year's course, a few were recruited due to academic achievement or other skills, some signed up because of interest in the subject, and still others were recommended by the school's guidance counselors who worked with me to place several "at-risk" students in the class who might benefit from the unique content, class structure, and assessment practices. The class composition included a diverse mix of students in terms of race, ethnicity, gender, religion, and traditionally high and low achieving students.

From the chosen theme for this year students chose seven topics for study:

- Bioethics/bioengineering
- Automation/robotics/computers/technology
- Public health
- Space exploration
- Global issues
- Race and Gender Relations
- Urban Planning

The students and I worked together to develop a curriculum around these topics. Once the topics were finalized, the students and I became a team that explored these issues together. Clearly, I was not an expert on each of these areas and, in fact, knew very little about space exploration and automation/robotics. On occasion we held a more traditional class with teacher-planned activities. However, more often than not the classes were student-centered or involved other specialists. Each student was placed on three committees: two content committees, choosing from the seven topics, and one planning committee to handle symposium planning and execution. A significant portion of class time was devoted to work in these committees. Students researched, discussed, wrote, and regularly presented to other members of the class. In addition, we had eleven guest speakers ranging from a *Sport Illustrated* reporter discussing race and gender relations issues to a hospital ethics director speaking about bioethics to the Consul General of the Israeli Consulate in Atlanta addressing various global issues.

In addition to the content exploration, the students planned for and ran a one-day symposium for 300 high school colleagues from ten schools throughout the Atlanta metropolitan area. Their responsibilities included:

- Researching, writing, and editing a "briefing book" about each topic, which was distributed to the 300 participants a month prior to the symposium to prepare the guests for active participation.
- Recruiting panelists from the local community for the symposium. Attending panelists included a Georgia state senator as the keynote speaker, Emory University professors of philosophy and medicine, ethics directors of two local hospitals, executives from IBM Corporation, an engineer from the Georgia Institute of Technology, professors from Georgia State University, professionals from the Center for Disease Control, a former Deputy Director for the North Atlantic Treaty Organization (NATO), the Consul General from the Mexican Consulate in Atlanta, producers from the Cable News Network (CNN), and representatives of the Anti-Defamation League, ACLU, the United States Department of Agriculture, and the Federal Transit Authority.
- Creating and running a simulation for all 300 guests.
- Planning, filming, editing, and producing a twenty-minute video on the topics discussed and shown at the symposium.
- Fundraising from corporations and local businesses to raise the $13,000 needed to run the symposium. Corporate support included the IBM Corporation (who hosted the event), The Carter Presidential Center, and others. The fundraising also included a 50-inning marathon softball game with people pledging per inning.

- Preparation for the trip to Tufts University and a role-playing simulation revolving around many of the same topics.

Clearly this was an enormous amount of work. Students (and their teacher) put in many hours after school and on weekends to ensure a successful symposium. Our principal was also extremely supportive and donated several hours per week of secretarial assistance from his office.

20/20 Assessment

This course reflected an interdisciplinary approach to learning that incorporated political science, history, biology, physics, math, language arts, fine arts, and other disciplines. The assessment practices relied almost exclusively on authentic assessment tasks. There were no exams. Assignments were partially designed by students and primarily created to contribute to the exploration of our topics, culminating in the summative assessments. The goals of the course were for students to develop a deeper understanding and knowledge base for each of our topics, analyze how these topics related to and built upon each other, evaluate how these topics may impact society by the year 2020, develop community outreach skills, and to evaluate the learning needs of their peers and develop appropriate and effective learning experiences both within the class and for the symposium. There were numerous formative authentic assessments for the students that supported the interdisciplinary curriculum including writing the briefing book, working with members of the local business, academic, and government community, role-playing simulations, and teaching their peers. The assessments all scaffolded the summative interdisciplinary assessments which were also authentic—running the symposium and participating in the workshop at Tufts.

Table 6.4 displays how the class and the specific assignments aligned with the participatory and justice-oriented citizen.

The interdisciplinary nature of the course combined with authentic assessments required students to actively participate in civic affairs and contemplate numerous conflicts and controversies immersed in issues of justice. The in-depth longitudinal nature of our study allowed for students to understand the complexity of ideas, events, and controversies. It also promoted an understanding of the intricate political nature of active participation in civic life. The activities of the class were based on real-life situations and clearly connected the students' school experience to the outside world. In addition, the students wielded significant influence as to the topics covered, the types of activities planned, and the ultimate outcomes for themselves and the symposium. This opportunity further augmented their participation. While the cloning unit was more focused on the justice-

TABLE 6.4 Two types of citizens and Visions of the future course

Type of citizen	Characteristics	How class addressed type of citizen	Specific assessment used
The participatory citizen	Actively participate in civic affairs at local, state, and national levels. Teaching how government and community-based organizations work and training to participate.	• Development of relationships with various stakeholders in Atlanta area. • Cooperation with the Atlanta Regional Commission, a regional planning agency • Partnerships with local corporations and businesses • Eleven guest speakers during the year • Culminating symposium for 300 peers • Preparation for role play at Tufts	• Writing and editing the briefing book • Research on various topics • Planning of symposium (recruiting panellists, inviting other schools, raising money) • Running of symposium including a simulation • Creating curriculum • Presentations to class • Working with media • Role-play at Tufts Inquiry Program
The justice oriented citizen	Importance of pursuing social injustice. Analyze and understand the interplay of social, economic, and political forces. Create social change.	• Exposure to multiple perspectives • Specific topics covered including bioethics/ bioengineering, public health, race and gender relations, and urban planning.	• Role-play at Tufts Inquiry Program • Research on various topics

oriented citizen, the 20/20 class may have favored the participatory citizen, particularly when it came to the assessments.

Over the five years I taught this course, it was clear that the interdisciplinary nature of our curriculum, combined with the focus on authentic assessment, was effective at meeting the courses' objectives and in developing better citizens. Students consistently applied what they were learning to their lives out of school, exhibited greater interest in issues of public policy, took strong positions on issues of social justice, and went on to pursue college majors and activities that continued the process of participatory and justice oriented citizenship, including careers in medicine, public health, journalism, education, and religion. Recently I received an email from one of the symposium participants who is now a high school science teacher and is creating his own symposium course.

Conclusions

The two models discussed illustrate two possible scenarios in which citizenship education could play out in classrooms. I believe that interdisciplinary units using authentic assessment, such as is the case with the Dolly unit and the 20/20 class, may be better able to address and promote both the participatory and justice-oriented citizen effectively.

Although state standards and district curriculum may include citizenship education as an important goal, these goals may not trickle down into daily classroom activities. Through interdisciplinary units or elective courses that utilize authentic assessment as the core of assessment practices, citizenship education could be brought more to the foreground and explicitly addressed.

There is some evidence that activities that more explicitly focus on citizenship education positively impact students. Westheimer and Kahne report two examples, including one that promoted participatory citizens and another that promoted justice-oriented citizens. In the first case students completed service learning (authentic assessment) projects. This experience "had significant success in making learning relevant to students, conveying practical knowledge about how to engage in community affairs, and demonstrating to students the ways that classroom-based academic knowledge can be used for civic working the community" (Westheimer & Kahne, 2004, p. 250). They concluded that the class activities developed students' interest in contributing to civic affairs. In the second case the class activities, connecting school-based academic work to educational experiences in the community, increased students' interest in politics and political issues. The program appeared to help students to recognize and critically address injustice in their community.

Westheimer and Kahne are quick to point out that programs that support participatory citizens do not necessarily promote justice-oriented citizens and vice-versa. What I propose is a series of interdisciplinary units and possibly course electives rooted in authentic assessment, that over the course of several years directly address both types of citizenship. Certain units may address one type of citizen or the other, or both, but the cumulative effect is for students to be better citizens through both participation and justice-oriented activities.

It is important to recognize that what I envision is not an easy task. Interdisciplinary units and authentic assessment do not solve every educational dilemma and could even aggravate issues such as debates about what to teach and how to teach it. All curricula do not need to be interdisciplinary and all assessments do not need to be authentic, but the more these two become part of standard operating procedure in schools the more likely we are to succeed in educating citizens. Clearly, the current focus on standardized tests, which emphasize subject-specific disciplines and non-authentic assessments, works against this vision of citizenship education. A central mission of schools is to develop citizens. Interdisciplinary teaching with authentic assessment is not only feasible, but with the increasing demands of *No Child Left Behind*, it is even more critical.

Ultimately, individual schools and the teachers who are the curricular-instructional gatekeepers (Thornton, 2005) must decide what is best for their school, classes, and students based on learning goals. As Barton and Levstik (2004) so aptly conclude, no one knows for sure what kind of education prepares students for participatory democracy because "there are no societies that currently exhibit the levels of participation, pluralism, and deliberation that we advocate, and as a result, there is no way to determine, empirically, which educational procedures most effectively develop the qualities needed for such citizenship" (p. 35).

The preservation of democracy will continue to be one of the primary functions of schooling; however, without a closer evaluation of whether or not we are meeting our citizenship goals, they are likely to continue to exist in name only. In his inauguration address, John F. Kennedy uttered his now famous words: "ask not what your country can do for you, but what you can do for your country." This seems like an excellent place to start.

Notes

1   For a more extensive discussion of these issues and dilemmas see *The Social Studies Curriculum* by E. Wayne Ross (1997).
2   Social Studies is both intra-disciplinary (history, political science, sociology, anthropology, economics, etc.) and interdisciplinary. The focus of this chapter is on the interdisciplinary nature of social studies.
3   California and Connecticut were chosen as examples because they are at various ends of the spectrum with regards to specific detail and required coverage. While California's standards specify content in detail, Connecticut's are much more broad with less specific content to be covered and instead provides general guiding goals and objectives. Both approaches have their benefits and pitfalls and are met with mixed review by teachers.
4   All school and teacher names have been changed for confidentiality.
5   Dolly was named after Dolly Parton and born at the Roslin Institute in Edinburgh, Scotland in 1996. Dolly died in 2003.
6   Units within the Bioethics segment of class ranged from a general exploration of morals, values, and ethics, to issues such as euthanasia, assisted suicide, and how to distribute limited resources such as money and organs.
7   See: www.epiic.org.

Bibliography

Banks, J.A. (1994). Transforming the mainstream curriculum. *Educational Leadership, 51* (8), 4–8.
Barton, K.C. & Levstik, L.S. (2004). *Teaching history for the common good.* Mahwah, NJ: Lawrence Erlbaum Associates.
Brandt, R. (1996). On authentic performance assessment. *Educational Leadership, 54* (4), 5.
California State Department of Education. *History Standards.* Retrieved June 1, 2005. Available at: www.cde.ca.gov/be/st/ss/hstgrade12.asp.

Center for Civic Education. *National Standards for Civics and Government.* Retrieved June 1, 2005. Available at: www.civiced.org/stds.html.

Connecticut State Department of Education. *History Standards.* Retrieved June 1, 2005. Available at: www.state.ct.us/sde/dtl/curriculum/currsocs.htm.

Cuban, L. (2001). *How can I fix it? Finding solutions and managing dilemmas.* New York: Teachers College Press.

Drake, F.D. & Nelson, L.R. (2005). *Engagement in teaching history.* Upper Saddle River, NJ: Pearson Education.

Evans, R.W. (1997). *Teaching social studies: Implementing an issues-centered curriculum.* In E.W. Ross (ed.), *The Social Studies Curriculum* (pp. 291–312). Albany, NY: State University of New York Press.

Evans, R.W. (2004). *The social studies wars: What should we teach the children?* New York: Teachers College Press.

Hirsch, E.D. (1988). *Cultural literacy: What every American needs to know.* Boston, MA: Houghton Mifflin Company.

Kaufman, D. (2003). Reading in the world and writing to learn: Lessons from writers about creating transdisciplinary inquiry. In D. Kaufman, D.M. Moss, & T.A. Osborn (eds.), *Beyond the boundaries: A transdisciplinary approach to learning and teaching.* Westport, CT: Praeger Publishers.

Nash, G., Crabtree, C., & Dunn, R.E. (1997). *History on trial: Culture wars and the teaching of the past.* New York: Alfred A. Knopf.

National Center for History in the Schools (1994). *National standards for United States history.* Los Angeles, CA: UCLA. Retrieved June 11, 2002. Available at: www.sscnet.ucla.edu/nchs/standards/.

National Council for the Social Studies Standards (1994). *Curriculum Standards for Social Studies.* Bulletin 89. Washington, DC: NCSS. Retrieved June 20, 2001. Available at: www.ncss.org/standards/exec.html.

Ross, E.W. (1997). The struggle for the social studies curriculum. In E.W. Ross (ed.), *The social studies curriculum* (pp. 19–42). Albany, NY: State University of New York Press.

Ross, E.W. (2001). Waiting for the great leap forward: From democratic principles to democratic reality. *Theory and Research in Social Education, 29* (3), 142–51.

Ross, E.W. & Marker, P.M. (2005). (If social studies is wrong) I don't want to be right. *Theory and Research in Social Education, 33* (1), 142–51.

Stearns, P. (1998). Why study history? Washington, DC: American Historical Association. Retrieved May 15, 2005. Available at: www.historians.org/pubs/Free/WhyStudyHistory.htm.

Stearns, P., Seixas, P., & Wineburg, S. (eds.) (2000). *Knowing, teaching, and learning history.* New York: New York University Press.

Thornton, S.J. (2005). *Teaching social studies that matters: Curriculum for active learning.* New York: Teachers College Press.

VanSledright, B.A. & Grant, S.G. (1994). Citizenship education and the persistent nature of classroom teaching dilemmas. *Theory and Research in Social Education, 22* (3), 305–39.

Vinson, K.D. (2001). Connected citizenship: Special issue introduction. *Theory and Research in Social Education, 29* (3), 400–4.

Westheimer, J. & Kahne, J. (2004). What kind of citizen? The politics of educating for democracy. *American Educational Research Journal, 41* (2), 237–69.

Wiggins, G. & McTighe, J. (1998). *Understanding by design.* Alexandria, VA: Association for Supervision and Curriculum Developments.

Wineburg, S. (2001). *Historical thinking and other unnatural acts: Charting the future of teaching the past.* Philadelphia, PA: Temple University Press.

Wraga, W.G. (1993). The interdisciplinary imperative for citizenship education. *Theory and Research in Social Education, 21* (3), 201–31.

CHAPTER 7

Language Learning as an Interdisciplinary Endeavor

TERRY A. OSBORN

I have argued that there could be an understandable position taken by educators to view the discipline of language education as the one example of a truly interdisciplinary discipline (Osborn, 2005b). We often include elements of political science, cuisine, drama, film, literature, cultural studies, history, mathematics, and even English grammar in the foreign language classroom, traditionally grouping all the facets into one of five categories: speaking, reading, writing, listening, and culture.

The *Standards for Foreign Language Learning*, similar to standards in other disciplines, call for interdisciplinary study when they suggest that:

> The conscious effort to connect the foreign language curriculum with other parts of students' academic lives opens doors to information and experiences which enrich the entire school and life experience. Those connections flow from other areas to the foreign language classroom and also originate in the foreign language classroom to add unique experiences and insights to the rest of the curriculum.
>
> (National Standards for Foreign Language Education Project, 1996, p. 49)

At the level of higher education, this interdisciplinarity takes many forms, including cultural studies. For example, in Kecht's and von

Hammerstein's (2000), *Languages across the curriculum: Interdisciplinary structures and internationalized education*, Heidi Byrnes (2000), noted that curriculum renewal is experiencing a sort of epiphany of late in the foreign language field, arguing that:

> [M]any departments have replaced a primarily philological or literary focus with what has been called a Cultural Studies approach. Second, departments attempted to expand a narrow disciplinary orientation to cross-disciplinary, at times even interdisciplinary, perspectives, involving not only the content foci of diverse fields such as anthropology, sociology, education, history, politics, and economics, but also their diverse methodologies and standards of scholarship. And, finally, the Languages Across the Curriculum movement and, more recently , various models for content-based language instruction (CBI) responded to broad changes in our field and society at large, often by at least rhetorically reasserting the inherent linkage between language, literature, and culture.
>
> (Byrnes, 2000, p. 155)

Swaffar (2000) argues that the approach prevalent in the field (that of spoken language being taught primarily at the introductory level of language courses followed by utilizing short texts in the second year) fails "to provide students with content and discursive continuity, that hierarchy illustrates few applications of context as bearer of meaning . . . textbook passages in beginning classes seldom link reading selections to the learner's knowledge base in other disciplines" (p. 125).

Foreign language educators have even attempted to draw on other models of language education, notable Teaching English to Speakers of Other Languages (TESOL) or bilingual education, to craft a more "interdisciplinary" content and language through dual language instructional programs, for example, which have as a foundation, "a complex mosaic involving theory, research, and discourse from several different areas of scholarship and inquiry" (Lessow-Hurley, 1996, p. xii). Shrum and Glisan (2000) point out that linking language with content in language courses is a worthwhile goal.

Contemporary and more critical insights into foreign language education suggest that the curriculum will need to move beyond the formula of "four-skills plus culture" to include issues of the ways in which languages function in a sociocultural context such as the United States democracy. A partial list of issues that would need to be explored would include:

- The social context of language use.
- The nature and implications of code-switching and code mixing.

- Bilingualism and multilingualism as individual and social norms.
- Ideology and language.
- Issues of language standardization and linguistic purism.
- The concept of linguistic legitimacy.
- The historical development of language.
- The nature of literacy, and the concept of multiple literacies.
        (See Osborn, 2000, 2002, 2005a; Reagan & Osborn, 2002)

Assessing interdisciplinary content in the foreign language classroom is another matter entirely. One could draw on Ackerman's (1989) time-honored, but rather abstract notions useful in all fields: the concepts of validity for, validity within, and validity beyond the discipline. These criteria require an interdisciplinary theme or organizing center to be important to involved fields of study, that is, not a contrived connection, to facilitate the learning of other concepts within the individual disciplines, and to give the student a "metaconceptual bonus" (Ackerman, 1989, p. 29; see also pp. 27–30). Beyond such a guideline, however, and a general approval of "alternative" or "authentic assessment" strategies such as portfolios and so forth, there is little guidance to aid the assessment of curricular, instructional, or student products that are "interdisciplinary" in a foreign language classroom.

In this chapter, I will outline a framework for beginning the analysis with a critically-oriented foreign or world language classroom. In my previous works, I have suggested that the Critical Inquiry Cycle can be an organizing vehicle for constructing curricula based on inquiry, and that this inquiry will be, of its very nature, interdisciplinary.

The Critical Inquiry Cycle (CIC) draws from qualitative research to suggest that inquiry is necessary in a foreign language classroom. Jacobs (1989), in her influential text on interdisciplinary curriculum, argues:

> Students should study epistemological issues. Regardless of the age of students, epistemological questions such as "What is knowledge?," "What do we know?," and "How can we present knowledge in the schools?" can and should be at the heart of our efforts . . . Relevance begins with the rationale for educational choices affecting the school life of the student.
>
> (Jacobs, 1989, p. 10)

Haynes (2002) echoes this position:

> Rather than view knowledge as certain and held by authorities, interdisciplinary students—in order to reconcile and synthesize the

differing disciplinary and nondisciplinary worldviews—must believe that knowledge is relative to a context and acquired through inquiry . . . How one understands knowledge is directly related to how one understands others and the self. In other words, inter-personal and intrapersonal awareness mediate the epistemological dimension of development. An individual's meaning-making undergoes changes that affect and are affected by his or her view of the self, relations to others, and understanding of experience . . . The interdisciplinary epistemology is not one that posits a pure relativism in which all knowledge claims are always equal. Instead it rests on the assumptions that disciplines and its practitioners, as well as their activities and concepts, are already socially consti-tuted. The task of the interdisciplinary investigator, then, is to invent a new discourse that critically combines key elements of several disciplinary discourses and that is in keeping with his or her own sense of self.

(Haynes, 2002, pp. xiv–xv)

Finally, Moran (2002) points out the relationship of interdisciplinarity as it ties to our historical divisions in education:

The critique of the academic disciplines as limited and confining is as long-standing as the disciplines themselves. Historically, this critique has often taken the form of referring back to an older, more unified form of knowledge, usually located in an undisci-plined subject such as philosophy. The term 'interdisciplinary' emerged within the context of these anxieties about the decline of general forms of education, being first used in the social sciences in the mid-1920s and becoming common currency across the social sciences and humanities in the period immediately after the Second World War . . . interdisciplinarity interlocks with the concerns of epistemology—the study of knowledge—and tends to be centered around problems and issues that cannot be addressed or solved within the existing disciplines, rather than the quest for an all-inclusive synthesis.

(Moran, 2002, pp. 14–15)

Students in language classrooms can explore local contexts, and can inquire into grand questions through the medium and content of a non-English language. Documents, videos, audio recordings, and other media are examples of sources that could be employed in such an endeavor. The language teacher, using those realia as communicative springboards, includes activities related to reading, writing, listening, or speaking as well as culture, involving the acquisition of relevant information in the target language.

In the past, language teachers have employed the techniques of culture capsules and culture assimilators to highlight cultural issues in the language class, but since these techniques tend to stress comparison and contrast of cultural differences, they rarely lead to the realization of metaconceptual whole. On the contrary, pursuing grand questions in a foreign language classroom may produce a more sophisticated (metaconceptually) whole. The use of resources in multiple languages will further add to the complexity of the whole.

Toward Assessing Interdisciplinary Sophistication

To be sure, though integrating sources in two languages and content from more than one "discipline" are markers of an interdisciplinary unit, there are two other issues that need to be addressed for the world language classroom: analytic integration and school/community integration. If inquiry becomes the framework of the unit, analytic integration, though not necessary for interdiscplinarity per se, does yield a more sophisticated product. Interdisciplinary work in the world language classroom can be coupled with a critical view of all disciplinary knowledge and should strive to incorporate the voices of the students and the community. Such an approach is consistent with Horton's work at Highlander and Freire's pedagogical insights, as explored by Freire:

> The more people participate in the process of their own education, the more the people participate in the process of defining what kind of production to produce, and for what and why, the more the people participate in the development of their selves. The more the people become themselves, the better the democracy. The less people are asked about what they want, about their expectations, the less democracy we have.
>
> (Horton & Freire, 1990, pp. 145–6)

I want to suggest descriptions of interdisciplinary complexity in the world language classroom in terms of a taxonomical heuristic although I am skeptical in general of taxonomies because of the positivistic underpinnings of them. For the purposes of this illustration, however, I suggest that this will allow for us to conceptualize a continuum or multiple continua that can be utilized to assess interdisciplinarity in a critical pedagogical frame-work. I base this argument in the claim that it is the process, and not necessarily the product, that should be of *primary* concern for critical education:

> 1st degree integration is Linguistic and/or Thematic only.
> 2nd degree is Linguistic or Thematic and Analytic.
> 3rd degree is Linguistic, Thematic, and either Analytic or School and community.
> 4th degree is Linguistic, Thematic, Analytic and School and community.

Let me draw on an example presented by Asher (2003) describing an interdisciplinary unit undertaken when I was on the faculty of the City University of New York. Oral history provides educators with an opportunity to transform textbook accounts to living lessons as the experience of people known to students take center stage in the classroom. Students can generate documents that serve as primary sources, reflecting the voices of those in the community whose personal stories not only may promote critical thinking and historical perspective, but may also help students obtain an *emic* perspective.

Asher (2000) describes initial research methods for the mural used in the interdisciplinary unit:

> Queens is significant to the history of immigration in New York City. In the 1900s this borough had a population of 152,099, and by 2001, the population estimate is more than three million. I wanted to illuminate this unique immigration history through the creation of a mural . . . Through artistic interpretation, the project offered the community a deeper understanding of the generations who came before us, with a goal that reflects tolerance of difference through an awareness of local history and values concerning cultural heritage and immigration. Students were encouraged to find their personal approach to qualitative, interdisciplinary, and multicultural teaching, and to understand the complexities of group activity in a cooperative learning environment. The aesthetic challenge for the class was to produce a professional and sophisticated work of public art collectively that tells a story.
> (Asher, 2000, pp. 161–2)

Utilizing oral history methods from the social sciences, mural creation from fine arts, and communicative skills from the foreign language classroom, I worked with Rikki Asher and David Gerwin to develop an integrated, interdisciplinary unit outline. The thematic organizing center (see Jacobs, 1989; Lonning *et al.*, 1998) chosen was *Migration Stories* (Alger, 1998; Hoerder, 1999). In history classes, students explored the power and methodology of oral history (see Ritchie, 1994). In art classes, creating a mural was to be the primary activity focus. In a subsequent work (Osborn, 2005b), I expanded our original design and tied it to the theme of *migrant (in)justice and liberty*. I suggested incorporating the case of Sacco and Vanzetti with an Italian class. On August 23, 1927, Sacco and Vanzetti were executed for the crime of murder by the State of Massachusetts. The evidence presented at trial was based on eyewitness testimony of eleven of the greater than fifty who saw the crime, physical evidence related to the weapon and bullets taken from one of the victims, and a behavior pattern that the state claimed showed a "consciousness of guilt." (Young & Kaiser, 1985).

On April 15, 1920, two men were gunned down in South Braintree, MA, as they transported a factory payroll. It was this crime for which Sacco and Vanzetti would stand trial and ultimately meet their demise. However, on August 23, 1977, some 50 years after their executions, Michael S. Dukakis, the then Governor of the Commonwealth of Massachusetts, pardoned them posthumously and declared that any stigma and disgrace should be forever removed from their names, their families, and descendants. The defendants, because of their Italian-American identities and anarchist views, were tried in an environment of xenophobia and paranoia related to immigrants that challenges the convictions of any tolerant person, and many who may even feel they were guilty.

Students in foreign language classes may extend from this study to oral history projects in which they interview migrants or immigrants and their families as a way of gathering more historical evidence. They could also create aesthetic, community, and creative projects, including a public mural. The language classroom activities could additionally include specific focus on language skills through interviews, transcription, composition, revision, and recording.

An Evaluation Strategy

Assuming that the class does engage in such a set of projects, how should it be evaluated? Remembering that for the critical language educator it is process, not product, that is of primary concern, so that the rubric presented in Table 7.1 can be adapted to evaluate the issues highlighted in this chapter.

At the same time, the National Standards for Foreign Language Learning are still applicable. The standards can be used to evaluate the process and product as shown in Table 7.2 . At some point, the instructor will obviously need to grapple with what constitutes acceptable accuracy, communicative

TABLE 7.1 Rubric to evaluate key issues

Assessing interdiscplinarity for world language education settings

Category	Excellent	Acceptable	Needs Improvement
Study across languages	Second language used exclusively for world language components	First and second languages used extensively	Primarily first language used
Study across disciplines	Multiple disciplinary perspectives integrated with team teaching	Multiple disciplinary perspectives integrated with limited or no team teaching	Multiple disciplines, little integration
Analytic tools across disciplines	Sociocultural analysis prevalent in each represented discipline	Sociocultural analysis represented in most disciplines	Sociocultural analysis either present in only one discipline or limited in multiple disciplines
School and community	School and community are integrated in the interdisciplinary unit	Community voices are regularly represented in the formation and assessment of the unit and its products	Community voices are limited to hearsay or printed documents

effectiveness, and style as well as what errors will be tolerated and to what degree. These questions are not unique to interdisciplinary units in the world language classroom, however, because they must be addressed in all assignments or activities in a language classroom.

Conclusion

Though world language educators have often anecdotally thought of the work they do as inherently interdisciplinary, the ability of language educators to articulate criteria that move beyond those currently in use in the profession will likely prompt more sophistication in our growth in this area. Interdisciplinary work in world languages provides students opportunities to examine the social and cultural worlds that they shape and are shaped by, specifically as it relates to language diversity and can be

TABLE 7.2 National standards for foreign language learning and evaluation criteria

National standards for foreign language education

Category	Standard	Acceptable	Unacceptable
Communication standards	Standard 1.1. Students engage in conversations, provide and obtain information, express feelings and emotions, and exchange opinions.	Two of three standards addressed	One or fewer standards addressed
	Standard 1.2. Students understand and interpret written and spoken language on a variety of topics		
	Standard 1.3. Students present information, concepts, and ideas to an audience of listeners or readers on a variety of topics.		
Culture standards	Standard 2.1. Students demonstrate an understanding of the relationship between the practices and perspectives of the culture studied.	At least one of the standards is addressed	No standards addressed
	Standard 2.2. Students demonstrate an understanding of the relationship between the products and perspectives of the culture studied.		
Connections standards	Standard 3.1. Students reinforce and further their knowledge of other disciplines through the foreign language.	At least one of the two standards is addressed	No standards addressed
	Standard 3.2. Students acquire information and recognize the distinctive viewpoints that are only available through the foreign language and its cultures.		
Comparisons standards	Standard 4.1. Students demonstrate understanding of the nature of language through comparisons of the language studied and their own.	At least one of the two standards is addressed	No standards addressed
	Standard 4.2. Students demonstrate understanding of the concept of culture through comparisons of the cultures studied and their own.		
Communities standards	Standard 5.1. Students use the language both within and beyond the school setting.	At least one of two standards is addressed	No standards addressed
	Standard 5.2. Students show evidence of becoming life-long learners by using the language for personal enjoyment and enrichment.		

effectively utilized in a critical approach to language education (see Osborn 2000, 2002, 2005a, 2005b; Reagan & Osborn, 2002). Students then can bridge arbitrary barriers erected by cultural misunderstanding, academic divisions of knowledge and the barrier that is the schoolroom door simultaneously as the vibrant diversity of languages within our own communities becomes part of the landscape of world language education.

Bibliography

Ackerman, D. (1989). Intellectual and practical criteria for successful curriculum integration. In H. Jacobs (ed.), *Interdisciplinary curriculum: Design and implementation* (pp. 25–38). Alexandria, VA: Association for Supervision and Curriculum Development.

Alger, C. (1998). Global connections: Where am I? How did I get here? Where am I going? *Social Education, 62* (5), 282–4.

Asher, R. (2000). The *Procession*: A mural about immigration in Queens. *Queens College Journal of Jewish Studies 2*, 161–5.

Asher, R. (2003). Murals as interdisciplinary teaching. In D. Kaufman, D. Moss, & T.A. Osborn (eds.), *Beyond the boundaries: A transdisciplinary approach to teaching and learning* (pp. 131–44). Westport, CT: Praeger Publishers.

Byrnes, H. (2000). Languages across the curriculum—intradepartmental curriculum construction: Issues and options. In M. Kecht and K. von Hammerstein (eds.), *Languages across the curriculum: Interdisciplinary structures and international education* (pp. 151–76). Columbus, OH: National East Asian Languages Resource Center.

Kecht, M. and von Hammerstein, K. (2000). *Languages across the curriculum: Interdisciplinary structures and international education*. Columbus, OH: National East Asian Languages Resource Center.

Osborn, T.A. (2000). Critical reflection and the foreign language classroom. In Henry A. Giroux, (ed.), *Critical Studies in Education and Culture Series*. Westport, CT: Bergin & Garvey.

Osborn, T.A. (ed.) (2002). *The future of foreign language education in the United States*. Westport, CT: Bergin & Garvey.

Osborn, T.A. (2005a). *Critical reflection and the foreign language classroom* (revised edition). Greenwich, CT: Information Age Publishing.

Osborn, T.A. (2005b). *Teaching world languages for social justice: A sourcebook of principles and practices*. Mahwah, NJ: Lawrence Erlbaum Associates.

Haynes, C. (2002). Introduction: Laying a foundation for interdisciplinary teaching. In C. Haynes (ed.), *Innovations in interdisciplinary teaching*. Westport, CT: Oryx Press.

Hoerder, D. (1999). From immigration to migration systems: New concepts in migration history. *Magazine of History, 14* (1), 5–11.

Horton, M. & Freire, P. (1990). *We make the road by walking: Conversations on education and social change*. Philadelphia, PA: Temple University Press.

Jacobs, H.H. (ed.) (1989). *Interdisciplinary curriculum: Design and implementation*. Alexandria, VA: Association for Supervision and Curriculum Development.

Lessow-Hurley, J. (1996). *The foundations of dual language instruction* (2nd edition). White Plains, NY: Longman.

Lonning, R.A., DeFranco, T.C., and Weinland, T.P. (1998, October). Development of theme-based, interdisciplinary, integrated curriculum: A theoretical model. *School Science and Mathematics, 98* (6), 312–18.

Moran, J. (2002). *Interdisciplinarity*. London & New York: Routledge.

National Standards in Foreign Language Education Project (1996). *Standards for foreign language learning: Preparing for the 21st century*. Lawrence, KS: Allen Press.

Reagan, T. & Osborn, T.A. (2002). *The foreign language educator in society: Toward a critical pedagogy*. Mahwah, NJ: Lawrence Erlbaum Associates.

Ritchie, D.A. (1994). *Doing oral history*. New York: Simon & Schuster.

Shrum, J.L. & Glisan, E.W. (2000). *Teacher's handbook: Contextualized language instruction* (2nd edition). Boston, MA: Heinle & Heinle.

Swaffar, J. (2000). Doing things with language: Acquiring discourse literacy through languages across the curriculum. In M. Kecht and K. von Hammerstein (eds.), *Languages across the curriculum: Interdisciplinary structures and international education* (pp. 119–50). Columbus, OH: National East Asian Languages Resource Center.

Young, W. & Kaiser, D.E. (1985). *Postmortem: New evidence in the case of Sacco and Vanzetti.* Amherst, MA: The University of Massachusetts Press.

CHAPTER 8

Rethinking Our Focus on the Future

Reading Assessment in the Transdisciplinary Secondary English Classroom

WENDY J. GLENN

What is done or left undone in the short run determines the long run.

Sydney J. Harris

American society currently offers an availability of written materials unprecedented in any previous era of human existence, yet only a surprising few pursue a passion for reading in their adult lives (National Endowment for the Humanities, 2004). Although our nation may boast an enviable literacy rate among its population, many of its citizens are growing up leaving school and leaving reading behind. We are creating an aliterate society, one in which citizens can read, but choose not to (Gallo, 2001). Despite our best intentions, our classroom assessment strategies may discourage young men and women from appreciating written texts. In too many classrooms, daily and weekly assessments are wedded directly to end of term tests. Students read excerpts out of context and answer multiple choice questions in preparation for what they are likely to see on exams. Real reading is not happening as often as it should in secondary English classrooms; assessment pressures and practices are largely to blame.

We must remember why we wish for kids to read in the first place and reexamine the methods we use (or fail to use) as we measure whether or not we are getting them there. It is true, indeed, that English teachers in an assessment-driven educational system are increasingly responsible for helping students pass reading comprehension tests. This goal would be more effectively reached, however, if we abandoned it and turned, instead, to a transdisciplinary approach to teaching and assessing reading that promotes genuine inquiry and exploration and thus makes the reading process relevant and real.

For the purposes of this paper, transdisciplinarity will be defined as an integrated instructional model grounded in a real-life context in which the subject areas become essential to the learning process rather than the focus of the curriculum. It is student-centered and grounded in efforts to promote personal growth and civic responsibility among students (Drake, 1998). In the transdisciplinary English classroom, (1) students engage in genuine inquiry and discussion by reading, writing, speaking, and listening unconstrained by content area boundaries in the pursuit of answers to complex questions they themselves generate, and (2) teachers provide ample time and opportunity for student choice, sustained scaffolding, and regular feedback, and employ assessment strategies that utilize a thoughtful management system, recognize and value process as well as product, and promote dialogue among teachers and students as a means to engender independent thought and a reflective stance in students.

As adults, why do we read? Not to have the capacity to recall the author of that 1789 classic tale of love and woe. Certainly not to pass an exam. We read to experience life in a way we cannot otherwise, to live in worlds that we are not likely or are unable to visit, to see in others the struggles we face in ourselves, to learn more about the world in which we live, to explore how to cope given the example of others, to feel as though we are not alone. Why do we assume that students are any different? When we focus our attention on reading only to succeed on exams administered at the end of the semester or year, we create mere imitations of real readers in our students. Sadly, we suck the joy out of reading when we limit our concerns to basic comprehension skills so often at the core of standardized tests. Yes, kids need to understand what they read, but there is so much more. They need to enjoy it, hate it, be angry with it, be empowered by it, revel in it, think critically about it, lose and find themselves in it.

Elementary school students readily display these behaviors. They are intrigued when they learn that Ramona Quimby struggles to make her way in the world just as they do, that the poems of Shel Silverstein deal with boogers and poop and gas, or that there is a book in the library that describes how to build a tree fort. These texts are real and relevant to this audience. Somewhere in the years of secondary schooling, however, this connection is severed; the student gets lost. In our attempts at the middle and high school level to help students read what we believe they are supposed to read and articulate what we believe to be the accepted critical response, we shut down their attempts at creative, unique, and divergent thinking. As students grow older, we treat them as more and more incapable of thinking for themselves. They are instead expected to read what we tell them to read and seek the answers that the great scholars of old have deemed good and right and true. We want them to be culturally literate, or at least prepared for the college literature classes they might face down the road, but, in the process, we deny students the freedom to think what they will of the literature they read.

> People seldom read simply for the sake of learning to read *better*. Yet a great many reading programs are based on the assumption that reading is done *for practice*. Students read passages and answer questions as a way of proving that they have understood; they read literary classics and write essay exams to show that they have mastered the central ideas. However, if we recall that the reader must be kept at the center of the process, we can see that unless reading serves a purpose, it is not likely to improve either reading skills or attitudes toward books.
>
> (Tchudi & Mitchell, 1989, p. 117)

Our purpose should be to create a climate in which the reader is seen as essential to the process of reading. We must foster an environment in which secondary readers can behave like adult readers and have the freedom to read texts of their choosing and use texts as a means to discover personal revelations, devise social questions, and conduct inquiry into their lives and those of others, each of which can be achieved through a trans-disciplinary approach to reading.

Re-envisioning Reading Through a Transdisciplinary Approach

A transdisciplinary approach, as argued in some of my related work and reviewed briefly here to provide context for the following discussion of assessment (Glenn, 2003a, 2003b), has the potential to place this freedom in the hands of secondary classroom learners, to allow and encourage young people to pursue answers to questions of interest to them as adolescents, as scholars, as humans. When we learn to let go and give students the means and opportunity to guide their own thinking, they do so much more than we could have imagined for them.

If we define learning as "the continuous integration of new knowledge and experience as to deepen and broaden our understanding of ourselves and our world" (Beane, 1995, 622), it becomes clear that our educational focus should be on enriching the knowledge and experience of each and every student. Instead, however, we often attempt to dictate student learning based on our own perceptions of what is important and worth knowing. In the creation of lessons that grow out of curriculum guides or our own visions of what kids need, our plans become so formalized that they do not allow students to formulate their own meaning, to imagine for themselves what they might gain through their reading. We attempt to predict the questions students have or the personal knowledge they possess without ever asking them. Rather than allowing students to imagine their own solutions to problems, we provide the answers through activities based on our own construction of knowledge. If we believe that "goals need to be flexible and that surprise counts, . . . that purposeful flexibility rather than rigid adherence to prior plans is more likely to yield something of value" (Eisner, 1992, p. 594), we must empower our kids as guardians of their own learning and honor their voices and those of their peers.

The transdisciplinary model, when applied directly to the teaching of reading, has the potential to free students from these constraints and defy the vision of the traditional English classroom in which the teacher serves as overseer and determines what texts will be read, how they will be interpreted, and what, ultimately, students will be expected to recite back come exam time. Rather than limiting students in their reading and thinking, and thus denying them access to knowledge beyond that considered assessable (and thus worth knowing) by the powers that be, a transdisciplinary approach opens the gate through which students might pass in their exploration and examination of texts that buy them cultural and social power, not to mention enjoyment. The teaching of reading when aligned with the theoretical foundation underpinning a transdisciplinary approach must hold true to the vision that students read for authentic purposes that ask them to reflect upon how the text might help them answer some larger set of essential questions that are compelling and complex and, ideally, student-generated.

The power of the transdisciplinary approach lies in the richness of content that it allows students and teachers to explore. No longer are they limited to canonical mandates or topics traditionally associated solely with the English curriculum. They instead can draw from multiple disciplines to ponder, discuss, and write about topics that are complex, weighty, and difficult or just plain interesting to them as young people and human beings. Rather than having all class members read Shakespeare's *Hamlet* and answering questions related to plot, setting, and theme, for example, a transdisciplinary approach asks students to generate questions they believe to be worth answering and use a variety of appropriate texts to get there. In the context of Shakespeare, students might choose to pursue a philosophical line of inquiry and examine the nature of good and evil in the author's works. They may look deeply into issues of historical under-standing and evaluate various interpretations of primary source docu-ments. They might even question the nature of reality and look to scientific treatises on the topic. Indeed, they might not read Shakespeare at all, opting instead to explore issues beyond the literary realm. Sacrilege? Not if we consider again the primary reading goals for our students. What do we hope they will achieve? The ability and desire to read independently as adults. Under a transdisciplinary model, students read with a purpose (not to find main idea). They gain exposure to unique perspectives that they must sort out and work through—just like real readers. They individually explore personal interests—just like real readers. They are forced to think deeply about texts and how they might help them make sense of questions they find engaging—just like real readers. And, once a passion for reading has been ignited, they just might pick up Shakespeare on their own.

Transdisciplinarity and the Reassessment of Reading Assessment

So, if we are to allow kids to read texts of their choosing and encourage them to formulate complex responses to that which they read as they engage in dialogue with the teacher and one another (all practices evidenced in a transdisciplinary classroom), how do we know they are learning anything or benefiting from this approach to teaching reading? In any classroom in which curriculum is designed around a transdisciplinary model, there are issues of assessment that complicate and enhance the experience of teachers and their students.

> Within more traditional models of teaching reading, assessment is easier. If reading becomes the domain in which we practice basic skills, then we may teach it simply as practice material, the exercises in which we teach skills of decoding, using context clues, iden-tifying techniques of characterization, and so on. We are likely to be concerned about measuring progress and about reading levels, and we may plan our teaching around specific skills, probably phrased as behavioral objectives, rather than around intellectual content or some organizing principle.
>
> (Probst, 1986, p. 60)

To prepare for such instruction:

> We select and assign a chapter or chunk at a time, to be read by the whole class as homework. We give tests to make sure kids did the homework, and we orchestrate discussions based on the

questions in the teacher's manual or old lesson plans. We present lectures on literary topics and require students to memorize various literary information—the Roman equivalents of the Greek deities, characteristics of the New Criticism, Latin roots, Old English and Greek prefixes, characters in *Macbeth*, George Eliot's real name—followed by exams in which students report back what we said or assigned them to memorize.

(Atwell, 1998, p. 28)

Here, there is uniformity, standardization, an opportunity to compare some aspects of performance across students by examining average scores earned on tests of comprehension. There is a correct answer for which students are held accountable and teachers are expected to teach.

In a transdisciplinary classroom, however, there is so much more. If we abide by the definition of transdisciplinarity laid out in the first section of this paper, assessment in the transdisciplinary English/Language Arts classroom must value multiple and varied responses and encourage the crossing of disciplinary lines. Students and teachers are partners in their learning, and their explorations of a piece may take them to places unexpected and uncharted and for which they are unprepared. Assessment in the transdisciplinary classroom must allow for individualization; not all students are interested in the same questions or texts or will pursue or experience their reading in the same way. While there might be times when it is valuable for all students and their teacher to pursue the same question at the same time (perhaps through a mini-lesson designed around common needs of those in the classroom community), opportunities for independent inquiry provide the backbone of the model.

In addition, the form of inquiry advocated by the transdisciplinary model is unpredictable and, thus, often messy. As students explore readings of interest to them, there is no way to determine at the start where their ponderings will take them. Designing instructional objectives that are aligned with final assessments relative to the class as a whole, then, is nearly impossible unless they are so watered down as to be nearly meaningless. Inquiry, too, does not guarantee that all elements of the scope and sequence will be addressed. Valuing depth over breadth, the transdisciplinary model requires thoughtful examination that takes time, likely resulting in lack of coverage of required content mandated by departments, schools, districts, and states. In terms of assessment, then, how do we deal with the multitude of educational outcomes that emerge for our multitude of students? If we cannot devise a singular objective to suit all students, how do we know if they are improving as readers and meeting the larger goal of developing improved literacy skills? Given these complications, assessment in the transdisciplinary classroom cannot be standardized or one-size-fits-all in nature.

Embracing assessment in the transdisciplinary classroom requires attention to three key components—*a unique management system, a recognition and valuing of process, and opportunities for genuine dialogue between teachers and students and students and their peers.*

Managing Multiple Readers and Their Many Texts

Given the individualized nature of the transdisciplinary model, we must find suitable ways to manage a classroom in which each student is reading something different and hold kids accountable for that reading. Several teacher-scholars have developed useful record-keeping models designed to help teachers maintain an organized system of tracking student reading (Atwell, 1998; Burke, 2003; Tchudi & Mitchell, 1989). Whether we draw from these models or design our own, we must reflect upon the form of management most appropriate for our students and our beliefs about teaching. In doing so, we might consider the following: Should we assess students based upon the number of texts read in a marking period, the number of pages read, the reading difficulty of the texts chosen, etc.? Should a minimum standard for success be established? If so, by whom? Should the standard vary for students of differing skills as readers? Should students be rewarded for growth over time? If so, how is that growth measured—through an increase in numbers of texts or page numbers read, written reflection in which students describe themselves as readers over time, our own professional observations of these young readers, or some other measure? Given the transdisciplinary goals of learning in a real-life context in which the subject areas become essential to the learning process rather than the focus of the curriculum, the desire to create opportunities for student-centered instruction, and an emphasis on personal growth among students, individualization of assessment practices is essential and will likely result in varied responses to these questions depending upon student needs.

Under a transdisciplinary model of assessment, however, one constant in the pursuit of answers to these questions would be the inclusion of student voices. If our goal is to help students develop the skills and interests necessary to maintain a commitment to reading in their adult lives, we must help them assess their own understanding and growth. Once students leave our classroom walls, they should not feel the need to depend upon a teacher to tell them what they have or have not learned. In fact, students know best what they know and don't know, and, "until we realize that the student is the best evaluator of his or her own learning, we will never know what our students really know or are able to do" (Rief, 1992, p. 131). The assessment process should give voice to those being assessed. To achieve this, students might be asked to set personal reading goals and compose self-evaluations that reflect upon how well these are being met.

In my former tenth-grade classroom, for example, students were expected to read independently a set number of pages on a variety of self-selected topics and in a variety of self-selected texts each quarter. Emma, a reluctant but growing reader, for example, was haunted by the experiences of Holocaust victims and survivors after visiting the Holocaust Museum. In her quest to better understand that which she saw, she generated a list of key questions she believed worth exploring. A few included: Why were some people (and not others) sent to the camps? In this survival situation, was there a different standard of right and wrong? How were the victims and survivors heroic? With my guidance and that of our school librarian, Emma developed a list of potential readings for the quarter and decided which would be read first, second, and so on and the dates for which she would aim to complete each. She decided to pursue answers to her questions by drawing upon novels (*Night* by Elie Wiesel, *Number the Stars* by Lois Lowry), diaries (*The Diary of Anne Frank*), and other nonfiction (*The Survivor: An Anatomy of Life in the Death Camps* by Terrence des Pres, "Arrivals and Departures" by Charlotte Delbo in *Voices of Experience*), looking to history, psychology, and philosophy, disciplines beyond those typically associated with English class.

In addition, she identified reading skills that she hoped to practice in the process of reading. While other students focused on summarizing a passage in a few sentences, identifying arguments, or identifying examples of author's craft, Emma selected vocabulary development. Midway through each quarter and again at the end, she drafted a three-page self-evaluation that asked her to report the number of pages read and from what texts, as well as reflect upon whether or not her goals were met and what she might try to achieve over the next four weeks. In a portion of her first end-of-quarter self-evaluation, Emma wrote:

> This has been a great and very scary experience for me. I have never really liked to read, except for books like *Sweet Valley High*, but I think I have become a better reader mostly because I have read so much . . . I liked how I had a chance to decide my topic and the things I wanted to read, although this was scary too, since I didn't know what was out there to read. As you know, I was interested in the Holocaust because I went to the Holocaust Museum with my family over the summer. I really wanted to know more about what happened to the people I learned about there . . . My reading goal for this quarter was to work on my vocabulary because that

has slowed me down in the past. I made a Vocab. Log [a technique discussed in class] and came up with 28 new words. My favorite is luminous. Although I still want to work on this, I think I am better at figuring out words while I read them and have had lots of practice using the dictionary.

As evidenced by this excerpt, encouraging students to set personal reading goals and compose self-evaluations allows teachers to learn from their students as they strive to understand how they might best help students meet their own needs as learners—the ultimate goal of any assessment system. The transdisciplinary nature of this reading task (drawing from texts grounded in various disciplines to answer student-generated questions) is well-suited for personal reflection as a means of assessment. Emma's words demonstrate an increased awareness of her strengths and needs as a reader; she is becoming autonomous in her learning. Student-generated evaluation allows students a say in how their learning takes place and how it will be measured, essential if we are to help students feel empowered in their textual (and personal) exploration of big questions, the crux of transdisciplinary instruction.

Valuing Process in a Product-Oriented Culture

Given the transdisciplinary belief that students must be afforded time to ponder how a text might help them answer some larger set of essential questions worth exploring, assessment must focus on the process of learning as well as a final product. As students work through issues in their reading, they must have the opportunity to interact with others and share their thoughts such that they can play with and revise the changing views as needed. Assessment in the transdisciplinary secondary English classroom, then, requires a willingness of teachers to share thorough, specific, regular, and useful feedback to each and every student, despite the fact that each and every student might be reading a different text and progressing at a unique rate. Rather than conceptualizing assessment as the evaluation of a final paper or project, we must take into account that which happened in the creation of that paper or product—if indeed we feel it necessary to assign such a paper or product at all.

When I first began teaching English, I supplemented the curriculum with an outside reading program. I asked students to read a set number of books of their choosing each semester and, at the completion of each novel, turn in a project that highlighted the text and their response to it. Whether this resulted in the drafting of an alternate ending, the creation of a vivid movie poster, or the reenactment of a particularly memorable scene, these products were often creative and very well done. I thought I was engendering in students a passion for reading. Ultimately, however, this assignment failed to allow students both ample time and opportunity to really reflect on what they were reading. Yes, they read some new books (maybe). Yes, they understood the books enough to create a project (maybe). But the work they did throughout the process was neither evaluated nor rewarded or valued in any meaningful way. I didn't (and still don't) know whether or not these students really grew as readers; I never thought to take time to find out.

Assessment is designed to provide teachers and students a sense of where they are and where they might need to go. It is not about final products or standardized test scores that realtors use to sell homes in select neighborhoods. I don't ever want my students to finish learning. A final product, then, is simply another step in the learning process, not the culmination or peak or end. This vision of assessment takes time, especially given the fact that secondary teachers often work with 100–150 students each week. There are no simple tricks to ease the load here. Teachers who believe in the inquiry approach to teaching reading will find and take the time to hold individual conferences with students, share written and oral feedback based upon observations over the term, or engage in other means of discussion, including dialogue journals, a method I have incorporated into my own classroom teaching and provide an example of below (see Atwell, 1998; Rief, 1992; and Staton, 1980 for examples of teachers who effectively manage the complexities of employing such a model with so many students).

In addition to having students conduct formal and informal conversations surrounding texts during class, I ask students to share (via email) their thoughts with respect to their reading with me each week. Students are encouraged to express their wonderings, frustrations, joys, etc. in an open dialogue format, writing approximately 250 words for each entry. Each week, I respond to each student personally. The following exchange provides a representative example of the dialogue exchange. It takes place between me and Elise, a twenty-one-year-old preservice teacher who, along with her peers, read and assumed various roles in her reading and discussions with other students who opted to read the same text. The various roles reflect unique content area perspectives, from the illustrator who utilizes a visual medium to the investigator who seeks resource information to supplement the fictional text to the connector who identifies links between the text and the self, other, and world. In the enactment of each role, students examine different ways to read a text, drawing upon multiple disciplines in their attempts to make sense of their reading.

Two-thirds through the novel, Elise writes:

Okay, now for some book talk. I just wanted to let you know that I love *Hard Love* so far. It is so hard to put the book down and not read ahead of the group. I just finished the next section tonight, and I wanted to share some of my thoughts with you through this entry.

This story is amazing! I like how you have us switching roles for the lit circles because, even though I am reading the same book, each time I am a different role (discussion director, connector, etc.), causing me to read the book differently each time. As the director, I began reading and formulating questions, and I actually questioned everything. My second role was connector, and I began taking the information out of the book and trying to apply it to a different context. My last role has been that of the illustrator, and I keep getting vivid imagery through the reading. I know what I want to illustrate, and I can see the characters in my mind quite clearly. I was just wondering, is this why you have us take roles and switch every time, so we can have different readings? Up to now, I have always read books and had a set way of thinking, but this time around, when my roles switch, I feel like three different people. In each role, however, I also have a personal reaction to the story as myself. For the first time, I am reading a book and viewing it with many perspectives, and I got so much out of this reading.

I have learned that I love to read books that deal with identity, and this book has great insight on the topic. I am so happy to see John growing through this book, and I actually cried when he calls his mom from Cape Cod and tells her, "I don't hate you, Mom." I was at work in the computer lab, and people must have thought I was crazy. I get really attached to characters in books and movies. I get really into both, and I live the action they are experiencing as I read the story.

One question, how do you think the ending will play out? I have mixed feelings about it. On the one hand, I want the story to have a fairy tale ending and have Marisol not be a lesbian so she and Gio can get together. When I read the part that Marisol says, "I lied to you," I thought for sure she was going to tell him, "Gio, I'm not a lesbian, let's get married and have a family." I watch too many Disney movies, I guess. I also want to see the mother and son reunite. At the end, I know Wittlinger is thinking of what happens with these characters. I would just like to know, too. Okay, well I can get carried away with this book, so have a great day.

In response to Elise's entry, I write:

> I am so glad to hear that you are enjoying *Hard Love* and under-
> stand completely what you mean when you describe feeling like
> you are reading the book from three different perspectives. Too
> often, readers think that reading critically is something that other
> people somehow know how to do. Lit circles, in my experience,
> allow readers to better understand the reading process by recog-
> nizing and practicing the various ways we can make sense of
> a text. We can garner different understandings and emotional
> responses with each role. It's a bit like the demystifying experi-
> ence we talked about with respect to writing last week. I also like
> to consider different literary theories—from Marxism to feminism
> to deconstructionism—and think about how these different lenses
> lead to very different readings of the same text. We can chat more
> about this, if you'd like.
>
> Hmm . . . the ending. I actually have come to enjoy novels that
> don't leave us with the ends all tied up neatly. Although I need to
> feel as though there is some closure, I like to imagine that the story
> goes on beyond the final pages. Ideally, by the end, I feel like I
> "know" the characters and can spend time pondering what I think
> they will do next. If Marisol professes her love for Gio, I personally
> will be disappointed. Admittedly, I want John to find love, but, if
> Marisol is the one to provide it, it wouldn't be a "hard love," one
> that helps John figure out who he is. I, too, love the scene in which
> he calls his mom, and I, too, balled my eyes out when I read it.
> Thanks, as always, for sharing your thoughts.

This exchange reveals deep thinking on behalf of Elise, both in terms of
herself as a reader and the text under consideration as she is reading it.
Through this glimpse into her mind, I, as an assessor, am afforded insight
into her comprehension of the text (its thematic treatment of identity), the
application of the author's craft (the ending of the novel), and her analysis
of herself as a reader (three different perspectives). This provides a much
richer view than would likely be afforded through a multiple choice or other
closed-ended response solicited upon completion of reading. In addition,
because this exchange happens in process, it allows me to probe her
understanding and push her in her thinking about the text (my vision of
endings) and her approach to reading (literary theories and the lenses they
provide) such that I can help her evaluate where she might go in her learning
(and begin the assessment cycle once again).

Encouraging Layered Perspectives

Although we want students to choose their own texts and make their own meaning, it is not enough to just give them texts, let them read, and record what they do and think in the process. There is also a need for social interaction surrounding what they read, opportunities for talk that involve students and teachers embodying what it means to exist in a democratic society. These conversations must allow for the genuine pushing and pulling of ideas in which multiple responses and interpretations are valued and respected. If, under a transdisciplinary model, we are asking students to work through complex and complicated issues, we cannot expect that the answers to which they come will be simplistic or singular.

To allow students to find themselves in the worlds and lives of others, transdisciplinary instruction is grounded in a reader-response approach to texts (Rosenblatt, 1938) that demands attention paid to the connection between a reader's experiences and the text he/she reads:

> At the center are readers' responses—to the world of the book, to the worlds of other books, to their own worlds, to the meanings they make, to the choices the author made, to the literature community of which they automatically become members the minute they lose themselves in a book.
>
> (Atwell, 1998, p. 30)

It is essential that students think critically about the works they read and recognize that the interpretation determined by a professor at X University is not the only interpretation. Our goal is not for students to guess what they think we are thinking but to think.

The dialogue that is essential in a classroom community:

> is inherent in a teaching approach that values all responses to a work, invites examination of those responses, and helps students find meaning in the literature [and other texts] they read. Teachers must become listeners and learners, refraining from imposing their own ideas and interpretations on their students. This does not mean that teachers must relinquish classroom authority, only that they must share that authoring with their students.
>
> (Monseau, 1992, pp. 87–8)

Many students can vividly remember a time when they read a work, came to their own conclusion about that work and its meaning, and were told by the teacher that they were wrong in their interpretation. Josh, a bright, thoughtful, young man and former tenth-grade student was reluctant to share his ideas at the start of the year. He noted that he hated poetry due to his ninth-grade teacher's insistence that Jarrell's "The Death of the Ball Turret Gunner" (1945) is about abortion. Although this may be a valid critical response, the fact that Josh did not see this in his reading and had developed an alternative impression made him feel as though he failed. Perhaps we need to remember, too, that literature possesses an affective component; "we sometimes diminish the sheer power of the stories by taking them apart, as if that were the reason we read them in the first place" (Burke, 2003, p. 46).

Kids must experience the risk-taking and negotiation that goes into a discussion surrounding texts. They must be allowed to venture a guess at the meaning of a certain passage, argue openly with teacher and students about author intention, and begin to trust in themselves as real readers capable of contributing to the conversation to which they have been denied access in their former quests for the "correct" response. Nancie Atwell (1998) has likened these social exchanges to that which might happen at a dining room table around which:

> people talk in all the ways literate people discourse. We don't need assignments, lesson plans, lists, teacher's manuals, or handbooks. We need only another literate person. And our talk isn't sterile, grudging, or perfunctory. It's filled with jokes, arguments, stories, exchanges of bits of information, descriptions of what we love and hate and why.
>
> (Atwell, 1998, p. 32)

From an assessment standpoint, use of a multiple choice format fails to capture the complexities of response likely engendered in a transdisciplinary classroom. Asking kids to identify the singularly correct answer undermines the transdisciplinary focus on asking and exploring questions that are compelling and relevant to individual students. Any assessment that we design ought, then, to remain open-ended and structured to elicit rich responses. This process is built into a transdisciplinary model in that it allows students to ask to examine multifaceted questions and seek compound answers. When we limit our assessment to questions that ask students to reveal the main idea of a passage they read in a text, we scratch only the surface of what students are able to contribute. Simple assessments yield simple responses. When evaluating student responses, we must look for depth and the extent to which students support their claims—whatever they are—with evidence supplied through the reading.

Revealing the Complexities of Reading Assessment

What is particularly difficult about reading assessment is the fact that all assessments of student performance in reading, transdisciplinary or not, remain one step removed from an evaluation of pure reading skills and could thus be seen as limiting, even inaccurate. Reading is a private act that takes place in the recesses of the individual mind; we cannot witness the act as completed by another and must depend instead upon the writing and talking that emerges from our reading. We do not see the student's mind decoding an unfamiliar word using context clues, deciding whether or not a particular character is admirable or believable, or navigating a complicated plot line.

If we were to design a rubric, for example, that assessed student performance on dialogue journals or in literature circle discussions, what might we evaluate? If we look at a students' ability to convey his/her interpretation or impression of a piece, are we really assessing reading? Or, are we assessing the ability of the student to write or speak articulately in the conveyance of that interpretation or impression? On the surface, it would seem that we might as well resort to using multiple-choice exams that ask students to identify correct answers in their demonstration of comprehension. This would surely eliminate the potentially time-consuming, messy, even potentially inaccurate forms of assessment touted by those who utilize a transdisciplinary approach. Where does this leave us, then? With students capable of reading but doing so for all the wrong reasons—or not doing so at all.

Reimagining a More Hopeful Future

When we reflect upon how we assess reading in schools, it would seem as though we do not wish for our students to develop any meaningful connections to texts or develop the skills needed to become life-long readers. We deny them opportunities to read self-selected texts, fail to consider the relevance of these selections to students' lives, and encourage them to seek the singularly "correct" answer in their analyses and interpretations. Why? Maybe we fear losing our expert status as guardians of literature. Perhaps we fear the unexpected, not knowing how students will respond. Probably we fear poor test results that others will assume reflect our skills as educators. Certainly, we are such lovers of reading that we want students to experience it as we do and fall in love with our own favorites.

The irony, however, is that if we let students follow their own lead, develop questions that are meaningful to them, and encourage them to pursue answers in a variety of texts, they will not only be engaged in the reading process, they will also carry the torch and defend the power of texts, teach us how to look at what they read from perspectives we might never have imagined, do just fine on district and state exams and, we hope, learn to love reading as we do. Ultimately, if we can help them read for now, the future will take care of itself. Translating these ideas into action requires a different approach to teaching and assessing reading than has been traditionally implemented in our schools. Although it might seem impossible in our era of accountability to take more class time away from covering the required material and break free from perpetual test preparation, the choice is essential if we hope to create lasting readers and break the cycle of aliteracy.

Bibliography

Atwell, N. (1998). *In the middle: New understandings about writing, reading, and learning* (2nd edition). Portsmouth, NH: Heinemann.

Beane, J. (1995). Curriculum integration and the disciplines of knowledge. *Phi Delta Kappan, 76,* 616–22.

Burke, J. (2003). *The English teacher's companion* (2nd edition). Portsmouth, NH: Heinemann.

Drake, S.M. (1998). *Creating integrated curriculum: Proven ways to increase student learning.* Thousand Oaks, CA: Corwin Press.

Eisner, E.W. (1992). The misunderstood role of the arts in human development. *Phi Delta Kappan, 73,* 591–5.

Gallo, D.R. (2001). How classics create an aliterate society. *English Journal, 90,* 33–40.

Glenn, W.J. (2003a). Learning to let go: Student participation in the development of an integrated English curriculum. In D. Kaufman, D.M. Moss, and T. Osborn (eds.), *Beyond the boundaries: A transdisciplinary approach to teaching and learning* (pp. 145–54). Westport, CT: Bergin & Garvey.

Glenn, W.J. (2003b). Imagine the possibilities. A student-generated unit to inspire creative thought. *English Journal, 92,* 5, 35–41.

Monseau, V. (1992). Students and teachers as a community of readers. In V.R. Monseau & G.M. Salvner (eds.), *Reading their world: The young adult novel in the classroom* (pp. 85–98). Portsmouth, NH: Heinemann.

National Endowment for the Arts (2004). *Reading at risk: A survey of literary reading in America.* U.S. Government Document. Available at: www.arts.gov/pub/ReadingAtRisk.pdf.

Probst, R.E. (1986). Three relationships in the teaching of literature. *English Journal, 76,* 26–32.

Rief, L. (1992). *Seeking diversity: Language arts with adolescents.* Portsmouth, NH: Heinemann.

Rosenblatt, L.M. (1938). *Literature as exploration.* New York: D. Appleton-Century.

Staton, J. (1980). Writing and counseling: Using a dialogue journal. *Language Arts, 57,* 514–18.

Tchudi, S. & Mitchell, D. (1989). *Explorations in the teaching of English* (3rd edition). New York: HarperCollins.

CHAPTER 9

Transdisciplinary Approaches to Bilingual Student Assessment

Creating Authentic Reflections of Meaningful Learning Opportunities

MILEIDIS GORT

In the United States, teachers and program administrators have struggled to identify appropriate procedures and instruments to assess the knowledge and abilities of students who are English language learners (ELLs). This endeavor has proved to be especially complicated because of the dual-language and culturally-specific nature of their understandings (Hurley & Tinajero, 2001), the realization that the purposes of assessment with ELLs are so varied and complex, and the lack of valid and reliable measures for students acquiring English as a second language (Lapp *et al.*, 2001). Assessment, hereby defined as a systematic approach for collecting information on student learning, understanding, and/or performance that is based on various sources of evidence, is generally used for five major purposes with ELL students. These purposes include:

- initial screening, identification and educational program placement;
- monitoring of student progress (both in learning English and in attaining grade level content area standards);
- accountability (English language proficiency and academic achievement);
- reclassification and/or program exit; and
- program evaluation.

In order to make informed decisions about their students, teachers plan, gather, and analyze information from multiple sources over time so that results are meaningful to teaching and learning. Because of the varying purposes and numerous stakeholders involved in this process, accurate and effective assessment of the bilingual student population is essential to ensure that these students gain access to quality instructional programs that meet their needs and that they are on course to becoming literate and able participants in classroom settings and beyond.

In the current context high-stakes testing accountability, there is a strong focus on adequate yearly progress for all students. The No Child Left Behind Act (NCLB) of 2001, in particular, places special emphasis on ensuring that English language learners make steady progress in acquiring English, as well as in reading/language arts and mathematics. But ELLs face many obstacles in existing assessment tools, including unfamiliarity with testing language, content, vocabulary, testing formats, test-taking skills, and cultural orientations of the tests (TESOL, 2000). Furthermore, existing measures are generally unable to separate language errors from academic errors (Hakuta & Beatty, 2000). That is, the language demands of content-area assessments may be so great for ELL students that they are not able to adequately or fully express their knowledge of the content being tested. Thus, it is difficult to determine whether the performance of ELLs on these tests primarily reflects their language proficiencies and abilities or their content knowledge.

Best practices suggest that assessment should be used to examine the nature of students' knowledge and the manner in which they learn best (Glaser & Silver, 1994). For bilingual learners,[1] this includes what they know (and how they know) and can do in each language. Because the bilingual student population represents such heterogeneity in cultural, linguistic and educational background and experiences, as well as socio-cultural, sociohistorical, sociopolitical, sociolinguistic, and socioeconomic factors that contribute to these experiences, the interconnected processes of learning, teaching, and assessment must move beyond traditionally fragmented practices and toward a transdisciplinary model of holistic understanding (Gort, 2003).

Transdisciplinary approaches move beyond a central focus on the disciplines (Meeth, 1978). This highest level of integrated study and understanding "start[s] with an issue or problem and, through the process of problem solving, bring[s] to bear the knowledge of those disciplines [including Western and other perspectives] that contribute to a solution or resolution" (p. 10). By connecting the visions of different disciplines into a more holistic understanding of the world, transdisciplinary perspectives have the potential to assist teachers of bilingual learners in (1) skillfully integrating students' work at mixed levels of linguistic and conceptual complexity, and (2) incorporating knowledge of the rules of appropriate behavior of at least two cultural and linguistic groups into the learning, teaching, and assessment process (Gort, 2003). Tapping into students' funds of knowledge (Moll, 1992; Moll *et al.*, 1992) and applying a multilingual lens[2] (Gort, 2006) to the teaching, learning, and assessment process, a holistic approach to bilingual student assessment provides a more complete picture of student needs and strengths and leads to more accurate, appropriate, and responsive educational decisions for English language learners.

A holistic approach to assessment integrates the complex relationship between languages, cultures, literacy, and conceptual understandings to:

1. examine the nature of student knowledge;
2. consider how students learn and come to understand;
3. monitor student progress;
4. guide individualized and classroom instruction; and
5.. improve student learning.

Miller (2001) describes three basic principles of holistic education: connectedness, inclusion, and balance. Connectedness refers to moving away from a fragmented approach to teaching and learning to an approach that facilitates connections at every level of learning, including connections between languages and cultures. Inclusion refers to including all types of students and providing a broad range of learning and teaching approaches to meet students' needs. Balance is based on the concept of complementary forces and energies that need to be recognized and nurtured. Because the goal of transdisciplinarity is a connected and comprehensive, inclusive and balanced understanding of the world, I propose that holistic assessment of bilingual learners is closely aligned with transdisciplinary approaches. These related approaches lead the way for authentic reflections of meaningful learning opportunities.

Although this chapter cannot possibly address all there is to say about assessment issues for bilingual learners, it builds on our collective knowledge base to propose a framework for bilingual student assessment grounded in multilingual and transdisciplinary perspectives. It begins with an overview of the problems and shortcomings related to monitoring bilingual student achievement and progress through traditional/current standardized testing practices. It then explores the application and development of inquiry-based, holistic assessment practices that apply transdisciplinary epistemological and pedagogical structures with bilingual learners and lead to the proposed framework for assessing bilingual learners. The chapter concludes with a brief discussion of the compatibility of such a paradigm with the TESOL standards for Pre-K through 12 grade students.

Defining the Bilingual Student Population

Over the past 30 years, language diversity has increased substantially throughout the United States (Crawford, 2004). The 2000 Census identified 9.7 million children aged 5–17 years living in homes where a language other than English is spoken, a 54 percent increase over the previous decade. Currently the fastest growing school-age population in the U.S., the K-12 ELL population exceeded 5 million by the 2002–3 school year (National Clearinghouse for English Language Acquisition, 2004).

By definition, English language learners are not proficient in English. English proficiency definitions vary by state, but generally refer to both productive (speaking, writing) and receptive (reading, listening) skills. English language learners have the challenging task of learning English at the same time as they are learning grade level academic content, which is usually presented in English. ELLs come from homes where a language other than English is the principal means of communication. These students are in the process of developing reading, writing, speaking, and listening skills in English as an additional language and have varying levels of native language oral and literacy skills.

With the exception of a single common defining educational characteristic of the use of a non-English language, the ELL population is incredibly heterogeneous. Some students were born and raised abroad, while others were born and raised in the U.S. Some students come from low socioeconomic backgrounds, while many are middle class or above. Bilingual students in the U.S. speak more than 384 languages (National Clearinghouse for English Language Acquisition, 2002). Spanish is the predominant home language of ELLs across the country (National Clearinghouse for English Language Acquisition, 2004), but this varies by school district and individual schools. The degree to which bilingual learners have been educated and are literate in their native language varies, as does the amount of academic instruction they have received in English. Similarly, their English reading and writing levels tend to vary considerably. While all ELLs are in the process of acquiring English, they are typically at different stages of acquisition with respect to conversational language (referred to as basic interpersonal communication skills) and to the use of academic language (referred to as cognitive academic language proficiency) in the various content areas.[3] Finally, ELLs who have had native language schooling acquire the language proficiency needed for academic achievement in English much faster than do their younger counterparts who have had little or no formal education in their home language (Collier & Thomas, 1989).

Standardized Tests and Bilingual Learners: Problems and Shortcomings

Bilingualism is a complex phenomenon that involves all aspects of communication, literacy, and social functions. For bilingual learners, any test *in* English is, to some unknown degree, a test *of* English language proficiency regardless of the stated purpose of the assessment. That is, since English language learners, by definition, have not sufficiently acquired the language of the test (English), results may not accurately reflect the qualities and competencies the test intends to measure in the first place.

The No Child Left Behind Act requires English language learners to participate in yearly districtwide and statewide tests in English proficiency, academic content areas and English reading/language arts for accountability purposes. State plans approved under NCLB rely heavily on English-medium standardized achievement tests. However, several leading professional groups of educators (e.g., American Educational Research Association, International Reading Association, etc.) oppose the use of such assessments with ELLs for various reasons. In addition to other assessment issues that come to bear on bilingual learners, major problems related to the use of existing standardized achievement tests include the mismatch between the tests' target and norming populations and the ELL population (i.e., most standardized tests have been developed in English, for monolingual native English speakers, and normed on native English speaking populations). As a result, these tests inadvertently function as English language proficiency tests for bilingual learners and not as holistic (i.e., connected, inclusive, balanced) assessment measures. The Joint Committee of the American Educational Research Association, American Psychological Association, and National Council on Measurement in Education (1999) suggest that:

> Test norms based on native speakers of English either should not be used with individuals whose first language is not English or such individuals' test results should be interpreted as reflecting in part current level of English proficiency rather than ability, potential, aptitude, or personality characteristics or symptomatology.
>
> (American Educational Research Association,
> American Psychological Association, &
> National Council on Measurement in Education,
> 1999, p. 91)

Because these measures fail to meet the criteria for holistic approaches to bilingual student assessment, they are in effect non-transdisciplinary.

Influence of Language Background on Standardized Test Performance

The research literature strongly suggests that the language background of students impacts their performance on standardized assessments. This has significant implications for English language learners who function in two or more languages. For example, we know that:

- a student's first language may influence his/her understanding of test items, vocabulary, directions, and/or general interpretation;
- English language proficiency level is associated with performance on content-based assessments;
- there is a performance gap in content assessment between ELLs and non-ELL students;
- the performance gap between ELLs and non-ELLs increases as the language load of the assessment tool increases;
- test items high in language complexity may be sources of measurement error;
- performance on content-based assessments may be confounded with English language proficiency level; and
- limited English-proficient students may perform less well on English tests because they read [English] more slowly (Abedi, 2003; Duran, 1989; Garcia, 1991; Mestre, 1988).

Native language issues. English language learners who are in the process of acquiring a basic knowledge of English vocabulary, syntax, and semantics may have problems understanding and interpreting content area assessment items that are language based. ELL students have to demonstrate not only content knowledge and skills, but also reading and writing skills in a language that they have not yet fully acquired. This poses a challenge since most standardized achievement tests do not differentiate between a student's content knowledge and his or her ability to demonstrate this knowledge in a second language. Linguistic issues in student responses may be related to native language influences, including the interpretation of English sounds; codeswitching or codemixing; English phonetics and spelling; punctuation and capitalization patterns; and English syntactic or semantic misuse (including false cognates). For example, ELL students may be influenced by sounds in their native language/dialect that differ from standard English sounds when reading English test items and writing responses in English.

Issues Related to Second Language Acquisition and Second Language Load

Most English language learners first develop a certain level of social communicative competency in English before developing the appropriate use of academic terms and ways to structure academic explanations and arguments. The basis of the distinction is that the language needed in the classroom, particularly as children move through the grades, is different from the kind of conversational language required to communicate on the playground, in stores, while watching television, or relaxing with friends. The language of the classroom becomes more formal, more technical, more abstract, and more specialized. Unfortunately, ELLs are often misplaced in standard curriculum, English-only classes when they achieve a certain level of social English proficiency but before they have developed grade-level academic language proficiency (which normally takes between 4 to 6 years to develop [Collier & Thomas, 1989]). This places ELLs at a disadvantage since instruction and assessment in these contexts are carried out with the assumption that students speak enough English to be able to cope and succeed in the mainstream (English) school curriculum without additional language support.

It becomes important, then, to separate what ELL students know from how well they can read and clearly and successfully articulate this knowledge in English. Certain standard patterns of misunderstandings that are related to second language and literacy acquisition and development influence ELL students' performance on English-language tests. For example, ELLs may misunderstand a test item because of dual word meanings in social language vs. academic content areas (earth vs. Earth), unfamiliarity with implicit questions, unknown vocabulary, literal misinterpretation, or a mismatch in cultural reference; homophones may also cause confusion. Other features of the second language and literacy development process include the production of developmentally immature or emergent sentence and paragraph structures, and the use of pictures and drawings as text in student responses (which is often unacceptable).

Accommodations during testing are sometimes provided for students with limited English proficiency. These may include translations of test questions and/or directions into the student's native language and the use of bilingual dictionaries. Unfortunately, these accommodations do little to alleviate validity and reliability problems. One reason is that native language tests and bilingual dictionaries are inappropriate for students who have limited literacy development in their first language. Even when native language tests are appropriate to measure ELL students' academic achievement, these are not readily available and are rarely aligned with state standards. Further, some "native language" tests are a direct translation of the original English version, a procedure that generally invalidates the test as the difficulty of vocabulary tends to differ across languages (August & Hakuta, 1997) and equivalent word forms differ across dialects, among other things.

Speededness. Time limitations on standardized tests also have adversely affected the test performance of English language learners. Bilingual students often spend too much time trying to understand what is being asked. The speededness effect is consistent with bilingual research that has demonstrated that bilinguals: (a) take longer to process either of the two languages than monolinguals; (b) read more slowly in their less proficient language; and (c) develop receptive competencies in their second language before they develop productive competencies (Garcia & Pearson, 1994).

There is no doubt that we must assess students in order to determine their educational progress and to be able to make instructional decisions that will impact and promote further learning. But, because existing standardized tests apply a monolingual perspective to a very complex and diverse multilingual/multicultural population [i.e., tests assume a relatively high level of academic English language skills (which, by definition, ELLs have not yet achieved) and were never designed for use with the ELL population], these measures cannot be counted on to meet the criteria for holistic assessment and thus do not generate meaningful information about the academic achievement of English language learners. Bilingual educators and researchers have warned that it is difficult to determine the language in which a bilingual student should be tested, just as it is almost impossible for any one formal test to capture what bilingual students know in their two languages (Garcia & Pearson, 1994). But, a holistic assessment system that is based on a multilingual perspective and oriented toward reforming instruction to reflect what is known about best practices in the classroom is inherently transdisciplinary as it applies multiple perspectives to student learning and understanding and provides a more complete picture of what bilingual students know and how they arrive at this knowledge. By examining the nature of bilingual student knowledge about languages, literacy, and conceptual understandings and considering how students learn and come to understand, a framework for assessing bilingual learners framed within multilingual and transdisciplinary perspectives has the potential to inform us about ways to more effectively teach and assess bilingual learners. This approach to assessment can lead to more accurate, appropriate, and responsive educational decisions for English language learners.

Assessing Bilingual Learners Through Multilingual, Transdisciplinary Approaches: Creating Authentic Reflections of Meaningful Learning Opportunities

Scientific and empirical evidence suggest that the bilingual is more than the sum of two monolinguals in one person and that his/her psychological profile indeed displays unique characteristics (Blanc & Hamers, 1989). The bilingual student brings to learning a linguistic repertoire that cannot be measured in a single language (Muñoz-Sandoval *et al.*, 1998). Regardless of the language they are using and their particular proficiency levels, bilinguals are influenced by their knowledge of another language and their cross-cultural experience. Considering that bilingual individuals can read the world in multiple ways based on their cross-cultural experiences and use of two (or more) languages to think about and express these multiple perspectives, one can argue that bilinguality itself is a transdisciplinary way of living.

Bilingual/bicultural education models, i.e., educational programs that use multiple languages and apply multiple cultural perspectives in the teaching, learning, and assessment process, have as a foundation "a complex mosaic involving theory, research, and discourse from several different areas of scholarship and inquiry" (Lessow-Hurley, 2000, p. xii) including linguistics, psycholinguistics, sociolinguistics, psychology, sociology, anthropology, and education. Quality bilingual/bicultural education programs apply a multilingual perspective to teaching, learning, and assessment that is holistic, comprehensive, longitudinal, reflective and reflexive in nature, and multi-dimensional (i.e., based on a variety of observations, in a variety of situations, using a variety of instruments in multiple languages and through multiple cultural lenses). Because bilingual education classrooms use multiple languages and apply multiple cultural perspectives in the teaching, learning, and assessment process, they are by definition transdisciplinary.

Best practices suggest that assessment is a continuous process of evaluating a student's progress toward their learning goals. For bilingual learners, in particular, progress toward learning goals is assessed through the products of student learning and understandings, the process of such learning and understanding, and the languages involved in those products and processes. A transdisciplinary approach to assessing bilingual students views the following goals as central to the assessment process:

Goal 1: Examining the nature of student knowledge about language(s) and conceptual understandings.

Goal 2: Considering how students learn and come to understand.

Goal 3: Monitoring student progress through multiple means and measures.

Goal 4: Guiding individualized and classroom instruction.
Goal 5: Improving student learning.

By connecting otherwise seemingly disparate aspects of the learning process and providing a comprehensive picture of student performance and understanding, a transdisciplinary approach to bilingual student assessment is inclusive, relevant, responsible, and responsive to student learning.

Examining the Nature of Bilingual Students' Knowledge: Language + Content

It is difficult, but necessary, to distinguish the conceptual understandings from the language abilities of bilingual learners. By providing multiple opportunities, mediums, and formats, a transdisciplinary approach to bilingual student assessment ensures that language proficiency does not interfere with the ability to demonstrate understanding of content. Although oral proficiency needs to be assessed in the language in question, literacy and other conceptual understandings (i.e., academic achievement) can be assessed in either or both languages. For example, to demonstrate comprehension of English text, a student can read the text in English but explain the content in the native language. In this way, a student's oral language proficiency in the developing language does not compromise his ability to demonstrate comprehension of text in that language. This is transdisciplinary in that it allows the student to apply the different lenses of each language in order to formulate a more accurate depiction of knowledge and proficiency. This kind of assessment is possible in bilingual/bicultural educational contexts, where the students, teachers, curriculum, and instructional materials share the same languages; it is especially appropriate for students at the early stages of English language development who may understand much more language than they can produce.

Unfortunately, most educational contexts are not bilingual (that is, although the students are bilingual, the teacher, curriculum, and instructional materials are monolingual English). In settings where English is the only language of instruction, teachers must purposefully and strategically integrate language learning with content learning, make use of learners' experiences, and focus on higher-level cognitive skills so that bilingual learners succeed academically. The English language becomes a medium of learning and the challenge becomes identifying effective ways in which instruction and assessment of language and academic content can be successfully combined. One of the most effective instructional innovations for bilingual learners in monolingual English educational settings is content-based language instruction, or sheltered content teaching.[5] Over the past ten years, researchers and practitioners have made much progress in developing, implementing, and refining strategies and techniques that effectively integrate language and content instruction. But, the challenge of assessing student comprehension of subject matter and student language development remains. The difficulty with assessment focuses on isolating language features from content objectives so that one does not negatively impact the other.

Although the proposed framework for bilingual student assessment asserts that the assessment process should be viewed holistically, it is important to separate language issues from conceptual understandings in integrated (English) language and content classroom contexts (Short, 1993). As previously discussed, assessments in the content areas are heavily language dependent and, thus, are likely to confound the assessment of English language and conceptual understandings for bilingual learners. In order to more fairly and validly examine the nature of bilingual students' knowledge, teachers can begin to isolate language features from conceptual understandings by reducing the language demands whenever possible and by providing contextual supports for meaning. Scaffolding techniques for reducing language demands in assessing language and content include:

- involving students in hands-on projects or exhibits that illustrate concepts or procedures;
- asking students to use graphic organizers to show their under- standing of vocabulary and concepts;
- asking students to present lists of concepts or terms and demonstrate how the concepts are organized or sequenced;
- asking students to construct and label tables and graphs showing they understand how data can be organized and interpreted; and
- accepting short answers or explanations (including illustrations) that focus on conceptual understandings.

These alternative techniques are transdisciplinary representations because they involve multiple mediums for demonstrating knowledge. By reducing the language demands of the assessments through such flexible approaches, teachers can increase the likelihood that bilingual learners will successfully reveal their conceptual knowledge and understandings (O'Malley & Valdez Pierce, 1996).

A second approach for adapting integrated content area assessments to the needs of bilingual learners includes using differentiated scoring. Differ- entiated scoring provides separate scores on written and oral responses for language conventions, literacy skills, and conceptual knowledge and understandings. That is, students can be scored once for language and/or literacy (including usage, accuracy, and fluency) and receive a separate score for the content of the written passage or oral response. Another option is to focus on a single objective that is related to either content or language. Some assessment activities can be used exclusively for evaluating content comprehension while others can be used to evaluate students' language development. Each score provides a different "lens" through which to view student progress and development; taken together, these multiple lenses lead to a more holistic and multidimensional understanding of the learner.

To evaluate oral language development, teachers can observe students as they carry out regular classroom activities or activities specifically planned to demonstrate knowledge of a particular language skill. Teachers can use protocols, checklists, or rubrics reflecting performance goals appropriate for bilingual learners at particular English proficiency and grade levels.[6] Literacy skills and conceptual understandings can be assessed by observing students directing a shared reading activity, discussing a book or chapter, or noting how well they use information from books for research projects. For example, while studying locally produced crops bilingual learners at early stages of English language acquisition can be assessed on their ability to:

- identify crops by pointing;
- match vocabulary terms to pictures of crops;
- sort by categories; and/or
- make lists following specified criteria.

In the same study of local crops, bilingual learners at the intermediate level of English language proficiency can be assessed on their ability to:

- identify relevant information about particular crops and copy this information from multiple resources;
- match target vocabulary terms with definitions;
- list key characteristics of crops that grow in their area; and/or
- produce phrases and short sentences about key characteristics of particular crops.

Examination of students' journals and learning logs provides additional data on students' language and literacy development. Journals can be analyzed for writing fluency, sentence structure, vocabulary, grammar, spelling, and ability to express complete thoughts. Numerous protocols, checklists, and other instruments reflecting performance goals that are appropriate for bilingual learners are available to facilitate the collection of relevant information.[7] Criteria used in the content scoring may include conceptual understanding, accuracy of response, and processes used to derive the answer.

These integrated learning activities provide multiple lenses into students' developing understandings in and across each of their languages. By providing multiple avenues and opportunities for demonstrating knowledge and abilities, including some that are not language-based, these transdisciplinary approaches to bilingual student assessment lead to more accurate measures of performance.

Considering How Bilingual Students Learn and Come to Understand

To assess bilingual students' performance accurately and meaningfully requires two other sets of data in addition to the evaluation of products. First, teachers need to become familiar with students' background characteristics. Basic student background information includes the amount of previous schooling, language and literacy levels in the home language, understanding of the school culture, personal interests, level of English proficiency, and parental and cultural attitudes toward schooling. All of these factors have an impact on student learning and are often ignored by large-scale accountability systems. Second, teachers need to consider the methods bilingual students use to arrive at an understanding.

Bilingual learners bring rich cultural background and prior knowledge to the classroom, which can be used by informed teachers to enhance student achievement. Considering the process will help teachers understand how an individual student arrived at a particular solution. For bilingual learners, especially, the process is as important as the product and can avoid incorrect assessments of a student's abilities and understandings. Observing students' process can also provide an immediate teaching opportunity while students are still engaged in the task.

Bilingual students' process can be bilingual and bicultural although the product of performance is usually in one language or the other. Bilingual students in my third grade class often wrote the most complete, organized, and interesting English stories when they were given the opportunity to rehearse their ideas in Spanish, their dominant language. They did this independently, by writing down ideas for a story on a story plan or similar graphic organizer. They also did this in small, heterogeneous discussion groups that included bilingual learners with varying language proficiency levels. Similarly, by looking at the process students undertake when solving a problem, a teacher can note students' language use, strategy application, and self-monitoring through observation and anecdotal records.

Monitoring Student Progress

A third goal of a transdisciplinary assessment system is to monitor bilingual learners' language development and academic progress. English language learners, in particular, are often assessed several times a year to determine progress in English language proficiency and whether they have learned "enough" English to be reclassified as English proficient (and thereby mainstreamed into a standard curriculum classroom). Multiple samples of students' work taken from a variety of authentic situations constitute valid evidence of what students can do. Performance assessment and portfolios are complementary approaches for reviewing student language development and academic progress. Together they represent authentic and continuous assessment of student progress, possibilities for integrating assessment with instruction, assessment of learning processes and higher-order thinking skills, and a collaborative approach to assessment that enables teachers and students to interact in the teaching/learning process. Provided that the purpose of the portfolio contents is to expand understanding of a student's growth based on multiple measures and time points, different kinds of data can be included in a portfolio. These can include specific work samples that show the content and language that students are learning, learning strategies used, and the progress students make over time. Artifacts that led to a published story, including drafts from all stages of the writing process, illustrations, and conferencing notes, provide information on students' language and literacy development. Tests can be included as an additional measure for both language and content as they may provide information to the teacher and other parties about students' test taking skills and demonstration of performance under pressure.

Data about students' sociocultural integration, collected through interviews, questionnaires, or student journal entries, should also be included. These measures provide insights into students' feelings about their languages and cultures, how they relate to their community, their attitudes toward English, and their developing friendships with peers from the majority and other cultures. Observations of student interactions with peers from their own culture and language, as well as with English-speaking peers from the majority culture, can reveal students' developing bilingualism and biculturalism (i.e., their ability to function in both cultures). Sociocultural integration must be closely monitored and supported in order to facilitate the development of healthy cross-cultural relationships and understandings.

Multiple assessments that are adapted to the language proficiency of bilingual learners can assist in cross-checking identified areas of strength as well as highlight academic and/or linguistic needs. As holistic, systematic collections of student work (and the processes that led to that work) that reflect specific learning goals and criteria, assessment portfolios provide transdisciplinary lenses through which teachers, students, parents, and other stakeholders can make informed instructional decisions that support future learning.

Guiding Individualized and Classroom Instruction

Transdisciplinary assessment strategies help teachers make timely instructional decisions by reflecting and allowing for critical inquiry into learning, instruction and the curriculum. Reflective and reflexive integrated assessment activities reveal insights into the effectiveness of certain teaching methods, classroom environmental features, materials selected to enhance learning, grouping strategies, and student learning of content and language. By examining *how* students solve learning tasks (a defining component of transdisciplinary assessment) through the integration of knowledge across disciplines and cultural perspectives, teachers can better understand different learning styles, unique talents, and instructional needs. Using a range of assessment information garnered from a variety of contexts also helps teachers modify or differentiate instruction more effectively. In this way, the distinction between holistic and systematic assessment and teaching becomes blurred and assessment activities become renewed and refocused opportunities to teach.

Improving Student Learning

Transdisciplinary assessment practices focus the purposes of assessment on documenting individual growth and providing instructionally useful information. When teachers understand what students know or how far their skills have developed in a target area and/or language, they can plan appropriately to extend student knowledge. The context of the assessment will contribute to its authenticity. Newmann & Wehlage (1993) suggest the following criteria for authentic achievement: "(1) students construct meaning and produce knowledge, (2) students use disciplined inquiry to construct meaning, and (3) students aim their work toward production of discourse, products, and performance that have value or meaning beyond success in school" (p. 8). Through the application of these criteria, transdisciplinary approaches to the assessment of bilingual learners have the potential to provide authentic reflections of meaningful learning opportunities and lead to more accurate, appropriate, and responsive educational decisions.

Compatibility of Transdisciplinary Approaches to Bilingual Student Assessment with the National ESL Standards for Pre-K-12 Students

In the current context of high-stakes testing to measure the attainment of standards and ensure accountability, there is a strong focus on adequate yearly progress for all students. The international association of Teachers of English to Speakers of Other Languages (TESOL) has developed a set of standards that specify the language competencies ELL students in elementary and secondary schools (Pre-K–12) need to become fully proficient in English and to have unrestricted access to grade-appropriate instruction in challenging academic subjects. As "a starting point for developing effective and equitable education for [ELL] students" (TESOL, 1997, p. 10), the ESL standards emphasize the importance of language as a principal means of communication; the development of language through authentic and meaningful use; the individual and societal value of multilingualism, the role of the native language in English and academic development; cultural, social, and cognitive processes in language and academic development; and assessment practices that respect and incorporate linguistic and cultural diversity as central to the learning and teaching process.

The ESL standards establish three broad goals for school-age bilingual learners, including personal, social, and academic uses of English. Each goal is associated with three distinct standards. The standards are guided by a vision of effective instruction and assessment for all students that are part of:

> . . . a comprehensive and challenging educational program that takes into account [ELL] students' social, educational and personal backgrounds as well as their existing skills and knowledge bases. [Assessment and instruction] must understand and respond appropriately to the interrelationships between language, academic, and sociocultural development. The linguistic, cognitive, and sociocultural competencies that [ELL] students bring to school are a solid base for building their future, in terms of educational and career success.
>
> (TESOL, 1997, p. 10)

A recognition of and emphasis on the interrelated nature of linguistic, academic and sociocultural development of bilingual learners provides a transdisciplinary foundation to the ESL Standards and demonstrates general compatibility with holistic, multilingual approaches to the instruction and assessment of bilingual learners.

TESOL's classroom-based scenarios for assessing the attainment of the ESL standards provide further evidence of the compatibility of the ESL standards with transdisciplinary approaches to bilingual student assessment. The assessment scenarios: (1) are directly linked to sample performance indicators and ESL standards; (2) elicit higher level thinking; (3) encourage the exploration of new ideas and concepts by students and teachers; and (4) present multiple ways to approach tasks and ultimately attain the ESL standards (TESOL, 2001). Built around a series of activities that are embedded in instruction, the assessment scenarios include relevant forms of documentation of student knowledge, performance, and progress (e.g., scoring guides, anecdotal records, checklists, rating scales, rubrics). In addition, suggested peer and self-assessment activities encourage bilingual learners to take an active role in their own learning.

In one scenario, a unit of study is described in which bilingual learners: (1) develop an increased awareness of their community and neighborhood resources, (2) elicit information and ask clarification questions, and (3) negotiate solutions to problems, interpersonal misunderstandings, and disputes that may arise in collaborative groups by researching and recreating their neighborhood map (TESOL, 2001). Students draw a large scale map of their community in collaborative groups, talk about the location of several important landmarks (e.g., the school, grocery store, post office, etc.), practice a dialogue between someone who is lost and a community member or official who provides directions, brainstorm names, and purposes of community businesses and resources, discuss walking routes with other students, and share the map they prepared though a group oral presentation (using the map as an additional visual support). Teachers can assess student progress and processes by:

- filling out a tally sheet that lists target phrases, prepositions of place, and question types used during the "asking for and giving directions" activity;
- observing and documenting student interaction patterns and interviewing students about how well they think they worked in groups; and
- taking anecdotal records of interactions during the map project development phases and final oral presentations.

By providing suggestions for broadly based, integrated methods of assessing language and academic achievement in the content areas that are appropriate to bilingual learners' developmental level, age, and level of oral and written language proficiency in students' first and second languages, the scenarios represent equitable assessment for bilingual learners framed within a transdisciplinary perspective.

Conclusion

The challenges of providing an equitable and effective education for bilingual learners are great. The proposed framework for assessing bilingual learners adopts a multilingual, transdisciplinary perspective that is based on a holistic view of the bilingual. Within this paradigm, students' cultural and linguistic backgrounds are validated as resources for learning; the role of primary language and literacy in the acquisition of a new language is understood; and sociolinguistic, sociohistorical, and sociocultural factors that contribute to the child's development, experiences, and competencies are considered in the assessment process. By addressing bilingual learners' unique characteristics, including systematic and multiple types of assessments of language proficiency and academic achievement, giving equal weight to both products and processes of learning, and informing instruction through reflective and reflexive practices, transdisciplinary approaches to bilingual student assessment legitimize students' experiences and are more likely to yield authentic reflections of bilingual learners' knowledge and understandings. With such powerful and comprehensive data, teachers can make appropriate and effective decisions that will support bilingual learners on their journey to becoming literate, active, and able participants in classroom settings and beyond.

Notes

1   I use the terms "English language learners" and "bilingual learners" interchangeably here as ELLs function in two languages, to different degrees and for a variety of purposes. I propose that the term "bilingual learner" more aptly describes these students' experiences and abilities, because "English language learner" and other terms used in the literature and legislation assume that language ability is measured by how much a person knows English.

2   A multilingual perspective is based on a holistic view of the bilingual learner including validation of students' cultural and linguistic backgrounds as resources for learning, an understanding of the role of primary language (including literacy) in the acquisition of a new language, and a consideration of sociolinguistic, sociohistorical, and sociocultural factors that contribute to the child's development, experiences, and understandings.

3   For a detailed explanation of basic interpersonal communication skills and cognitive academic language proficiency, visit Dr. James Cummins' website at: www.iteachilearn.com/cummins.

4   Validity refers to whether assessments actually test what they are designed to test (i.e., whether results are confounded by lack of proficiency in the language of the test). Reliability is an assessment's ability to produce consistent results (i.e., whether results vary because of unrepresentative sampling of the populations being tested).

5   For a more detailed description of sheltered content approaches, see Gort (2003).

6   For useful oral language and literacy checklists, rubrics, and protocols designed for bilingual learners see O'Malley & Valdez Pierce (1996).

7   See Gottlieb (2006), Griffin *et al.* (2003), and O'Malley & Valdez Pierce (1996) for useful assessment instruments designed for bilingual learners at different levels of English language proficiency.

Bibliography

Abedi, J. (2003). *Impact of student language background on content-based performance: Analyses of extant data* (CSE Report 603). Los Angeles: University of California: Center for the Study of Evaluation.

August, D. & Hakuta, K. (eds.) (1997). *Improving schooling for language-minority students: A research agenda.* National Research Council. Washington, DC: National Academy Press.

American Educational Research Association, American Psychological Association, & National Council on Measurement in Education (1999). *Standards of educational and psychological testing.* Washington, DC: American Educational Research Association.

Blanc, M. & Hamers, J.A. (1989). *Bilinguality and bilingualism.* New York: Cambridge University Press.

Crawford, J. (2004). *Educating English learners: Language diversity in the classroom* (5th edition). Los Angeles, CA: Bilingual Educational Services.

Collier, V.P. & Thomas, W.P. (1989). How quickly can immigrants become proficient in school English? *Journal of Educational Issues of Language Minority Students, 5,* 26–38.

Duran, R.P. (1989, October). Assessment and instruction of at-risk Hispanic students. *Exceptional Children, 56* (2), 154–8.

Garcia, G.E. (1991). Factors influencing the English reading test performance of Spanish-speaking Hispanic children. *Reading Research Quarterly, 26* (4), 371–91.

Garcia, G.E. & Pearson, P.D. (1994). Assessment and diversity. *Review of Research in Education, 20,* 337–91.

Glaser, R. & Silver, E. (1994). *Assessment, testing, and instruction: Retrospect and prospect (CSE Technical Report No. 379).* Los Angeles: National Center for Research on Evaluation, Standards, and Student Testing (CRESST), University of California.

Gort, M. (2003). Transdisciplinary approaches in the education of ELLs. In D. Kaufman, D.M. Moss, & T.A. Osborn (eds.), *Beyond the boundaries: A transdisciplinary approach to learning and teaching* (pp. 117–30). Westport, CT: Praeger.

Gort, M. (2006). Strategic codeswitching, interliteracy, and other phenomena of emergent bilingual writing: Lessons from first-grade dual language classrooms. *Journal of Early Childhood Literacy, 6* (3), 327–58.

Gottlieb, M. (2006). *Assessing English language learners: Bridges from language proficiency to academic achievement.* Thousand Oaks, CA: Corwin Press.

Griffin, P., Smith, P.G., & Martin, L. (2003). *Profiles in English as a second language.* Portsmouth, NH: Heinemann.

Hakuta, K. & Beatty, A. (eds.) (2000). *Testing English-language learners in U.S. schools: Report and workshop summary.* National Research Council. Washington, DC: National Academy Press.

Hurley, S.R. & Tinajero, J.V. (eds.) (2001). *Literacy assessment of second language learners.* Boston, MA: Allyn & Bacon.

Lapp, D., Fisher, D., Flood, J., & Cabello, A. (2001). An integrated approach to the teaching and assessment of language arts. In S.R. Hurley and J.V. Tinajero (eds.), *Literacy assessment of second language learners* (pp. 1–26). Boston, MA: Allyn & Bacon.

Lessow-Hurley, J. (2000). *The foundations of dual language instruction* (3rd edition). New York: Longman.

Meeth, L.R. (1978). Interdisciplinary studies: A matter of definition. *Change, 10,* 10.

Mestre, J.P. (1988). The role of language comprehension in mathematics and problem solving. In R.R. Cocking & J.P. Mestre (eds.), *Linguistic and cultural influences on learning mathematics* (pp. 200–20). Hillsdale, NJ: Erlbaum.

Miller, J. (2001). *The holistic curriculum.* Toronto, ON: OISE Press.

Moll, L.C. (1992). Bilingual classroom studies and community analysis: Some recent trends. *Educational Researcher, 21* (2), 20–4.

Moll, L.C., Amanti, C., Neff, D., & Gonzalez, N. (1992). Funds of knowledge for teaching: Using a qualitative approach to connect homes and classrooms. *Theory Into Practice, 31* (2), 132–41.

Muñoz-Sandoval, A., Cummins, J., Alvarado, C., & Ruef, M. (1998). Research in bilingualism: Implications for assessment. Paper presented at the Annual Meeting of the American Educational Research Association, San Diego, CA.

National Clearinghouse for English Language Acquisition (2002). *Language backgrounds of limited English proficient students in the U.S. and outlying areas, 2000–2001.*Washington, DC: National Clearinghouse for English Language Acquisition. Retrieved May 2005. Available at: www.ncela.gwu.edu/stats/4_toplanguages/langsalpha.pdf.

National Clearinghouse for English Language Acquisition (2004). *The growing numbers of limited English proficient students: 1992/93–2002/03.* Washington, DC: National Clearinghouse for English Language Acquisition. Retrieved May 2005. Available at: www.ncela.gwu.edu/...data/2002LEP/Growing_LEP0203.pdf.

Newmann, F.M. & Wehlage, G.G. (1993). Five standards of authentic instruction. *Educational Leadership, 50,* 8–12.

O'Malley, J.M. & Valdez Pierce, L. (1996). *Authentic assessment for English language learners: Practical approaches for teachers.* Reading, MA: Addison-Wesley.

Short, D. (1993). Assessing integrated language and content instruction. *TESOL Quarterly, 27* (4), 627–56.

Teachers of English to Speakers of Other Languages (TESOL) (1997). *ESL standards for Pre-K-12 students.* Alexandria, VA: TESOL.

Teachers of English to Speakers of Other Languages (TESOL) (2000, June). *Assessment and accountability of English for Speakers of Other Languages (ESOL) students.* Alexandria, VA: TESOL. Retrieved March 2005 from www.tesol.org/s_tesol/sec_document.asp?CID=32&DID=369.

Teachers of English to Speakers of Other Languages (TESOL) (2001). *Scenarios for ESL standards-based assessment.* Alexandria, VA: TESOL.

CHAPTER 10

Interdisciplinary Assessment

A System at the Heart of Teaching and Learning across Domains

JACQUELINE KELLEHER

Maura Kennedy is a second year teacher at Polar Elementary, a K-6 institution in an urban setting. Maura loves her job. She prepared as a teacher in a rural state, but felt she was ready for the challenge and adventure she would find in a big city. She has found the multi-cultural, bustling New England setting is constantly alive with activity and excitement. The State Department of Education Strategic data indicate that Polar Elementary has a demographic breakdown of significant diversity:

- 84 percent of students are from under represented groups.
- 65 percent are at or below the poverty level established by the federal government guidelines.
- 25 percent have been identified with special needs under IDEA.
- 56 percent come from a single parent home.
- 60 percent are at or below grade level in math as measured by the state exam.
- 45 percent are below grade level in literacy as measured by the state exam.
- 54 percent speak another language other than English.
- 27 percent have a household with one parent holding a degree.

Maura is often busily preparing for her day 90 minutes before the first pupil arrives and stays until 6:00 pm tutoring children, researching learning strategies, and developing meaningful educational activities. She donates her time to support the after school tutoring program as well as the Saturday Reading Power initiative. She has twenty-eight pupils, but rarely has full attendance in this fourth grade classroom; she is constantly creating instructional packets for her students who cannot or do not make it to school. She has been known to personally hand deliver packets door to door.

Maura's school is not meeting proficiency goals on the statewide assessments and the district has mandated that the focus of instruction and professional development be on building literacy and numeracy skills across all grades. There is a tremendous concern that the school will be slated for restructuring next fall. Maura's students have been working tirelessly on preparing for the statewide test. Her heart goes out to these children who seem to approach mastery on informal assessment activities, but struggle on the bubble sheet, pencil-based practice tests the administration requires every other week. They are making incredible progress as a class; despite inconsistent attendance she has changed her own assessment strategies to be more in line with the state tests. The sense of pride in their classroom community is strong and they are working well in collaborative groups for the first time all year.

It's test day. Juan, a recent immigrant from Puerto Rico, is approaching his ninth month in the U.S., so he is no longer exempt from the state assessment due to State rules; his brow furrows as he struggles to read the directions, and he gives up quickly, keeping his head down on the desk for the remaining sixty minutes of practice testing. Anesha day-dreams throughout the assessment; she has documented learning disabilities and reads at the first grade-level, she does not qualify for the 1 percent special education exemption and needs to take the same grade-level assessment as her fourth grade peers. There are other pupils with similar challenges, but they remain a part of the testing process. Maura rallies them through the experience, but she is personally frustrated. Aside from her personal feelings about the assessment mandate, she is annoyed that she does not get her student results for up to one year after the assessment has been administered. Her plan for using these criterion-referenced assessment results is to inform her practice and provide necessary support for her kids before they move on to fifth grade; her plans are thwarted due to the slow turnaround of reporting. Still, she understands that each child needs to be a part of the assessment protocol and looks forward to the day when her test scores are delivered sooner so she can make appropriate accommodations for individual learners. She wishes the assessments captured the spirit of interdisciplinary activities and the learning connections across subject areas. She's discovered that using inquiry methods have facilitated critical thinking and deeper written and oral responses that cannot be captured on a multiple-choice test or edited task.

Recently, Maura came into school and received shocking information at the district level. The new superintendent implied in a statement to the schools that all untenured teachers were expected to have their students perform at grade level on the statewide assessments or they would be let go. There was a sense of alarm and panic among the new teachers at Polar and across the district. Testing was set to begin in just a few weeks! Many of the new teachers began looking at the Sunday classifieds, knowing that there was not a lot they could do to get their pupils prepared to meet proficiency although they'd been preparing all year. Maura was irate and deeply saddened by this situation. She had received approval to loop with her class and work with the same kids in the fifth grade. She was doing everything she was supposed to do—collecting regular formative assessment data to shape her instruction and make decisions about the learning. She was differentiating instruction to match the needs of her diverse learners, keeping abreast of the latest research-based practices in literacy. She was involving her students in the assessment process and keeping communication open with parents and guardians. She was determined to find the right solution to fit her students' unique learning needs. Under NCLB, she was a highly qualified teacher and deserved the opportunity to continue her work at Polar. Now, however, she was likely to lose her job when she was just getting started. Her evaluations were strong, her commitment evident; yet, the word throughout the district was clear: mastery or bust.

Assessment Defined

Why does the word *assessment* send chills immediately down the spine of the innocent or conjure up images of high stakes tests constructed to penalize teachers and injure students? Why do the terms standard, bench-mark, measurable, evidence-based, value-added, and outcome strike terror in the heart of many educators and students? Maura's story is one real world example that illustrates the tensions that exist in our era of accountability. Perhaps this is not experienced directly by all educational professionals, but it is undisputable that practicing educators and students are deeply affected by the accountability movement. Situations like those illustrated in this chapter are a reminder to the field that best practice in assessment is being challenged by the current climate of accountability and it's imperative we find a balance between holding schools accountable and engaging in positive assessment practices used to facilitate teaching and learning.

No Child Left Behind currently serves as a national blueprint for educational reform:

I. Improving the academic performance of disadvantaged students.
II. Boosting teacher quality.
III. Moving limited English proficient students to English fluency.
IV. Promoting informed parental choice and innovative programs.
V. Encouraging safe schools for the 21st century.
VI. Increasing funding for Impact Aid.
VII. Encouraging freedom and accountability.

The principles seem reasonable enough. High quality teaching, improved academic performance, safe schools—all of these efforts lead to strong learning environments. Somehow, however, the original flavor of the blueprint has been masked by an emphasis on statewide proficiency levels and mean scale scores. Parents, teachers, pupils, teacher candidates, higher education, K-12 administrators, and others are influenced by this legislation and the current focus. Holding people accountable in meeting outcomes affects how future teachers are prepared; hence, assessment becomes an important component in teacher education especially as we consider how to move ahead as a nation, enhance our educational system, and identify assessment practices that allow us to monitor attainment of NCLB principles.

There are immediate issues and there are long-term challenges that have not been fully articulated or even anticipated until recently. Overall, the act's intent is to assure that children in every classroom sit before well-prepared teachers, are engaged with research-based curriculum, and are learning in safe environments. At the center of NCLB is the idea of accountability, and assessment is used widely to determine the successful design and implementation of programs and activities developed in response to NCLB principles. Still, there are tensions related to identifying adequately yearly process, defining the notion of a highly qualified teacher, statewide report cards, and funding issues to support all of these new initiatives. The true irony lies in the fact that the last bullet under NCLB emphasizes *encouraging freedom and accountability*. The dilemma has become a dichotomy for many educators: freedom in the classroom versus accountability shackles.

The key to long term progress is understanding how to make assessment work for our institutions rather than have it drive programs in a way that causes us to lose our grounding in who we are as professionals and school communities. Assessment, when understood, planned well, and implemented with care, is a powerful tool. When assessment is used as a continuous feedback loop embracing the tenets of collecting meaningful information using credible tools, evaluating and making sound judgments based on this information, and communicating results to stakeholders with the intent of sharing strengths and weaknesses, it becomes a rich and powerful mechanism for improvement. Despite the feeling that the field struggles to define an agreed-upon definition for assessment, there are many who concur that assessment is a strategy for understanding mastery, effectiveness, and impact based on sound methods of collecting information that describes an outcome. Educators judge and evaluate based on these data and communicate this evaluation back to those being assessed and to those involved in the assessment system (Hinkle, 1993; Schalock, 2002; Tanner, 2001).

Using Assessment Results

Dr. Craig Daniel is a program coordinator for the Special Education division of a rural School of Education in Oregon. Despite a depletion of human, fiscal, and physical resources at his university, he is tasked with developing an assessment system for all programs preparing K-12 professionals as part of NCATE re-accreditation requirements. His colleagues are excellent teacher and principal educators as evidenced by high faculty ratings and placement data on graduates for all programs. The NCATE standards are part of their commitment to excellence. While faculty know they are preparing all of their graduates to have the knowledge, skills, and dispositions necessary to support pupil learning, Dr. Daniel is struggling to document when and where faculty and other decision-makers are using assessment results across disciplines to understand how all of the courses and program experiences are contributing to this excellence. His institution has always collected data: demographic, incoming test scores and GPA's, grade ranges in required courses, and feedback from internship hosts. But Dr. Daniel can't seem to find evidence that programs are actually using assessment results in their strategic planning, resource allocation, or accountability efforts. Most faculty members are tenured and used to "the old ways of doing business." Dr. Daniel anticipates a great deal of tension, confusion, and skepticism. He appreciates using information to get an understanding of the current situation of candidate competencies and how programs are effectively enhancing proficiency levels. Data are a tool that can ground all the different contributors to the development of candidates. But it's a lot of work to promote and implement strategies and infrastructures that enable a diverse faculty new to assessment to use assessment results.

There's the challenge of getting this operationalized before the NCATE visit two years away and getting faculty across disciplines to engage in this practice because it's a good thing to do. Dr. Daniel is struggling with an action plan and rationale for moving this forward. It's hard enough to get a faculty across campus to connect through scholarship, and service-building a data-driven feedback loop seems impossible!

Many institutions and organizations grapple with the challenge of knowing what to do with all these assessment data once they have collected them. As early as 1974, the idea of interfacing learning systems with looping strategies that channeled critical information back to governing bodies and people guiding the development of action strategies for learners was proposed to enhance reflective thinking and decision making (Argyris & Schon, 1974). The continuous feedback loop is a critical component to effective assessment systems. This is the dynamic relationship between what gets done with the information collected, how it is evaluated, by what methods results are shared with those affected by the assessment, how instruction or programs are modified, and how learning outcomes are applied to benchmarks established by a community. An ongoing system that involves representative stakeholders with clearly stated expectations, criteria, and modes of communication is the type of infrastructure necessary to feed meaningful data back to decision-makers. Then, an interdisciplinary community examines not only data but the tools and procedures in place. Does this information help us understand mastery? Can we generate a plan for program effectiveness? Do these tools help us create the culture of evidence that we need to make appropriate decisions? Information about performance, measures, and potential considerations for moving forward are reviewed and decisions are made. While monitoring the outcome of such decisions, the assessment overseers attend to the next set of goals, objectives, and activities within this cycle. What makes for a strong system is looking regularly at multiple measures and data indicators. Making decisions based on data as opposed to anecdote can be an uncommon prac-tice for professionals across the disciplines. Data guide assessors and allow for stronger evaluation techniques of pupils, candidates, and programs. However, without the proper training opportunities, connection to a big picture, or promotion from school leadership, using assessment results and communicating action plans are never completely successful.

Interdisciplinary Assessment

Defining interdisciplinary assessment is nebulous at best. Entering the words into a web-based search engine reveals an array of explanations, from medical intakes and scientific interactions to risk assessment systems. The idea behind interdisciplinary assessment is grounded in the notion that it is a measure of educational impact on personal, social, and cognitive knowledge; attitude; and skills leading to recommendations of improvement for the learner, the instructor, learning events, and curriculum. Additionally, it is an assessment opportunity that taps into different domains that have been identified as relevant by the school, teacher, or class. Integrating assessment activities allows pupils, candidates, and faculty to work through the learning process while engaging in multiple disciplines, and it is a rich opportunity for growth.

For K-12 pupils, offering or facilitating lessons and assessment activities that cross multiple subject areas can lead to deeper connections. For example, a middle school math activity on probability might include having pupils work through a scientific research or evaluation question on a community issue using skills needed for data collection and analysis, literature review, interviewing community members, and writing a letter to the editor after the formal results are written. This allows for many competencies to be assessed by the teacher and may be a rich opportunity to partner with other school team teachers in creating an assessment scoring guide and involving multiple raters in these authentic assessments. As teachers, we are able to look across different domains and expected outcomes all in a focused task. We are able to assess a more global part of the pupils' learning experiences with the tools we create to measure performance. The activity crosses disciplines for both learners and teachers.

The same approach is appropriate in higher education, whether in teacher education, liberal arts/sciences, or any other discipline. Many institutions such as The University of Connecticut, UCLA, The University of Michigan, University of Texas-Austin, University of Oregon, University of Southern California, and Oklahoma are examining general education requirements using an integrated curricula to prepare students for a global world; this restructuring and emphasis on preparing graduates to make connections across subject areas and to experience learning that crosses disciplinary lines is apparent whether the institution is public, private, large, small, or nationally-ranked. Teacher preparation programs are charged with accreditation expectations that direct how they assess the general education experience as well as other aspects of the program where candidates are exposed to these curricula designs. Places like Western Oregon University, Old Dominion, Virginia, UMass, and UConn are organizing opportunities to look at cross discipline experiences for their candidates by modeling these experiences in interdisciplinary classes. Programs are beginning to strategize ways of monitoring if these approaches lead to graduate effectiveness in these areas. Not only are candidates being exposed to interdisciplinary curricula, methods, and activities, but they are learning how to evaluate pupils using tools that capture interdisciplinary information about the learning. The assessment, activity plan, and system designed to capture multiple data indicators that emerge across subjects and outcomes are used with candidates, but also serve as a model for candidates to use in their own practice with PK-12 pupils.

Good Assessment Plans

While the definition of interdisciplinary assessment was just described as a process that allows us to look at multiple competencies and make judgments about proficiency, I would also like to introduce the notion of interdisciplinary assessment as one that is interdisciplinary if the assessment data are reviewed and used for understanding and change by decision-makers who represent multiple disciplines. This next section will describe best practice in planning and implementing for assessment, leading to an overview of making decisions through interdisciplinary lenses.

For those who prepare preservice and in-service teachers, it comes as no surprise that one of the keys to success as a teacher is instructional planning, and consistently organizing and managing the environment. Similarly, when planning your assessment program or system at the coordinator and administrative level, it takes the same amount of care and attention. We look at ways we can assess before, during, and after instruction rather than having it serve as a punitive means of motivating a student, serving as an extra task not connected to the instruction but just as a means to an end (Popham, 1995). Whether this is for a school or district, an assessment plan to meet the needs of accreditation, or a plan to guide how you will assess students on their learning within a particular unit, the following characteristics are important in designing an assessment plan and system.

The assessment design needs to take root in the conceptual framework, mission statement, or set of agreed upon guidelines that are defined at the department or program level. The assessment plan can be crafted and driven at the program level, but it does need to link and align with the overarching initiatives and outcomes determined at the national, state, or institution level. Successful assessment implementation should be overseen by an assessment coordinator or designated person within the department or school who monitors how plans and systems align and argues for the unique needs of the organization to the state or national constituencies if the plan deviates in any way from the regular expectations. Assessment systems and activities are unique and should reflect the individuality of the program and/or discipline.

Assessment activities should be clearly communicated to all stakeholders affected by the assessment system. For example, those who impact or who are impacted by your program (school of education), project (increasing content knowledge for Praxis II), product (program completers/teacher candidates), resources (curricula/materials), or personnel development (employees, volunteers, evaluators) should be included in the development of measures, examination of data, and process of creating action plans. Involving others provides a comprehensive look at the complete data picture and gets at the heart of understanding interdisciplinary approaches in assessment. It would lead to invalid judgments if assessors did not try to gather as much information as they could from any entity that could be or should be involved in the assessment measures. Bringing multiple disciplines and perspectives to the table ensures representative insights and deeper perspectives. Planning for this configuration in advance will help assessors develop and implement better assessment practices, allowing for better judgment.

In my practice as a higher educational assessment coordinator, I repeatedly see programs and school districts behaving like teenagers procrastinating before the big exam and cramming with the hopes of passing a test! There is a frantic rush to begin collecting assessment data without a clear rationale or plan, but with the intent of passing an accreditation visit. The purpose of a test as a tool for learning becomes lost and does not enter into these candidates' minds because neither the plan nor system of measures has been presented in a way that promotes best practice in teaching and learning. There should be a commitment to program or institutional assessment as an ongoing, useful practice in which we engage to strengthen programs and experiences. If we perpetuate the notion that it is a practice performed during accreditation, program review cycles, or other high stakes periods, the positive use of data for growth will never be a part of the organizational fiber. Programs need to make assessment a part of the everyday culture and not use it to jump through hoops, giving the illusion they are a data-driven community.

Assessment needs to be a fully supported practice. Easy to say, but how is this accomplished? Leadership and resource allocation. Administrators need to endorse assessment practices and provide funds to support programs that are planning to engage in developing assessments and systems. Leaders need to include assessment goals in their communication with target groups, through writing, speeches, and scholarship. Assessment coordinators need to develop strategic marketing tactics to get programs on board in developing assessment protocol that reflect their unique qualities. Internal grant opportunities should help faculty and teachers get started so that they have the resources necessary to engage in thoughtful work. Teacher educators and practicing leaders need to model best practices, present at national conferences, and write articles for clinical and scholarly journals. A quick and fast implementation of an assessment plan and tools may backfire and create that feeling of suspicion and frustration. As with any type of cognitive or paradigm shift, how assessment is introduced and implemented within a community is an important component. Assessment needs to become a part of the organization over time, beginning with assessing only a few goals or outcomes at the outset. Great care and sensitivity to feasibility should be employed.

Assessment plans and developing systems should provide a clear rationale with respect to why assessments are being done, what assessors hope to gain from the data, and what implications the implementation and results have for those being assessed. Plans should clearly articulate how the assessment data will be shared and acted upon. In crafting mission or goal statements, documenting the rationale or guiding principles will help the assessment coordinators and teachers focus and commit to a valid practice. The few assessment activities I have developed that were not aligned with a clear rationale generated data that could not be used as well as a feeling of resentment from those being assessed. No one wants their time wasted. Communicate results as often as possible after data have been collected to assure that time invested was worthwhile.

To assess an interdisciplinary curriculum or practice, the tools or procedures to gather evidence should be sensitive to competencies that are interdisciplinary in nature. In other words, matching an assessment to a purpose and in a way that is congruent with the learning event or context takes critical thinking about the task at hand. Paper-based, multiple choice response data will not and should not reflect learner competency or program impact in many cases. Interdisciplinary teaching and integrated learning should have innovative data collection efforts reflective of these pedagogies. Products and processes such as making connections across multiple disciplines, taking different perspectives, and demonstrating a deeper understanding of content need to be captured using other tools such as reflective journal activities with credible rubric criteria, self-assessment exercises, or reactions to relevant case studies with scoring guides grounded by the interdisciplinary domain. Another powerful way to look at change, impact, or movement as a result of the practice is to employ pre-post assessment techniques.

These are areas to consider in developing your assessment plan for your particular program, department, classroom, or institution. I write from the perspective of one who has implemented similar plans for a school of education, a university learning outcomes committee, a study skills program for secondary education, and for my own middle-school classrooms.

Here are some suggested procedures for setting up the assessment plan in your classroom, department or program, or institution when it comes to involving many perspectives and skill sets in working with data. These strategies follow models found in many assessment textbooks and assessment courses in schools of education (Lewin & Shoemaker, 1998; Popham, 2001; Stiggins, 1998):

- Program, department, teacher, institutional goals, or targets need to be cited. Critical standards necessary to the discipline should be clear and used to guide instruction. (Carr & Harris, 2001). A clear definition or mission statement for the organization, course, or experience needs to be crafted to focus the plan.
- Identify student learning outcomes. As a result of being in your class, program, or institution what can one expect a student to be able to know or do as a result of experiencing an intervention? This can take a lot of time and debate in terms of articulating these outcomes in meaningful ways. Yet, this is where the power of bringing interdisciplinary groups into the conversation can positively shape the way we prepare our learners.
- Benchmarks or critical points in the development of the student or unit should be identified. We have assessment data, but what do we compare it to in order to make a decision about the learning? Is it a cut score? A proficiency? Are there percentages we are trying to shoot for in order to quantify "excellence"? Are we comparing along target variables each year as a program? There should be a justification as to what makes these important benchmarks or milestones for a program, candidate, or pupil, and why these are essential in the development of the learner. Benchmark configuration allows groups to explore where they are and what they aspire to be.
- Identify specific evidence to seek out about the learning, environment, attitude, perceptions, knowledge, skills, and whatever else is important to those developing the assessment plan. Determining evidence is an opportunity to collaborate with others in and outside of your field. This practice, again, is what lends itself to becoming interdisciplinary assessment. The assessors develop standards and criteria for benchmark performances and a description for what evidence looks like. Data take many shapes, sizes, and meanings when offering quantitative and qualitative information into the system. The tools should be conceptualized to measure knowledge, skills, behaviors, and attitudes elicited as a result of working with the target curriculum or experience. There is a tremendous amount of

creativity and inquiry involved in identifying sources of evidence reflective of outcome and developing innovative or strategic ways to collect such information.

- Collect evidence that serves decision-makers. What are reliable and valid procedures to measure the learning, environment, attitude, perceptions, knowledge, skills, and whatever else is important to those developing the assessment? Are there tools and techniques already in existence? Do you need to develop an original tool to tap into an area specific to your unique situation? We described *what* the evidence might look like—now implementing the protocol becomes the focus. Develop a timeline for tool development and revisions, data collection, data analysis, evaluation, and sharing results with stakeholders. Whether at the individual classroom or institutional level, having an organized scheme or map that keeps the assessment plan on target and moving as a comprehensive system is essential.

- Analyze credible data, write up results, and make recommendations for change or sustaining the positive aspects that emerged through the investigation. There should also be an emphasis on assessing the credibility of tools or procedures that are used to collect this information. The data are only useful if the assessment tools have been designed and evaluated to collect the right information in response to the target questions. Finally, key people, including school leaders, need to insure a monitoring system for regularly reviewing any changes made as a result of the recommendations.

Good Assessment Information Gathering

Gathering information in multiple and varied ways can be initially time consuming and overwhelming; still, in this diverse world, looking beyond a "one size fits all" mentality in assessing outcomes is critical if we want to make meaningful decisions. Many people hear that they have to be involved in assessment or outcomes-based practices and jump to the idea of a paper-based test or standardized, commercial measure that assigns a number, label, or value and somehow reflects a culmination of grouping experiences over time. In many ways, using a manufactured or published test is an easy method to quickly collect information that may or may not inform teaching and shape student learning. Such a monocular view of assessment, where one relies primarily on one measure to make a decision, can become a barrier to understanding the achievement of outcomes and effectiveness of instruction.

Using assessment pieces such as mastery test scores, Praxis outcomes, GRE results, and the like, may give some useful information, but it would be a perilous journey for students and teachers to be guided by an assessment plan that simply uses one or two similar instruments as the sole indicators of performance. One instrument alone does not fit all instructional aims or learning outcomes. One instrument is more like a snapshot of a particular day at a particular time on a particular topic. Was a candidate feeling ill on the day of the Praxis? Was a pupil unable to read the literacy portion due to an E.L.L. challenge? Was the learner struggling with the bias inherent in many of the items? Without other pieces of evidence to help flesh out the picture for decision-makers, we run a grave danger of assuming someone has not learned when indeed they have but were not able to demonstrate. On the other hand, a decision-maker could look at a high score and infer mastery when it has not occurred; rather, the test taker has savvy test taking skills or can manipulate an instrument to give the appearance of learning (Popham, 2001).

Multiple, varied assessment tools and unique activities reflective of the different domains contribute to an interdisciplinary perspective on two levels. First, faculty and decision-makers are able to look at performances across different domains and evaluate program design and impact. Second, students are able to reinforce the synthesis of disciplines if assessment activities reflect multiple areas in one event or across events. We need to offer multiple opportunities using different methods in order to make decisions, inform our own practice, encourage student responsibility for their own learning, and monitor development. Published tests have their place, but so do other formal and informal ways to collect information: portfolios, authentic tasks, reflections, questioning, interviews, observations, pre- and post-tests, self-assessment, teacher-made pencil tests, essays, role playing, group activities, and other performance opportunities, just to name a few. These varied methods should be used across one discipline and multiple disciplinary assessment activities should reflect what we take as the learner's performance from an interdisciplinary perspective.

Beyond Classroom and Courses

In addition to developing typical assessment opportunities that reflect or determine academic mastery of objectives, in order to truly experience assessment as a creative, artistic, interdisciplinary entity, teachers and faculty can also assess the climate of their learning communities. Through surveys, interviews, focus groups, pre-post means, and observation, teachers can collect information from their own communities to help shape how they are teaching and having an influence beyond the classroom doors. By putting assessment measures out in public—visible to all who are affected—and soliciting regular feedback, the teacher also models a positive assessment climate for students as an opportunity to regularly collect information for improvement. We are modeling that assessment is a natural, important aspect for teaching and learning. We are not afraid of it. We regard it as an essential ingredient to any practice and demonstrate that we care enough about our craft and discipline to monitor strategically.

At the University of Connecticut, as part of the Neag School of Education Assessment Plan, the following instruments and techniques have been regularly employed with the goal of monitoring and adjusting in response to using a feedback loop. Interdisciplinary stakeholders work to understand how multiple data indicators can be used, make group decisions, engage in critical dialogue, and identify resources necessary to develop a program using data to guide their planning. Here are some of the assessment tools:

> Faculty self-assessments or goal statements, alumni survey, employer survey, focus groups, pencil- and performance-based tests or projects, teacher candidate and faculty self-assessment, clinic evaluations, portfolios with artifacts reflective of growth and/or performance at pre-set benchmarks, program evaluation online surveys, state or national tests, climate evaluations, mentor surveys, assessment checklists, professional development surveys, admission tools, conference/workshop evaluations, hour logs, attitude/affective/disposition tools, pre and post, rubrics, exit interviews, previous grades or grades earned through a particular program.
>
> (Kelleher, 2003, accessed July 2007)

A Note on Credibility

Most teachers and education professionals know that in designing or selecting an assessment instrument, one needs to take great pains in recognizing issues of reliability and validity. Often, teacher preparation programs offer initial classes in assessment to teacher candidates that address reliability and validity issues in creating and selecting instruments; there are professional development opportunities to learn more about the importance of using tools that allow us to make reliable and valid decisions about mastery and understanding. Techniques in controlling for reliability and validity go beyond the scope of this chapter, but are critical to assuring that the decisions one makes as a teacher are credible. Having this knowledge of understanding common measures of reliability and validity also prepares us to be better consumers of information that we encounter in the media, journals, and even our faculty meetings. It is important to conduct curriculum audits of our teacher prep programs and identify the quality of this assessment experience. When bringing those with multiple disciplines to one table and developing an overarching assessment protocol capturing interdisciplinary principles, investigating the soundness and credibility of tools or procedures become critical.

Good Assessment Evaluation and Curricular Decisions: Interdisciplinary Tactics for an Interdisciplinary World

Evaluation is making a judgment based on the information collected; it is using professional expertise to make an evidence-based decision and determine the merit and worth of a performance, product, or behavior (Hinkle, 1993). Good curriculum design linked to sound assessment plans may vary from the dynamic, to the ideal, to the linear, to simply what is comprehensive and manageable (Carr & Harris, 2001). How one looks at data and uses set criteria and/or standards to determine the value of a performance, product, or environment is already an integral part of many professional disciplines. So why should education be any different? Is this different in interdisciplinary assessment? Interdisciplinary assessment is grounded in the same design principles, only being particularly sensitive to assessing target learning outcomes and competencies matched appropriately to an interdisciplinary curriculum, lesson, or activity.

When asked to write a chapter in a book dedicated to interdisciplinary assessment, the vision I had in addressing what interdisciplinary assessment *is* encompassed the role of the feedback loop, the idea that all stakeholders affected in some way by the assessment should be involved. There should be multiple ways to tap into understanding the learning while collecting information on the cognitive, personal, social, and moral development of learners across multiple disciplines. It is a powerful model and is easy to articulate on paper, but it is increasingly more challenging within this era of accountability. In many ways, it supports or reinforces many of the central ideas practiced through the integration of interdisciplinary curriculum (Jacobs, 1990). It also brings together interdisciplinary teams and procedures to come to a complete decision about performance. Assessment is a strong component in medical, business, pharmacy, and law schools, to name just a few. Schools of education are also professional institutions shaping a professional learning community. It's critical that we recognize interdisciplinary assessment as something that aligns our field with other professions.

However, judgment can become complicated when compiling data from multiple sources and learning events. Judgment can become clouded due to our emotions and subjectivities as we become influenced by variables that are not part of the objectives or learning outcomes: effort, behavior, attitude, political tensions, parental pressures, or personal biases. The bottom line is that we must make decisions based on the evidence without undue influence of outside variables and based on data elicited through sound methods. The following practices are necessary to engage in when developing the interdisciplinary assessment plan and system:

Instrument Design. The instrument used to enable the assessor to collect information needs to be clearly aligned with the objectives for the learning that one has set in advance (Popham, 1995; Lewin & Shoemaker, 1998). If that learning experience has been designed to have outcomes reflective of the interdisciplinary intervention, the instruments to collect data need to capture those critical components. The first question one asks before designing an instrument or procedure is what do I need to know about the said performance? In the spirit of good interdisciplinary assessment, assessors need to move beyond solely using content-focused objective, pencil-based assessments. Although these have their place and should be one measure of mastery, the assessor needs to look for multiple tools reflective of both the content and processes. Some examples include performance-based assessments, self-assessment, observation, exit interviews, developmental portfolios, group work, and opportunities for multiple correct responses (Popham, 1995; Schalock, 2002).

Models of different gradations of performance or target scores should serve as the benchmark or comparative structure for teachers or students, especially when more than one discipline is to be measured. It is important to make sure that the purpose of the performance is clearly defined as are the criteria; also, the activity selected to represent a performance should be considered and decided with care (Stiggins, 1998).

Proficiency. Using appropriate tools and explicit criteria to determine mastery of a performance, quality of instruction, or the effectiveness of an experience is critical. Determining mastery or learning proficiency as a result of a particular experience allows teachers and decision-makers to understand which practices to sustain and which others to revise or omit from the protocol. A key piece to this type of decision-making lies with linking assessment to instruction by including mastery learning aligned with curricular expectations. A set of expectations is established by a teacher, district, committee, or other authorizing bodies, and a decision is made regarding the expected amount or degree of performance in relation to these expectations (Tanner, 2001). In mastery learning, a curriculum is developed and broken down into a set of sub-skills, which are then ordered in a hierarchy of instructional objectives, or of importance, as indicated in a guiding standard or goal (Glickman, 1985).

Quality of Instruction. Ultimately, the assessment feedback loop should provide critical information about how the instruction went and where the instruction should go in the future. Assessors need to reflect on learner mastery or the lack of learning evidence and examine if this may be a result of instruction. Assuring that objectives were presented and covered in ways that were comprehensible to students, good assessment/data collection should provide clear information about what might need to be covered again or how a new strategy might be introduced to facilitate the learning. In our own heads we might think that we know the best way to share our content, but regular assessments can serve as a gauge by which we can determine mastery of information (Popham, 2001). When someone does not master content, we need to look at delivery, content, and assessment tactics to determine if we collected the most valid information (Glickman, 1985). Changes need to be made in case it is clear that the instruction or the time spent on a topic was inadequate.

Tanner (2001) suggests using teacher self-assessment formatively and summatively within a content unit or across a quarter or semester. We can examine student achievement and consider it a reflection of the teaching and learning dynamic. Additionally, if teachers incorporate the use of self-assessment to examine variables that indicate how the instruction led to the achievement of objectives, whatever the information collected led to an increased understanding of the needs and progress of learners, and whether or not the methods complemented the learning environment, the instructor will have critical information about his or her own personal performance. It allows for regular assessment of how students are making personal connections across disciplines and synthesizing them into a unified concept.

Attitude. What is an affective indicator like attitude doing in this chapter? I placed it here for two reasons: to draw attention to assessing attitude of students and other stakeholders as part of the information collection process and to help you recognize your own personal attitude toward assessment and instruction. We should consider having instruments or procedures for assessing attitudes and perceptions of our students as well as for the content and the instruction. We might look at change over time or we may just want to weigh that information when making a decision about mastery. We also want to understand our own belief systems with respect to assessment since our strong opinions are often evident to our students, faculty, and parents. This is not a cry for a national attitude adjustment; however, it is an argument that our own beliefs about assessment can affect how we incorporate it into our classroom and use it to make decisions. Understanding the attitude of a student or group or organization toward a particular topic or event can help an educator or learner understand opinions or foundations that ground choices, behaviors, responses, or decisions. There is an affective piece to learning that can be assessed.

Collaboration. In addition to analyzing data on your own you have the opportunity to recognize the spirit of interdisciplinary curriculum and assessment: colleagues or committees can review data with you and provide input on the outcomes, activities, and measures that are part of the experience. Perhaps you have an assessment group at your higher education institutions, or maybe you have an assessment team at your K-12 school that shares your love of inquiry and serves in the role of advisory board for your new tools and methods. Results can then be fed into your personal or team feedback loop and shape your subsequent teaching, planning, monitoring, intervening, and decision-making. You are creating an individual plan or strategy for your pupils, teacher candidates, program, or project through this rigorous process. This is science. This is art. This is making evidence-based decisions about the nature of teaching and learning. The amount of creativity involved is enormous and critical for success.

Communication of Assessment Findings

How does one communicate achievement, mastery, opinions, and the judgment made based on the data? The assessor might conclude that communication is a grade or narrative that articulates the judgment and is translated into words or symbols like "A" or "F" or "100%" or "Great work!" Information collection and judgment are most often, as Tanner writes, "an abbreviated form" of evaluation called grades (Tanner, 2001, p. 101). There's a challenge to squeezing and translating our data into something comprehensible for multiple audiences. We strive to find a common language for a particular audience to understand. We often take on symbols like letters, numbers, P/F, credit, or no credit. We may write qualitatively to describe the performance and convey a sense of strengths and weaknesses. We may have a checklist with all the behaviors necessary to indicate mastery. However we choose to translate the learning and the data, the audience needs to know what the symbols mean, how we arrived at our decisions, and what can be done to improve upon areas of weakness

(Popham, 2001). Depending on the audience, other ways to communicate using data include presenting results comprised of frequencies, measures of central tendency, gain scores, trend analyses, categories, themes, bullets, and charts/graphs. Often, graphical displays of data are important to employ when working with stakeholders. In looking at data from the macro-level, teachers and assessors can explore connections and disconnections across multiple areas. Perhaps groups of students are consistently performing well in content area courses that are more practical and factual, but experience issues in more abstract, theoretical courses. What can be done at different points in the program to support students with the skills necessary to improve performance? Data need to be shared in ways that allow for themes to emerge, trends to become apparent, and patterns to become clear.

Whereas one concern is how we convey mastery, the other area to consider is with whom we share this information. Using an interdisciplinary approach to assessment as described in this chapter is only effective if the results are clearly communicated and recommendations are generated for the student, project, program, or whatever else is being assessed. Part of the communication process that is integral to interdisciplinary assessment is identifying modes to transmit your tools, criteria, findings, and plans for adjustments in response to the information collected and judgments made about the learning. I am providing some examples to consider with respect to clear communication with various stakeholders.

Instructors can anticipate communicating to students, parents, administrators, and, to some extent, the community at large. Instructors should conduct a needs analysis to find out exactly to whom they will be reporting and the best mode of communication. I recall that, as a new assessment coordinator, I had grandiose ideas of using a discriminant function analysis or logistic regression to describe performance. Who wouldn't be amazed if I could predict what category of performance someone would fall into based on the data profiles? I learned very quickly that my sophisticated statistical techniques did nothing to help others understand the learner. My aggregated data were fine for administration and a research presentation, but did nothing for the assessment feedback loop. I had not communicated in a language that was meaningful for most of my audience. Know your audience and find out in advance what they need to do with these data. Also, prepare yourself by understanding any local or state privacy legislation before defining to whom you are communicating.

Communication may take different shapes for different people. Your students should have the criteria communicated in advance and models of what you are looking for whenever possible. When you have evaluated the work, the symbols or rubric or other ways you scored the assessment need to be taught to your students. You need to provide guidance in showing how their work aligned to your standards and how you weighed their performance against your criteria. In addition to the symbol, you need to provide adequate written or verbal feedback that praises the positive attempts and clearly identifies areas of weaknesses with strategies toward improvement (Popham, 2001). This communication should be shared as soon as possible. Withholding feedback for weeks after the learning was assessed does not provide the swift, immediate reinforcement one needs in learning.

The more visibility you give your assessment plan and the more you share it with people affected by your teaching and classroom, the greater degree of understanding and positive regard that will emerge. Teachers can develop an assessment handbook outlining practices and descriptions of assessment throughout the year, to be signed off on by pupils and caregivers; regular newsletters with updates, reminders, and disclosure of initial findings can keep your stakeholders informed; reports to administrators and professional development partnerships can help inform others and allow for more sound decision-making; writing scholarly articles about how you are engaged in assessment and how you are using results to inform your practice can have a lasting impact on others in this profession and across other disciplines; and presenting at local, regional, and national conferences would not only help others in your professions, but would buffer the agenda of having the field regarded as a legitimate social science and field of inquiry.

The Current Climate of Assessment

The climate of assessment for educators, administrators, parents, and students has not been formally assessed as far as I have been able to determine. Looking through *The Chronicle of Higher Education*, sitting through faculty meetings, reading statewide initiatives online and listening to my teacher candidates as they make their way through the student teaching trenches gives me a sense that the current climate is tumultuous at best. Issues that have surfaced as a result of states and districts scrambling to meet the requirements of No Child Left Behind or of teacher preparation institutions responding to the latest accreditation hoops have made it difficult to be a teacher and learner in this era of accountability. In our current climate, in many instances, the emphasis of assessment is on mastery test scores in grades 3–8, the connection to federal dollars, shaming schools that are not passing the appropriate tests, and assessing K-12 pupils in more or less a uniform way. There seem to be many people who feel that the current assessment demands are a top-down mandate that doesn't consider those directly affected by new regulations. A big question that lingers for me is who is holding the accreditors accountable? Who is monitoring and evaluating progress of NCLB? What unbiased, skilled evaluation team is making sure children are not left behind despite these new rules, regulations, mandates, and expectations? The current climate in this new era seems nebulous at best since there is no clean evidence of impact at this point. There is, however, great hope held onto by assessment experts such as me. If we focus on assessment as a process that enables professionals to engage in inquiry, faculty and students will deepen their understanding of mastery across multiple domains and the impact of exposure to interdisciplinary experiences as reflected by relevant data sources. Assessment is a critical component in schooling across all levels and the current climate is not always conductive to supporting the best practice in assessment.

How to Change the Climate of Assessment

I hope that readers get the sense from this chapter that assessment can be a positive, necessary, and natural aspect of everything we do if we take the time to develop thoughtful assessment opportunities and use the collected information for the greater good of our classroom and communities. Assessment does not have to be a painful exercise in futility. If one believes in these important principles of sound assessment practice, the next part of the process involves a little strategic marketing. Assessors need to be approachable, have their assessments visible, and engage in regular, open dialogue with those affected by the assessment and its results. By highlighting the positive aspects of an informative feedback loop used to assess teaching and learning simultaneously, the assessor can generate enthusiasm through this open communication.

Concluding Remarks

Assessment is challenging, creative, frustrating, and rewarding. At times, the amount of responsibility that goes into developing a plan, implementing, monitoring, and adjusting in response to data collection seems daunting and unmanageable. Still, if you break down the components into meaningful chunks, it can be accomplished; if you do not try to measure every goal and objective overnight, the assessment practice will be more logical and sequential for learners and others being assessed. The benefits that emerge as a result of having this system in place affect teachers and learners. It leads to the development of greater collaboration, stronger programs, enhanced opportunities for learning, and increased support as your entire community becomes involved with your assessment system. It makes goals, objectives, and anticipated outcomes more clearly and readily understood. It provides data on impact that our administrators are requesting while allowing practitioners to remain grounded in what they value. This approach of merging the knowledge of measurement, evaluation, communication, content, pedagogy, learning, and mastery raises standard assessment to the next level: an interdisciplinary art.

If more organizations take part in this method of assessment as a form of inquiry, as noted in the opening paragraphs of this chapter, perhaps the Maura Kennedys of the profession will continue on as teacher leaders who build a culture of evidence in best practice that will lead to those proficiency goals under NCLB. Perhaps if we use an assortment of approaches in our teaching and assess the learning with an interdisciplinary lens, we will truly prepare future citizens with valuable tools to strengthen our world.

Postscript: Revisiting the Case Studies

Maura Kennedy can be a change agent for Polar Elementary. She can take an assessment class, lobby school leaders for professional development opportunities in assessment, serve on a school-level assessment task force, or get involved in assessment efforts at the state level. She can encourage her community to become more informed about assessment expectations, best practice methods in preparing students for assessments, and how to use results from multiple areas. Maura can lead the way in modeling grade-level or subject-level assessment reflection sessions that keep student learning at the forefront. Maura feels out of control and driven by assessment rather than feeling professionally equipped to navigate her students through the current wave of accountability demands. She needs to be proactive; however, the school leadership in her building has to change on several levels to support a data driven environment.

This, too, is reflective of what needs to happen in Dr. Daniel's world. He needs to turn to school leaders for support while becoming involved at the state and national levels to make sure that the assessment of students across disciplines captures accurate and representative information about teaching and learning. Additionally, both Dr. Daniel and Maura need to model practice so that it becomes tangible and visual to all involved. If we are to use assessment results generated from multiple data opportunities and make sense of program design and impact, viable examples of this implemented practice and data gathering instruments need to be available to those seeking change.

Bibliography

Argyris, C. & Schon, D. (1974). *Theory in practice: Increasing professional effectiveness*. San Francisco, CA: Jossey-Bass.

Carr, J.F. & Harris, D.E. (2001). *Succeeding with standards: Linking curriculum, assessment, and action planning*. Alexandria, VA: ASCD.

Glickman, C.D. (1985). *Supervision of instruction: A developmental approach*. Needham, MA: Allyn & Bacon.

Hinkle, D.E. (1993). *Outcomes assessment and program evaluation: What are they—and for what purpose?* Washington, DC: AACTE Publications.

Jacobs, H.H. (1990). The growing need for interdisciplinary curriculum content. In H.H. Jacobs (ed.), *Interdisciplinary curriculum design and implementation* (pp. 1–11). Alexandria, VA: ASCD.

Kelleher, J.P. (2003). *The Neag School of Education assessment system*. Storrs, CT: University of Connecticut. Available at: www.education.uconn.edu.

Lewin, L. & Shoemaker, B.J. (1998). *Great performances: creating classroom-based assessment tasks*. Alexandria, VA: ASCD.

No Child Left Behind. Retrieved August 23, 2004. Available at: www.whitehouse.gov/news/reports/no-child-left-behind.html.

Popham, W.J. (1995). *Classroom assessment: What teachers need to know*. Boston, MA: Allyn & Bacon.

Popham, W.J. (2001). *Classroom assessment: What teachers need to know* (3rd edition). Boston, MA: Allyn & Bacon.

Schalock, M.D. (2002). Assessing teacher work samples. In G. Girod (ed.), *Connecting teaching and learning: A handbook for teacher educators on teacher work sample methodology* (pp. 65–89). Washington, DC: AACTE Publications.

Stiggins, R.J. (1998). *Classroom assessment for student success*. Washington, DC: National Education Association.

Tanner, D.E. (2001). *Assessing academic achievement*. Needham, MA: Allyn & Bacon.

CHAPTER 11

In Praise of Complexity

Moving Interdisciplinary Assessment in Education from Theory to Practice

DOUGLAS KAUFMAN, DAVID M. MOSS, AND
TERRY A. OSBORN

The other day, a friend of ours, in contemplating the political state of our nation, observed that "the age of reason is now officially dead." He now sees a country run by a federal administration that rules by the "gut"—by a *feeling* of what is right or wrong—and that seems to ignore any evidence that contradicts its participants' belief systems or desires. Commensurately, policy mandates "evidence based research," but only when that research appears to support a narrow political agenda. Our friend's remarks struck home even more pointedly given our Chapter One discussion of the current educational era as the "age of assessment." The question we pose is this: if the age of reason has experienced its demise and the age of assessment is upon us, has the federal government shaded the definition of the latter to such an extent that it can now be recognized as *diametric* to the former? Instead of seeing assessment as a natural and *reasonable* way to collect evidence in order to learn and then act upon what we learn, promoting new learning and growth, we now use it as a way to test whether or not a certain school, teaching method, or child supports a narrow, preconceived agenda. We may use unfavorable data to punish and deprive, an eminently *unreasonable* endeavor, especially when those who are most punished are children, who are just as often as not held to account when a school is identified as "failing." The responsibility of meting out this punishment has become unreasonable as well, with the decisions of those who interact daily with classroom students being superseded by those who have no grassroots contact with them at all.

The authors of this volume have endeavored to bring reason back into assessment: to create and describe systems within interdisciplinary or trans-disciplinary frameworks by which children and their work are valued and to expand the definition of what counts in schools so that they align with what counts in productive lives. In reading their chapters, rich in their diversity of viewpoint and voice, we nevertheless recognize common threads that tie them together into a consistent challenge to the status quo that currently pauperizes our nation's larger educational agenda.

The Acute Tension Between Sound Interdisciplinary Practice and High Stakes Testing Mandates

Reading these chapters, we came away with the clear sense that the writers agreed, for the most part, that the tenets that define interdisciplinary and transdisciplinary practices and curricula inevitably contradict the goals of high stakes testing and the implemented policy that results from those goals. While professionals who support interdisciplinary and transdisciplinary approaches and those who support high stakes testing can both insist that they do what they do to promote better, more comprehensive, more equitable learning for students, their conceptions of what can count as learning are very different.

The differences that separate the desired ends of these two entities are stark. Standardized tests almost necessarily "draw distinct disciplinary lines and emphasize facts over critical thinking and complex problem solving" (McGivney-Burelle *et al.*, this volume, p. 72). The wider the scale of the test, the narrower its focus must be, if only for the logistical reason that it is too expensive and time-consuming to look at more. Resultantly, we continue to isolate the content areas from one another in order to preserve the validity of the tests by keeping the scope of the content pure and to a manageable size.

When we accept these structures and procedures that necessarily limit the scope of the standardized test's focus we commit ourselves to a clear philosophical stance: we acknowledge that the breadth of coverage is more valuable than the depth of knowledge that any individual possesses. We affirm the value of expediency. In doing so, we also define what we accept as important to children and to society. As we narrow the knowledge that counts to specific content matter and we isolate that content into neatly prescribed packages, we also narrow our definition of the *student* to a lowest-common denominator: we standardize the child to fit the individual subject area and the test. Simplification in this case leads to the simplistic.

Our current national and state assessment systems in no way reflect the richness and diversity that define our nation and its children.

This simplification makes it impossible to actually use the tests for their purported purpose: to offer evidence that can help schools and districts revise their curricula and pedagogy based on revealed need. The wide-scale nature of the tests, their narrow definition of learning, and their narrow definition of the learner inhibit the promotion of change. Too, these tests cannot promote response that addresses the immediate needs of learners—that allows for quick revision on the daily or even minute-to-minute basis that is so often necessary. We were struck by Jacqueline Kelleher's story of Maura Kennedy, the new urban teacher who engages her students in activities and assessments designed to promote critical thinking, independent learning skills, and continual revision of her practices based on her students' needs, but who runs the danger of losing her job because her students are not yet performing up to speed on the only tests that count: the state standardized tests. However, she does not get the score results of these tests until a year after they are administered, far too late to use them to inform her practice with that group of students. We also see these stark effects in Mileidis Gort's discussion of creating authentic assessment systems for bilingual learners. The promise of authentic interdisciplinary practice is readily apparent in bilingual classrooms, where students inevitably bring diverse knowledge and talents informed by different languages, cultural backgrounds, and world perspectives. But yet again, we see the diminishment of possibility in the wide scale nature of high stakes testing, which cannot value the benefits of different language and culture. English Language Learners' "unfamiliarity with testing language, content, vocabulary, testing formats, test-taking skills, and cultural orientations of tests" (Gort, this volume, p. 136) quashes interdisciplinary possibilities because the different facets of these learners' profiles—their understandings of other languages, content, vocabulary, testing formats, testing skills, and cultural orientations—cannot be valued without undermining the narrow goals of the test.

Interdisciplinary and transdisciplinary practices, in contrast, define themselves by their attempts to *connect* disciplinary structures and even blur the lines among them. At the same time they draw their power from the varied perspectives of individual students, who are required to examine not only content matter, but the discipline itself and the connections among disciplines, drawing on their own varied backgrounds, experiences, and proclivities to understand and shape the different way of seeing that individual disciplines bring to the fore.

When we recalculate what counts in education in this way, our definition of assessment also shifts radically. The philosophy behind interdisciplinary studies rests resolutely on the ability of both teacher and student to know how to make independent and informed decisions. This is, in fact, a primary reason for having an interdisciplinary or transdisciplinary curriculum in the first place: it teaches decision making and interpersonal interaction as outcomes above and beyond important subject matter learning. Thus, we see hope residing within these chapters, and along with hope comes a true reconceptualization of assessment. In these chapters, student knowledge and student need drive evaluation; assessment becomes a tool to build new knowledge, not just judge the quality of prior knowledge. While assessment must provide feedback to both teachers and students about their specific performances in order to legitimize itself as a tool of *teaching*, it, just as much, becomes a tool for *learning*. Assessment redefines itself as an active component of the learning process, imbued within all the choices students make over time, the products they are creating, and the communication in which they engage with others.

Within this bustle of interaction and intensive activity lies the power of interdisciplinary and transdisciplinary studies, and within it we see a vision of assessment that does more than synthesize information on a massive scale. Instead, it attends to the individualizing of the curriculum—the attempts to value and build off of the work of each and every learner.

The Embrace of Complexity

The clearest theme arising out of the chapters as a whole is this: we need more *complicated* conceptions and models of assessment rather than simpler, more easily quantifiable ones. These authors take as a given that the real world is complex. Living and growing within the world, therefore, require approaches that acknowledge and even welcome complexity. This is what interdisciplinary and transdisciplinary approaches do as they:

> swell to encompass multitudinous perspectives, activities, and challenges, and the assessment that is integral to the mission— and is, in fact, one of its defining terms—must follow suit. The assessment must be as complex as the actions it examines or else we have no transdisciplinarity at all.
>
> (Kaufman, this volume, pp. 48–49)

At the very core of interdisciplinary and transdisciplinary learning models is the welcoming of complication—the very fact that we bring together multiple subject areas and the multiple perspectives that emanate from their study indicates the inevitable introduction of complexity, subtlety, interdependence, and holism.

The result is a description of teaching assessment systems across chapters that expand the options for both the tools of teaching and the tools of evaluation. Presentations of isolated subject materials and tests that measure discrete, short answer responses fail to suffice; hands-on projects, independent student inquiry and reflection, performances, and assessment modes that evaluate longitudinal, comprehensive conceptions of learning fill the void. The curriculum shifts away from uniformity and simplicity and instead embraces the inevitability of a complex, dynamic, and fascinating world in all its multitudinous facets. This expansion into variety that is nonetheless unified by a philosophical focus ties this book together, and its embrace of complexity reveals itself in a number of the chapters' sub-themes.

A Shift from a Content-Driven Curriculum to a Process-Driven and Inquiry-Driven One

The simplest acts of assessment are those that ask students to relay back to the assessor content information: *Question*—what is the capital of Japan? *Answer*—Tokyo. While none of the writers in this volume argue against the essential value of subject area knowledge, they agree that this knowledge by itself is an insufficient aspect of education. Our love of teaching content material stems from our own love of our respective subject areas. But in teaching, we often neglect to answer the important questions that students must pose: "How are we supposed to find information independently?" and "What are we supposed to *do* with content knowledge once we acquire it?" Our authors answer that we must shift the focus of our instruction and personal learning to commensurately recognize the processes of learning and the inquiry that leads to product creation and a *deeper* understanding of content. While reform efforts have been attempted, an either/or conundrum continues across virtually every subject area in which process remains a focus separate from its relationship to product and content knowledge.

The authors in this volume highlight several new conceptions of the relationship between product and process, content and inquiry. They define the subject areas variously as ways of reading the world, as landscape for exploration, as process itself. In essence, they have *activated* content, blurring the line between it and the processes that both examine and create it. Teaching process for these authors is eminently practical: it helps students learn how to navigate the world, making clear sense of the landscapes (read "content") that they inhabit. Teaching process—exploration, use of tools, strategies that make learning more efficient, states of mind that reveal previously unrecognized possibilities—is a given in the effective interdisciplinary or transdisciplinary classroom. Ultimately, it makes content learning much more relevant because students can now use content to chart the courses of their own lives.

A Shift to Promoting (and Assessing) Authentic Student Experience

Real lives are not disciplinary: different themes, ideas, interests, experiences, and problems overlap and intertwine. More often than in subject-specific units, interdisciplinary or transdisciplinary projects focus on real world problems and open up opportunities for students to explore them in authentic situations. Living, learning, and creating within a world of others is more complicated than the traditional academic theme, and throughout these chapters one sees their authors focusing in on the complexity of real life, casting interdisciplinarity and its commensurate assessment processes as media for addressing real world problems and finding real world solutions. Alan Marcus in his chapter describes the potential for interdisciplinary studies to offer activities that are "more realistic and similar to a citizen's societal existence. These units may create opportunities for inquiry into real-world dilemmas in a more holistic manner" (p. 95). Jean McGivney-Burelle, Katherine McGivney, and Jane M. Wilburne, in arguing for an interdisciplinary curriculum that can expand students' understanding of math content, state that this real-world focus leads directly to real-world assessments: classroom discussion, journals, case studies, interviews, observations, performance assessments, project manuals, and presentations that simulate authentic, real world experiences, and are more relevant to students. Scott Brown cites several examples where this type of work takes place in more authentic situations, which he states helps students learn to transfer their learning to situations outside the original learning context.

Outside the *original* learning context is where these authors want to lead us, into a landscape where we all inevitably reside—a landscape beyond the comfort of the classroom walls where responsible independence and self-sufficiency is required.

Creating Learning and Assessment Systems that Put Responsibility on Students

This attention to real life creates another inevitable shift in focus. When our definition of education, through an embrace of interdisciplinary or transdisciplinary studies, changes to acknowledge our responsibility of helping learners *think* and *do* in complex, real world arenas, we—sometimes only tacitly—affirm that we are putting students at the center of the curriculum and offering them all the rights, privileges, and responsibilities therein. Complexity increases as we abandon earlier conceptions of our roles as deliverers of only compartmentalized content material. As we compel participants to examine who exactly is learning, who is processing, and how he or she is doing it, we necessarily acknowledge the active agent and the activities that he or she introduces. If we define content material as a landscape within which learners explore, we must attend to the nature of the explorers and the equality of the exploration. The Irish philosopher George Berkeley once famously asked, if a tree falls in the forest and there is no one there to hear it, does it make a sound? Similarly, we might ask: if we create a classroom world full of rich information and there is no one there who knows how to examine and use it, is it really there?

Thus, we now have the added responsibility of helping students learn how to take their *own* responsibility for learning. To do so through interdisciplinary and transdisciplinary studies, the teacher considers that any academic responsibility that he or she might assume during the normal course of the day must be taught to students so that they can assume the responsibilities for themselves. This does not mean that students are left to their own, still incompletely formed devices, unilaterally creating the curriculum and deciding independently what will work best for them. Instead, it means that we help them to develop the tools of independent responsibility so that they might not only *share* in classroom operations, but also be able to move forward as competent, creative, and independent agents once their formal scholastic careers are over.

Paramount among these responsibilities, say many of the authors, is the responsibility for self-evaluation. These chapters offer detailed examples of what self-evaluation looks like within interdisciplinary and transdisciplinary frameworks. We posit that this self-assessment is, in fact, at the center of independent learning. The authors here expand self-assessment into what comes before and during a learning act—acts of goal setting and generating questions that drive the learning forward. They promote the concept of reflection upon one's own written work in order to discover themes and problems that can help guide students during future projects.

Creating Curricula and Assessment Systems that Promote Democracy

But what is the upshot? Upon reading this volume, the answer that resonates most strongly with us is the power of the interdisciplinary or transdisciplinary curriculum to help students establish themselves as knowledgeable, reflective, able citizens within a strong democracy. A democratic view of the world again introduces and champions complication. It explores the multifaceted relationships among different points of view and different ways of interpreting the world, and it explores the connected influences among all of them. We suggest that interdisciplinarity and transdisciplinarity help students learn how to engage in public discourse, understand how and why dissenting viewpoints are established, accept differing viewpoints as valid if based upon sound premises, and engage with the world in a way that expands rather than narrows physical, intellectual, emotional, and moral possibilities.

The theme of democracy surfaces throughout this volume. Terry Osborn sharpens his focus on the need to expand the language curricula to study "the ways in which languages function in a socio-cultural context such as the United States democracy" (p. 108), while David Moss advocates that we specifically teach science so that citizens may fully participate in public environmental discourse, such as issues underpinning global change, which is central for a thriving democracy. Others take a wider perspective, seeing in interdisciplinary and transdisciplinary approaches the potential to create a more knowledgeable and engaged citizenry "who actively participate in civic affairs, understand how our democratic society functions, can think about social issues and problems, and take action when necessary" (Marcus, this volume, p. 93).

Overcoming the Barriers to Interdisciplinary Work

Despite the very real possibilities for interdisciplinary or transdisciplinary work to strengthen, even revolutionize the classroom curriculum, there are still weighty barriers in place. We have already discussed how content area learning, especially in the secondary school, is still bound into prescribed units that completely isolate the subjects from one another, and how federal assessment mandates promote this isolation. Authors describe the overwhelming logistical constraints of developing an interdisciplinary curriculum and the added work of compiling data from multiple, data-rich sources. Other obstacles include the loud arguments of subjects-specific proponents about what counts as necessary content to be learned and the need to be aware of subjectivity and bias when we welcome students' personal lives into the curriculum.

Yet the very nature of interdisciplinary and transdisciplinary work may mitigate some of the apparent intractability of those overwhelmed by these barriers. In reading these chapters, we see natural, if sometimes hidden points of overlap that suggest that the nature of each discipline is not as self-contained as some of its inhabitants might imagine, or even hope for. We see, for instance, social studies described as "naturally interdisciplinary, easily connected to and overlapping with science, language arts, fine arts, and other subjects" (Marcus, this volume, p. 89). We learn of the inevitable interdisciplinary nature of the bilingual classroom. In fact, we see virtually all the subject areas redefined as complementary ways of seeing phenomena that, when used together, create a more holistic understanding.

TABLE 11.1 Guide to promote interdisciplinary or transdisciplinary assessment

In the interdisciplinary or transdisciplinary unit, what do you want to evaluate?

Ability to analyze
Ability to choose topics
and themes
Ability to defend positions
Ability to develop well-
supported claims
Ability to embrace
complexity
Ability to evaluate
Ability to find value in
things
Ability to fundraise
Ability to generate
questions
Ability to interpret
Ability to organize events
Ability to recruit
Ability to self-evaluate
Ability to synthesize
information
Ability to plan travel
Academic independence
Amount of text being
read/Amount of time
spent reading
Application of knowledge
to real world situations
Attitudes
Behaviors
Change over time
Citizenship understanding
and skills:
personal
participation
justice

Collaboration
Communication skills
Community values,
beliefs, and practices
Conditional knowledge
Content area knowledge
Content area literacies
Curriculum development
Declarative knowledge
Deduction
Divergent thinking
Drawings and
illustrations
Film-making skills
Foreign language skills
General knowledge
Growth over time
Historical
understandings
Inductive thinking
Inquiry skills
Listening skills
Memorization
Moral development
Nature of knowledge
Nature of the disciplines
Note-taking skills
Participation
in the community
with individuals
with groups
Personal growth
Practical knowledge
Prior knowledge

Performance
Process
Problem-solving
Products
Proficiency with
technologies
Reading comprehension
Reading fluency
Revision skills
Risk-taking
Role-playing
Self-efficacy
Skills of managing
research questions
Speaking skills
Sociocultural integration
Student well-being
(social, emotional,
physical, intellectual)
Task-solving
Understanding of
concepts
Understanding of
connections among
disciplines
Understandings of
democracy
Understanding of
language conventions
Vocabulary development
Writing skills
Other

At what times do you want to evaluate it?

Before a project begins	During a project	At the end of the project
Evaluating prior knowledge and/or skills and/or dispositions and/or behaviours	Evaluating the process of creating	Evaluating summative knowledge, skills, dispositions, and/or behaviors
Evaluating goals and plans	Evaluating the evolution of the learner's ability to learn	Evaluating the final product
Evaluating questions	Evaluating the product as it is being created	Evaluating questions

What form of evaluation do you want it to be?

Formative	Summative
Formative assessment is assessment that is usually performed before and during a learning act. It usually involves reflection on the part of the learner and teacher. It rarely involves grading or comparisons of students' performance. Instead, it is designed to enhance learning, teaching and curriculum and is designed to improve a student's self-regulated learning. Formative assessment is also characterized by its role in the learning process itself—in other words, the assessment itself can contribute to growth and learning. Formative assessments include analysis to set goals and make plans, observations of classroom activities, interviews, self-reflections, and ongoing record keeping. It is designed to revise learning and teaching while they are actually occurring. Formative assessment as an actual aspect of practice, and students should be directly involved in formative assessment as it provides feedback to students while they are in the act of learning.	Summative assessment is assessment that identifies and summarizes the development of knowledge/skills, attitudes, and/or behaviours of a student at a certain point in time, typically after a teaching-learning event has occurred or a specific time period has elapsed. It is used to determine if students have met the objectives of the teaching-learning event. Traditional summative assessments include tests (including standardized tests), quizzes, judged performances, projects, and portfolios that document learning. It is not always assumed to have a role in student learning except in that it evaluates it. Summative assessments are often used as an accountability measure.

Have you considered implications underscored by the two common assessment paradigms?

Qualitative	Quantitative
• Reality is socially constructed	• Facts have an objective reality
• Primacy of context	• Primacy of method
• Variables are complex, interwoven, and difficult to measure	• Variables can be identified and relationships measured
• Emic (insider's) point of view	• Etic (outsider's) point of view
• Understanding participants' perspectives	• Tests theory
• Generates theory	• Generalizability sought
• Naturalistic	• Predict and show relationships
• Inductive	• Emphasizes formal instruments
• Embraces subjectivity	• Deductive
• Longer-term	• Numerical
• Theme and pattern based	• Seeks objectivity
• Multiple realities	• Statistical
• Making meaning	• Experimental
• Interpretive	• Positivist
	• Establish facts

What are the most effective instruments and activities for assessing the things that you want to assess?

Anecdotal records	Laboratory reports	Questionnaires
Checklists	Learning logs	Question-of-study
Concept maps	Mock trials	forming
Conferences	Multiple choice items	Rating scales
Created products	Mural creation	Real-time monitoring
Debates	Observations	Response scales
Essays	Peer assessments/feedback	Rubrics
Experiments	Performance-based	Self-assessments
Focus groups interviews	evaluations	Self-efficacy scales
Dialogue journals	Plan making/charting a	Short answer questions
E-mail correspondence	course of action	Surveys
Focus groups	Portfolios	Statistical data collection:
Goal setting	PowerPoint presentations	Descriptive
Graphic organizers	Pre-/post-tests	Inferential
Journaling	Products	Worked problems
KWL/KWHL charts	Projects	Writing assignments

In essence, in reading these chapters we came to view interdisciplinarity and transdisciplinary as more natural aspects of the disciplines than we had previously.

However, these assumed barriers still hold sway and must be addressed. One of the ways to begin to overcome them is to start with a direction in which to move and a framework within which to ground our subsequent work. Part of the problem is the seemingly overwhelming task of managing so much new information, so many new viewpoints, so much discussion, so many *voices* that the interdisciplinary or transdisciplinary approaches invite into the classroom.

To this end, we offer a modest beginning: a simple, non-prescriptive organizer with which to conceptualize assessment among the multitudinous possibilities inherent in interdisciplinary and transdisciplinary teaching and learning. This guide is derived from our interpretation of the authors' work within this book. It provides a focus for what to account for while considering practical assessment systems that allow interdisciplinary and transdisciplinary inquiry to flourish.

Concluding Remarks

To ensure equitable, superior educational opportunities for all students, nothing is more vital than a motivated and well prepared professional teaching workforce. This book was envisioned with the notion of nudging the assessment pendulum away from an overbearing and castigatory trajectory toward a course characterized by thoughtful and responsive models in which such talented individuals could thrive. A renewed pathway in which teachers are afforded the autonomy to leverage assessment strategies to promote learning, thus each and every child may approach their potential as young citizens.

The principal proposition from this book for inservice and preservice professional development providers, program and research design personnel, policy makers, and curriculum developers is clear: assessment matters—but that is not all that matters. It is far too easy to forget that real children live each and every day with the consequences of our decisions. The educational milieu is, to a large extent, in a defensive and responsive mode characterized by chaotic responses to assaults on our professional autonomy. We hope this book assists educational activists in the reclaiming of assessment as a positive and fully integrated element of learning in the real world.

Bibliography

Glesne, C. & Peshkin, A. (1992). *Becoming qualitative researchers: An introduction.* White Plains, NY: Longman.

Kaufman, D.K., Moss, D.M., & Osborn, T.A. (eds.), *Beyond the boundaries: A transdisciplinary approach to learning and teaching* (pp. 47–67). Westport, CT: Praeger Publishers.

About the Contributors

Scott W. Brown is a Professor of Educational Psychology in the Neag School of Education and the Director of the Teachers for a New Era Project at the University of Connecticut. Professor Brown received his bachelors degree from Boston University in psychology, his Master's of Science degree from Montana State University in psychology and his Ph.D. in psychology from Syracuse University where he specialized in educational and school psychology. Professor Brown has served the University of Connecticut as the department head for Educational Psychology and Director of the Bureau of Educational Research and Service. He is the author of over 100 journal articles, book chapters, and monographs focusing on issues of learning, assessment, instructional processes, and cognitive psychology. Professor Brown has directed grants and contracts totaling over $7 million with funding from NSF, the U.S. Department of Education, the Carnegie Corporation of New York and the U.S. Centers for Disease Control and Prevention. He has been awarded visiting professor positions at universities in New Zealand and Taiwan where he lectured on topics related to teacher education, assessment procedures, and educational psychology.

Wendy J. Glenn is an Assistant Professor in the Department of Curriculum and Instruction in the Neag School of Education at the University of Connecticut. In her role as Coordinator of English Education, she teaches undergraduate and graduate courses in the theories and methods of teaching language, literature, and composition. She is the author of *Sarah Dessen: From Burritos to Box Office* (Lanham, MD: Scarecrow, 2005) and *Presenting Richard Peck* (Lanham, MD: Scarecrow, forthcoming) and co-editor of

Portrait of a Profession: Teachers and Teaching in the 21st Century (Westport, CT: Praeger, 2005). She has published articles in *The ALAN Review, English Journal, Journal of Adolescent and Adult Literacy, SIGNAL, Teacher Education Quarterly,* and *Peremena/Thinking Classroom.* Her authored book chapters appear in *Censored Books: Critical Viewpoints, Vol. II* (Lanham, MD: Scarecrow, 2002), *Beyond the Boundaries: A Transdisciplinary Approach to Teaching and Learning* (Westport, CT: Praeger, 2003), and *Boys, Girls, and the Myths of Literacies/Learning* (Canadian Scholars Press, in press). She currently serves on the editorial review boards of *The ALAN Review* and the *Journal of Literacy Research,* has been elected to the ALAN Executive Board Member, and works as the Literature and Literary Analysis section editor for the *Journal of Literacy Research.*

Mileidis Gort is Assistant Professor of Literacy and Bilingual Education in the Department of Teaching and Learning at the School of Education, University of Miami. Her research examines the early bilingual and biliteracy development of English- and Spanish-speakers in dual language programs, as well as faculty-initiated efforts toward culturally- and linguistically-responsive teacher education. Her work has been published in peer-reviewed journals such as *The Journal of Early Childhood Literacy* and *Educational Policy,* as well as numerous edited books, and serves as a section editor for the *Journal of Literacy Research.* Dr. Gort worked as an elementary bilingual teacher in Lawrence, Massachusetts before becoming a teacher educator.

Douglas Kaufman is an Associate Professor of Curriculum and Instruction at the University of Connecticut's Neag School of Education. His areas of expertise are writing, literacy education, and teacher education. Doug currently researches the organizational structures of literacy workshops. Other research interests include the influence of teacher-student affective relationships on literacy learning, the effect of social talk on literacy development, the influence of teachers who write with their students, and student writing in urban classrooms. Doug is the author of *Conferences & Conversations: Listening to the Literate Classroom* and co-editor of *Beyond the Boundaries: A Transdisciplinary Approach to Learning and Teaching.*

Dr. Jacqueline Kelleher is Director of Content at the Beginning with Children Foundation in New York City, focusing on program development, quality assurance, assessment, and evaluation for BWCF schools and Foundation-level initiatives. Additionally, she provides technical assistance to departments, school leaders, K-8 teachers, and governing boards with respect to guiding them toward their vision, mission, and goals; creating systems and using data to make decisions focused on continuous improvement. She has worked as a professor and administrator in higher education specializing in accreditation, assessment systems, and teacher education. Her consulting in evaluation has taken her to numerous K-12 schools, universities, and government agencies including NASA. Dr. Kelleher has presented globally in the area of positive assessment practices and has had articles of the same theme published in peer-reviewed journals including the National Honors Collegiate Journal. Her most important work, however, was serving as a secondary educator in special education and English Language Arts. Dr. Kelleher's areas of interest also include learning strategies, differentiated instruction, teacher stress management, service learning, and teacher preparation.

Catherine M. Koehler is currently an Assistant Professor of Secondary Science Education at the University of Cincinnati. Her area of expertise in science education involves training preservice and inservice science teachers with strategies to foster the nature of science in the secondary science classroom through inquiry-based activities. She is currently exploring behaviors that describe the notion of pedagogical content knowledge for the nature of science and means to measure it. She is a frequent presenter of original research at the annual meetings of the National Association for Research in Science Teaching and the Association for Science Teacher Education.

Katherine McGivney is an Associate Professor of Mathematics at Shippensburg University. She received her Ph.D. in 1997 from Lehigh University in Probability Theory. She has published probability articles in peer-reviewed journals and is currently interested in the use of technology in under-graduate discrete math and statistics courses. Kate is an active member of several state and national mathematics organizations and for the past two summers she has co-directed a large-scale professional development program for K-12 mathematics teachers.

Jean McGivney-Burelle is Assistant Professor of Mathematics at the University of Hartford where she serves as the Director of Secondary Mathematics Education. She teaches undergraduate mathematics and mathematics education courses and is actively involved in professional development activities with area K-12 mathematics teachers. Her current research interests focus on the use of technology in teaching mathematics at the college-level. Jean has published numerous articles in peer reviewed journals, conference proceedings and edited books. She is actively involved in several state and national mathematics and education organizations and presently serves as an editor of the Calendar Department in the NCTM journal the *Mathematics Teacher.*

Alan S. Marcus is an Assistant Professor in the Department of Curriculum & Instruction. His research and teaching focus on social studies education and teacher education with a dual emphasis on the benefits and dilemmas of film and television as pedagogical tools in the history classroom, and on museums and historic sites as representations of the past. Alan earned his Ph.D. from Stanford University in curriculum and teacher education. Prior to attending Stanford he taught high school social studies for seven years. He recently completed an edited volume on film, history, and pedagogy and he serves on the Board of Directors for the Connecticut Council for the Social Studies.

Dr. David M. Moss is an Associate Professor in the Neag School of Education at the University of Connecticut, Storrs, CT. His faculty appointment is in the Department of Curriculum & Instruction in environmental education. His current research interests are in the areas of international education, environmental education, and teacher education reform. Dr. Moss has authored over 50 articles, book chapters, and reviews on such diverse topics as student understandings of the nature of science, interdisciplinary education, teacher education, and forest ecosystem health monitoring. He is co-editor of *Portrait of a Profession: Teachers and Teaching in the 21st Century* (Westport, CT: Praeger, 2005) and *Beyond the Boundaries: A Transdisciplinary Approach to Learning and Teaching* (Westport, CT: Praeger, 2003). He earned his Ph.D. from the University of New Hampshire and completed his undergraduate work at Alfred University. He has extensive curriculum development and assessment experience on large-scale projects funded by the National Science Foundation (NSF) and the National Aeronautics and Space Administration (NASA).

Terry A. Osborn, Ph.D., is Professor and Chair of the Division of Curriculum and Teaching in the Graduate School of Education, Fordham University. Dr. Osborn taught public school German for six years at the high school level, including one year also at the middle school level. Dr. Osborn is co-editor of *Critical Inquiry in Language Studies: An International Journal* (Lawrence Erlbaum Associates), series editor of the Praeger Publishers *Contemporary Language Studies* series and former editor of the Bergin & Garvey *Contemporary Language Education* series. He co-authored *The Foreign Language Educator in Society: Toward a Critical Pedagogy,* and edited *The Future of Foreign Language Education in the United States.* He also authored *Critical Reflection and the Foreign Language Classroom,* winner of the 2001 American Educational Studies Association Critics' Choice Award, and as awarded the Stephen Freeman Award by NECTFL for the best published article on foreign language teaching techniques. Dr. Osborn served on the Executive Board of the International Society for Language Studies, and his work has appeared in *Educational Foundations, Educational Studies, Foreign Language Annals, Language Problems and Language Planning, Multicultural Education, SchoolArts,* and *NECTFL Review.* Dr. Osborn is a featured keynote speaker at education conferences in the United States.

Raised in the verdant Midwest, **Dr. John Settlage** has spent a lifetime within science education pursuits. His father, a science educator, relied upon John and his three siblings as field test subjects for the varied science curriculum materials being generated in the post-Sputnik heyday. Beneficiary of astute mentoring and infused with unwavering idealism, he is now Teacher Educator and Educational Researcher at the University of Connecticut's Neag School of Education. It is from this vantage point that he strives to promote equity in learning opportunities for K-12 students across Connecticut and beyond. He has recently published a text on diversity and science teaching methods (*Teaching Science to Every Child,* Routledge, 2007).

Jane M. Wilburne is an Assistant Professor of Mathematics Education at Penn State Harrisburg. She teaches mathematics and mathematics education undergraduate and graduate courses and facilitates many professional development programs. Her research interests focus on problem solving, assessment, writing in the mathematics classroom, and effective professional development programs. She has publications in many of the NCTM journals and serves as a reviewer for the *Mathematics Teaching in the Middle School* journal. She was the author and PI for several large professional development grants for K-12 mathematics teachers in the areas of algebra, geometry, measurement, modeling and problem solving. She taught middle and high school mathematics prior to receiving her doctorate from Temple University.

Author Index

Subject Index